THE LONDON MONEY
MARKET

The London Money Market

E. R. SHAW
M.A. (Econ.), A.I.B., M.B.I.M.

Midland Bank Senior Lecturer in the Practice of Banking,
Loughborough University of Technology

HEINEMANN LONDON

William Heinemann Ltd
10 Upper Grosvenor Street, London W1X 9PA

LONDON   MELBOURNE   TORONTO
JOHANNESBURG   AUCKLAND

First published 1975
Second edition 1978
Third edition 1981
434 91833 4

Printed and bound
in Great Britain by
REDWOOD BURN LIMITED
Trowbridge, Wiltshire

To

Doris, Jacky, and Peter

'be careful in teaching, for error in teaching amounts to deliberate sin.'

The Mishnah, Pirekei Avot, 5

Acknowledgements

It is impossible for me to single out everyone who has contributed in some way to this book. Over the years I have made many friends in a wide variety of City institutions who have all contributed in no small measure to the success of the two previous editions of the book as well as the present one. I wish particularly to thank Graeme Gilchrist of Union Discount Co. Ltd for reading and commenting on much of the re-written text and his patience in discussing numerous contentious points. Similarly Dick Turpin and Jane Clarke of C.I.P.F.A. Services Ltd for their guidance and assistance in the preparation of the Local Authority chapter and Charles Ferrier of the Finance Houses Association and Mick Redgewell of Butler Till Ltd. I am also indebted to Allan Nichols, Tim Clarke and Simon Eccles of Grieveson, Grant & Co. and Peter Morley of Phillips & Drew for their generous help and opinions.

Many institutions have also given generously of their time and access to data including the Bank of England, National Westminster Bank, Midland Bank and the Department of Trade. I also owe thanks to my captive audience of students and the University of Loughborough who have suffered my banking classes in recent years and to academic colleagues, especially Chris Gill for his unstinting help in the detailed preparation and Geoff Dennis and Professor David Llewellyn for their advice and assistance.

Finally, my thanks go to my secretary Daljit Nandra and Mrs Su Spencer for their speedy and accurate typing of the manuscript. To my wife Doris and children, Jacky and Peter, who suffered my crises of confidence as only a family can, I give my sincere thanks.

I hope that all these kind people have successfully steered me clear of major errors of omission and commission. If not I accept the responsibility myself.

Preface

When I completed my original research work into the operation of London's money markets in 1971, little did I realize the speed with which the markets were to grow or the importance that they would achieve in the financial system. Two papers by the Bank of England which were introduced in 1979 and 1980 have highlighted the importance of the money market as the fulcrum of credit and regulatory control. The Bank's papers were 'Monetary Base Control' and 'The Measurement of Liquidity' (the second of these proposals is outlined in Appendix III). It remains unclear (February 1981) precisely what form the new control measures will take but they are certain to bring about major changes in the financial markets over the next decade.

This book attempts to chart the growth and development of London's various markets for money over the last fifteen years. It is a complicated story because of the constantly changing nature of the market which in turn is influenced by government economic policy, banking controls, taxation and major international impacts. A particular difficulty in amending and up-dating much of the material for the book has been the many changes in official and other statistical series which create major discontinuities in the data and render close analysis a somewhat tenuous task. Nevertheless, every section of the book has been brought up-to-date and many chapters such as the euro-dollar, inter-bank, finance house, certificate of deposit and the whole of Part IV, have been completely re-written.

There has always been an element of mystery about the workings of certain institutions in the City and this is particularly true of the money markets. The main thrust of this book is directed towards helping the reader view the operation and growth of these markets as a logical process with the hope that those unfamiliar with financial institutions will gain a better understanding of why they are so important to the continuing development of the U.K. economy.

The book is divided into four parts, each of which has a brief introduction which describes its scope.

This book is designed primarily for use in undergraduate money and banking courses and by students studying for the finals of professional examinations such as Chartered Accountants, Institute of Bankers, Chartered Secretaries, Diploma in Public Administration, and also those following Higher National Diploma courses.

Students continuing their studies at universities, polytechnics, and colleges of further education will generally have a background of at least one introductory economics course and should have little difficulty in following the text. Those readers who have no previous knowledge of economics are advised to read one of the many basic economic texts currently available.

Every textbook writer hopes that he may have done some things which are different, and perhaps some that are better than those in books already in existence. My objective was to write a book that would take the motivated and advanced student a long way along the road to a thorough understanding of the London money markets, their practical and theoretical probelms, together with some historical and institutional background. The book will also provide the average student with a logical and reasonable non-technical discussion of the subject. I am also hopeful that the book will prove of interest to those who work in the City, to practical bankers, accountants, corporate treasurers, and all those who have an interest in money.

AUTHOR'S NOTE

At the time of writing the Bank of England is formulating new methods of monetary control and fresh banking liquidity measures to replace arrangements which have existed since September 1971. Readers are, therefore, asked to bear these new proposals in mind, particularly when reference is made in the text to reserve ratios, reserve assets, defined assets, public sector debt ratio (of the discount houses) and eligibility of bills. Reference should be made to Appendix III which describes the latest known position. This note is intended to obviate the frequent need for footnotes on individual pages throughout the book.

Loughborough   E. R. Shaw

Contents

CONTENTS

Tables

Figures

Part I

Introductory

Chapters 1 and 2, which form the first part of the book, endeavour to provide the reader with the basic concepts which underlie the functioning of a money market.

If the development of the present function of the discount market is to be clearly understood, it must be seen in relation to the whole U.K. monetary system. The money market is an intergral part of our monetary system and it plays a dominant role in the working of that system, having particular significance for the main problems of monetary policy.

Chapter 1 lays down the basic criteria necessary for the formation and operation of a money market. Chapter 2 describes the theoretical working of a modern centralized banking system, outlining the chief characteristics of the British system with the discount market as its centrepiece.

1 The anatomy of a money market

A money market simply defined is a grouping of financial institutions which facilitates the borrowing and lending of short-term money. The transactions carried out are motivated by considerations of profit and usually cater for the demands of a complex industrial economy.

For a money market to exist in a highly developed industrial economy there are certain basic conditions which must be met. Firstly, there must be a central bank capable and willing to act as a lender of the last resort. Where such a facility exists it enables the banking system to operate to lower levels of liquidity, making full use of available resources. It also has the advantage, for the central bank, that its influence over the banking sector is that much greater when the banks work to finer margins. Thus, when the central bank wishes to influence the amount of cash and other liquid assets available by creating shortages or surpluses in the money market, then its effects are felt much more rapidly, and a given intervention has larger repercussions. There must also be grouped about the central bank an integrated structure of institutions of a financial nature who hold a variety of assets of differing liquidity and profitability. It is, of course, only in large national financial centres that such organizations exist and money markets are seen to develop. In Britain there is a highly centralized banking system with the central bank and the head offices of the main banking groups all located in London. Moreover, the principal offices of other financial institutions such as the merchant banks and acceptance houses, insurance companies, and the Stock Exchange are close at hand.

The significance of an integrated structure must also be emphasized since this is essential to the development of any money market. Integration implies the free movemnt of money and financial assets so that funds can be moved from sectors in the economy where there are surpluses to points where deficits occur. The importance of integration lies in the fact that influences which affect one sector of the market will be transmitted fairly quickly to other related markets so that a consistent pattern is maintained for the cost of money within each sector. The essence of this structure will be the continuous links which are created as between one market and another and their several prices. In other words, there will be some sort of equilibrium situation created between the markets as any inconsistencies are rapidly adjusted.

Secondly, if the market is not to be limited in scope, there must be a larger number of organizations comprising the market with the desire to switch their assets, whether they be in cash or other liquid or near liquid form, to meet the public's demand for the supply of cash. The holding of idle balances is, therefore, kept to a minimum and in practice it means that the banking system employs its cash reserves economically and establishes a stable and effective reserve ratio. It is also important that the assets dealt in should be of a known quality and maturity. The presence of such a condition is not vital to a money market but, for example, in a new and under-developed market it would materially assist its growth and development, whilst in a mature market it would ensure that a high turnover in various assets were maintained. In a market in which profit margins are narrow the rate of turnover attains particular importance.

Thirdly, a system of control and classification of market assets must be formulated and implemented to inspire confidence in the system. In the London market the balance sheets of the banks and the operators in the market come under the scrutiny of the Bank of England to ensure that the type of investment held is of appropriate quality and liquidity. Since the fringe banking crisis of 1974 far more detailed information has been required on the composition and maturity of both assets and liabilities and far more institutions have been subject to Bank of England supervision. Furthermore, it is essential that the number of participants in the market is sufficiently large to ensure both an effective market together with adequate lquidity for the investor. Both of these factors have been shown to have very practical applications in recent times. The growth of the market for sterling Certificates of Deposit was inhibited for a time because the number of banks issuing Certificates was limited until the participation of the clearing banks in September 1972.

Other considerations which have expanded the size and importance of the London market during the last century are the steady internationalization of the City as a financial and trading centre, the enormous growth of the Treasury bill as a means of government borrowing, and the emergence of the sterling inter-bank, local authority and Euro-dollar short-term markets. These factors have been especially significant in widening the scope and importance of the London market, the ramifications of which are fully discussed in the following chapters.

It cannot be postulated that where these pre-conditions do not apply, or apply only in part, a satisfactory money market cannot function. Money markets exist in many parts of the world, and it is not uncommon for economists and others to distinguish between 'developed' and 'underdeveloped' money markets in an attempt to be specific in their description of the conditions which should be met in the various patterns of organizations. However, the line of demarcation is blurred by the wide diversity of type and size of the world's markets stemming from their different origins and environments. Nevertheless, we have endeavoured to set out certain pre-requisites, the elements of which provide a viable working framework for a money market.

THE NEED FOR SHORT-TERM FINANCE

Not all countries have markets in short-term money and short-dated securities; indeed, many advanced countries operate in an entirely satisfactory way without such a mechanism. The commercial banks in these countries are required to maintain specific cash reserve ratios with their central bank. When they need to replenish their cash supplies they rely on their rediscount facitilites with the central bank. The commercial banks receive direct assistance from the central bank or surplus finds may be passed to the central bank thus completing the equalization of surpluses and deficits within the system. In Great Britain there is a fundamental difference in the operation of this equalizing function. This is carried out through the intermediary of the money market which comprised, until comparatively recently, the traditional discount market only. Since the early 1960s, however, responsibility for this liquidity function has been shared to an increasing degree with the sterling inter-bank market. In September 1971 the Bank of England stipulated that all banks should maintain a reserve ratio of $12\frac{1}{2}\%$* which comprises certain specified reserve assets. Included among these

---

* Reserve ratio abolished August 1980. See Appendix III for details of revised arrangements.

reserve assets is call money with the discount market and the banks, both clearing and secondary, have chosen to maintain approximately 50% of their reserve assets requirement in this form. Substantial sums of money which are surplus to the banks' requirements are still, however, placed in the inter-bank market and, in fact, may well be attracted to the market when a profitable interest arbitrage exists.

It is an almost invariable rule amongst British commercial banks that they do not borrow directly from the central bank. This policy has been followed since 1825 except in times of national emergency such as the two world wars or the monetary crisis of June 1972 when the Bank gave direct assistance to the banking system, bypassing the money market. The Bank does, from time to time, give assistance to the clearing banks, but only on its own initiative. The intermediatry role of the discount houses is a unique mechanism in world monetary systems which is now well established.

The role of the central bank and of its operations in the money market are highly complex, so much so that the Bank of England has a multiplicity of conflicting aims which will motivate its actions.

(1) It must finance and administer the National Debt as cheaply as possible, facilitate funding and arrange maturities and redemptions.
(2) It must provide the banking system with its cash requirements.
(3) It must influence the level of commercial bank borrowing consistent with the needs of the economy and government policy.
(4) It must establish a chosen level of interest rates through operations in the money market, the pattern of which must attempt to reconcile short-term and long-term interest rates, bearing in mind domestic as well as international economic pressures.

Central to these Bank of England aims are the operations of the London discount houses, and it is to this process we must now turn.

The succeeding chapters of the book analyse each sector of the money market in detail so that for the moment only a brief outline of the role of the discount houses will be given. It follows from the aims of the central bank given above that there is at any one time a considerable ebb and flow in daily monetary requirements. For example, the National Debt is being 'turned over'; that is, redemptions and maturities are met and new bond tranches issued to the order of some £8,300 M. on the year 1979/80. The government will also wish concurrently to borrow on Treasury bills, which in turn affects the liquidity of the banking system as a whole. The needs of the commercial banks and secondary banks (i.e. the Common-wealth, overseas and foreign banks, merchant banks and accept-ance houses) will naturally be influenced by these overriding government requirements, and also by the level of economic activ-ity. It can be seen then that the cash requirements of the banking system fluctuate to a wide degree. It may seem surprising that the discount houses carry out their equalizing function with the aid of very modest capital resources amounting to some £160 M. Their ability to do so stems from the knowledge that their working capital is provided by extensive borrowing from the banking system, underpinned by their exclusive last-resort facilities at the Bank.

The implicit reliance placed on the discount houses by the banking system is demonstrated by the fact that in 1971 70%* of all bank reserve requirements are held in the form of call money with the discount† market. The flexibility of the British system is clearly provided by the Bank of England which operates to mop up surplus funds, or by covering deficiencies as they arise. When meeting a liquidity shortage the Bank exerts its influence by charging penal rates and by varying the term of the loan. The authorities can, of course, create a shortage of liquidity in the market if they so wish, through the medium of open market operations in bonds. The mechanism also enables the Bank to prevent or moderate fluctu-ations in short-term money rates. The detailed practices of the authorities in this connection are described in Chapters 4 and 5.

THE INTERNATIONALIZATION OF THE LONDON MONEY MARKET

Before we begin to examine our theoretical model of central bank operations in the money market, there is one further aspect of the development of the London market which should be noted. The gradual internationalization of the City's money markets since the late 1950s and throughout the 1960s has probably been the greatest single influence in London retaining its pre-eminence as an inter-national financial centre.

Until the mid-1950s the market for money in London was largely conducted in sterling, whilst its techniques, expertise, and experi-ence ensured that the City was without equal. From both the politi-cal and economic point of view sterling was the predominant

---

* Since then this percentage has declined somewhat and in December 1979 stood at 50%.

† See Appendix III for revised arrangements.

currency throughout the nineteenth century, and even into the 1930s the trade of the overseas sterling area countries was transacted with Britain. Following the departure from the gold standard in 1931 sterling suffered from recurrent troubles until the second world war and after. By 1946 the United States was the significant economic power and consequently the relative importance of the U.S. dollar increased substantially. Even though sterling no longer occupied its former strategic role the pound continued to dominate the financial scene in the City. In 1958 external convertibility came to Western Europe which, combined with the relaxation in exchange controls, gave banks and business firms greater freedom to conduct foreign exchange transactions and foreign capital operations. At the same time the U.S. balance of payments deficit was emerging to provide Western Europe with increasing holdings of dollars.

It was probably the sterling crisis of 1957 which gave the impetus to the growth of the use of the U.S. dollar to finance foreign trade, when the availability of sterling for such purposes was severely restricted. Up to that time the use of Euro-dollars for trading and liquidity purposes merely supplemented the traditional money market in the international sphere. The Euro-dollar was looked upon more as a vehicle for foreign exchange transactions than a money market in its own right. The Bank of England, however, were quick to appreciate that although sterling was no longer the leading international currency, and that this was detrimental to London's prestige as a world financial centre, by encouraging the growth of the Euro-dollar market in the City, valuable foreign business could be retained.

In 1958 the emergent and developing nations needed an international mechanism that could tap existing sources of finance. Subsequently, the 1960s witnessed a great expansion in international trade. There is no doubt that easy access to short-term capital through the medium of the Euro-dollar market in London contributed significantly to the supply of world liquidity and expansion in trade. Such developments through the media of the merchant banks overseas and foreign banks, were stimulated by the overt encouragement of the Bank of England which reasoned that if such operations were not carried out in London, then they would be in other foreign financial centres.

THE ABOLITION OF U.K. EXCHANGE CONTROLS

Another move which still further enhanced the claim of London to be the foremost financial centre in the world occurred in November 1979 when forty years of exchange controls were abandoned. It is now possible for non-residents to have complete access to U.K. credit markets and U.K. residents are free to invest or borrow overseas.

It became clear that following the increasing contribution of North Sea oil to the U.K. balance of payments, a new approach to exchange rate policy was required. Moreover, the Conservative government was committed to a strategy of encouraging the strengthening the free market economy and the step was also necessary to fulfil Britain's E.E.C. membership obligations.

The continuing appreciation* of sterling on the foreign exchange market coupled with the U.K. interest rates at generally higher levels than those of other countries, presented the authorities with two unwanted alternatives, so long as exchange controls were retained. First, the authorities could allow sterling to appreciate even more and jeopardize the competitiveness of the non-oil trade sector. Secondly, they could intervene in the foreign exchange market and risk the resulting domestic monetary expansion with its inflationary implications.

The precise effects of the abolition of exchange controls are far from clear but most certainly have significant influences on monetary control, and financial markets and the reserve role of sterling. The most important implication for London as a financial centre is that its money and capital markets are now fully integrated into the world financial markets. Thus London could become a major international source of capital in addition to its present role as an entrepot for funds.

---

* Clearly sterling will fluctuate from time to time on the foreign exchange markets as the sharp depreciation of sterling in the spring of 1981 showed.

2 Central bank operations

The object of this chapter is to describe the basic concepts which underlie the central bank's operations in the money market. A word of caution is, however, appropriate at this juncture because most descriptions of such a system imply a degree of precision in the mechanism which does not exist in practice. If our only goal were the control of credit within the economy by the central bank, then the theoretical blueprint which we are about to construct would indeed be reasonably accurate. We saw in the previous section, however, that the central bank must bear in mind at least four considerations when formulating monetary policy. These considerations are seldom compatible as one aim frequently conflicts sharply with another. The art of central banking lies in the reconciliation of these conflicts. We are to concern ourselves with a purely mechanistic model of central bank operations in the money market.

DEFINING THE PROBLEM

The significant economic function of the monetary system is that it influences and partially, together with fiscal policy, controls the level of effective demand in the economy. At one time it was thought that the total quantity of money, that is notes and coins in circulation and demand bank deposits, was the sole element in determining the level of effective demand. Since the Radcliffe Committee sat in 1959 the more widely accepted view has been that it is the whole liquidity position that is important, that is to say the total supply of liquid assets available to the banking sector. So the problem had moved from the purely cash base argument to the wider issues involved in controlling the liquidity structure of the lending institutions.* We must, therefore, focus our attention on the chief institutional groups, which operate a series of related markets in highly liquid monetary assets.

The first institution we must describe is the central bank itself which exercises a number of important functions. It is a government controlled non-profit making agency which acts as banker to the government, maintaining the accounts of government departments, receiving the proceeds of taxation, and making payments on their behalf. It administers the National Debt by issuing new bond tranches and repaying and converting maturing ones. In carrying out this process it creates a strategic link between the public and private sectors of the economy. It controls the issue and replacement of notes and coin. It makes short-term loans to the government and acts as the commercial bankers' bank, influencing their activities. It controls the government's international monetary transactions by operating on the foreign exchange market, and administers the foreign currency and gold reserves. Finally, it shares with the government the responsibility for formulating and implementing these various monetary functions.

Secondly in our list of institutions come the commercial banking groups which include the five clearing banks. Scottish and Northern Ireland banks, Commonwealth, overseas and foreign banks, merchant banks, and acceptance houses. These banks are profit-earning commercial companies motivated by operating in competition with each other. Broadly speaking, they take deposits and deal in a variety of assets of differing liquidity.

Lastly, we have that interrelated group of companies which comprises the London discount market. This consists of the eleven discount houses who derive their working capital from money lent on a day-to-day basis, mainly from the banking system. They are dealers in short-dated government and local authority bonds, Treasury bills and commercial bills as well as in the complementary markets. They employ their borrowed funds by purchasing Treasury bills, commercial bills and other assets which may be either sold to the banking system or held to maturity. Traditionally, the discount houses stand between the Bank of England and the commercial and other banks in the system. On any given day the banks may have to meet heavy demands from the public whilst

---

* 1979 and 1980 have witnessed a tremendous resurgence of interest by the authorities in the possible introduction of a monetary base control system. At the time of writing (February 1981) no firm decisions has been made but an outline of the proposed mechanism will be discussed in Appendix III.

at the same time they will also be receiving money from many different sources. There is no certainty, however, as to when or if these funds will be received. Consequently, they must maintain sufficient liquid funds to cover possible withdrawals. Surplus funds are, therefore, lent to the discount houses who will pay the current market rate for short-dated loans. This arrangement enables the banking system to make the most economical use of its liquid resources in the knowledge that these monies can be called in from the discount market if required. If only a few banks call up their loans then the discount houses can probably replace these funds by borrowing from other banks within the system. If the demand for liquidity is general, that is all banks within the system are short of cash, then the discount houses will be forced to exercise their traditional privilege to borrow from the Bank of England in its rôle as a lender of the last resort. The central bank then lends to the discount houses, usually for seven days at whatever rate of interest it chooses to impose. In practice this means the Minimum Lending Rate (or Bank rate as it was known prior to 1972) which for a time was based on the current market rate plus $\frac{1}{2}$% and rounded off to the nearest $\frac{1}{4}$% above.* It can be seen that such a rate is a penal one so far as the discount houses are concerned since the houses usually obtain their funds from the banking system at a cost below that which they earn on the assets they hold, such as Treasury and commercial bills for example.

If the authorities only render assistance to the discount market on the above terms, it is an indicator that the Bank wishes to see a general increase in short-term money rates. Indeed, the monetary authorities can engineer shortages of cash in the money market by engaging in open market operations in government securities which have the effect of reducing bankers' deposits at the Bank of England. This may, in turn, result in the commercial banks' reserve asset† ratio falling below the prescribed limit of $12\frac{1}{2}$%. Equally, it is possible that the authorities do not wish to see an increase in interest rates when a liquidity shortage appears in the money market. In such circumstances assistance will be given to the discount houses at market rates instead of at the penal Minimum Lending Rate. The market rate in these conditions is usually the Treasury bill rate. In practice such open market operations are carried out very frequently as the Bank wishes to prevent sudden fluctuations

---

* The formula approach has been suspended and the Bank of England once again makes discretionary changes as it did with the old Bank Rate.

† See Appendix III for revised arrangements.

in the flow of funds from the public to the private sector which could increase bank liquidity at an inopportune time. The authorities, therefore, endeavour to purchase from the money market (and sometimes the banks themselves) bills and bonds due for maturity at that time.

The purpose of the mechanism is to influence the cash and liquid assets base of the banking system and thereby control the creation of credit. This is the essence of a centralized banking system. At the beginning of the section we expressed the generally accepted belief that one of the important elements in determining effective demand was the availability of credit in the economy and, as a corollary of this, the liquidity of the banking system. We have, therefore, established the importance of central bank control in the economy. To complete our simplistic model of the Bank of England's operations in the money market we must now briefly examine these influences from the standpoint of the banking sector. We will see what effect the transactions have on the commercial banks' asset structure.

The commercial, merchant, and other banks which make up the banking sector, earn their profits by investment of deposit liabilities in various kinds of assets. Generally speaking the more liquid the asset the lower its earning capacity; conversely, the less liquid the asset then the more profitable it becomes. Clearly, being profit-seeking organizations they will wish to maximize the yield on their investments by so distributing their assets as to hold those which produce the greatest profit. They are restricted in their choice of asset mix by the central bank requirement that a minimum percentage must be retained in certain prescribed reserve assets. If we examine a simplified commercial bank balance sheet we see that there are four main categories of asset:

Liabilities		Assets	
Deposits	6,000	Cash	1,000
		Bills	3,000
		Investments	1,000
		Loans	1,000

The assets are purchased in return for deposit liabilities so that at all times the total of assets equals the deposit liabilities. The significance of the bank deposits is that they add to the stock of money and, therefore, constitute an addition to purchasing power in the economy. In our example the bank concerned would be in a highly liquid position since it is holding £4,000 in liquid assets against deposits of £6,000. This is far higher than would be required to meet the claims of depositors for cash. The bank is therefore in a position to switch a proportion of its liquid assets to other more profitable but less liquid forms of asset such as bonds or loans to customers. It could do so by expanding its loans by a further £4,000 and purchase additional bonds of £2,000 giving an amended balance sheet as follows:

Liabilities		Assets	
Deposits	12,000	Cash	1,000
		Bills	3,000
		Investments	3,000
		Loans	5,000
	12,000		12,000

The important factor is that only when liquid asset backing for deposits has been provided can a bank carry out this process. We now have a reserve ratio of 4:12 and a cash ratio of 1:12. Thus, it is the central bank reserve requirement, which we will say for our purpose must not fall below 4:12, that provides the safety factor and prevents the bank from continuing to increase its assets, thereby creating more deposits.

It is important to understand that our example cites only one bank in the system and it does not create deposits to a multiple of its base. In the process of credit creation it is the banking system as a whole which creates the new money. An example will illustrate the point: if a bank is working to a reserve ratio of 1:10, then it creates credit to the extent of $\frac{9}{10}$ of its deposits. This is because for each deposit taken it must retain the prescribed proportion, i.e. as a reserve, distributing the remainder in income earning assets. In acquiring its new assets it makes payments which form deposits of the other banks in the system. New money in the system as a whole is therefore created as the sum of a geometric progression $1,000 \times [1 \times \frac{9}{10} (\frac{9}{10})^2 + (\frac{9}{10})^3 \ldots$ until £10,000 in further deposits is produced. The theoretical bank credit multiplier made would therefore predict that the rate of deposit creation is equal to the liquid assets held by the banking sector multiplied by the reciprocal of the reserve ratio which we can write as follows:

Creation of total deposits

= Total liquid assets created by the central bank $\times \dfrac{1}{\text{Reserve Ratio}}$

Under the British system of central bank control, every bank must hold a minimum reserve asset ratio of 12½% including balances at the Bank of England, call money with the London discount market, Treasury bills, British government stocks and nationalized industry stocks with one year or less to maturity, local authority bills, and commercial bills eligible for rediscount at the Bank. This would imply that banks are able to create deposits up to a multiple of eight times the amount of any extra reserve assets they obtain.*

Clearly, the Bank of England can exercise control of the banking sector's ability to create credit for two reasons: firstly, it controls the proportion of total assets which the banks hold in liquid or near liquid form against deposits. Secondly, it controls the constitution and availability of these liquid assets. The significant thing about the Bank's specified list of eligible reserve assets is that most are short liabilities of the State and consequently the authorities effectively control, for example, the quantity of Treasury bills in issue or short-dated bonds, thus setting a limit on the deposit creating activities of the banking sector. The question of shortages of reserve assets arising was a very real problem for the banks and discount houses in the U.K. during 1972.

There is, of course, a good deal more to the theory of the multiple creation of bank deposits and the theory of central banking than we have outlined here. Readers who wish to acquaint themselves more fully with these mechanisms should consult one of the many excellent text books which are available.†

What we have done is merely to outline the general theory surrounding the Bank of England's operations in the money market to enable the reader to understand the more detailed analyses of the various processes which appear throughout the book.

---

* Reserve ratio abandoned August 1981.
† J. R. S. Revell, *The British Financial System.*

Part II

The Traditional Markets

The London discount market provides a distinct commercial and financial service in its own right which has great significance and is quite separate from its importance in the overall financial system. Indeed, the market is unique in that its origins lie in commercial bill discounting and broking during the 1800s. It was not until the late nineteenth century that it dealt in Treasury bills and even later before it purchased and sold short-dated government bonds. Part II of the book describes the discount market's participation in the three so-called traditional markets—the commercial bill, the Treasury bill, and the short-bond market. The finer points of bill and bond dealing are examined and some of the discount market's difficulties in operating within the constraints of the Treasury and Bank of England official policies are highlighted. These chapters provide the necessary background to an understanding of the more complex problems faced by the market during the 1970s.

3 The Commercial Bill

Despite the prognostications of the Radcliffe Report,* when it noted the 'irreversible shrinkage in the relative supply of commercial bills', the commercial bill had in fact shown a truly remarkable resurgence. During the 1950s borrowing on commercial bills doubled while in the first part of the sixties a similar pattern was established.

The Bank of England in 1961 stated that 'the relative importance of commercial bills in the London market has diminished during this century', and whilst that was substantially true the revival was well under way by 1961.

This expansion has subsequently continued (although not at quite such a rapid pace, as is evident from Table 1) despite official strictures which operated from 1965 until 1971. The total of commercial bills outstanding in December 1971 had reached £1,572 M.

For reasons of clarity and convenience it is proposed to divide this chapter into two parts: first, to show the reasons for the revival of the commercial bill since 1959; second, to trace the decline of the Treasury bill.

Before embarking upon an examination of the individual sections of the chapter it would be helpful to summarize the types of bills found in the discount market. They can be divided into two main groups—bills which bear one name only and bills bearing two or more names. The one-name bills may again be sub-divided into two main types: British Government Treasury bills, and promissory notes of local authorities. The second group or 'two-name bills' are bills of exchange proper, as distinct from financial promissory notes, and have several sub-divisions. These are (1) bank bills accepted by British banks or acceptance houses, (2) fine trade bills,

---

* The governor of the Bank wrote to the Discount Market Association requesting that the houses limited their intake of bills of exchange.

Table 1

HOLDINGS OF COMMERCIAL BILLS

End of	London Clearing Banks	Discount Market	Total
1960	155	117	272
1961	252	183	435
1962	268	189	457
1963	305	249	554
1964	426	302	728
1965	454	339	795
1966	474	404	878
1967	489	437	926
1968	525	560	1,085
1969	608	629	1,237
1970	764	697	1,461
1971	986	586	1,572
1972	557	565	1,122
1973	604	684	1,288
1974	675	1,370	2,045
1975	483	980	1,463
1976	551	1,019	1,570
1977	862	1,213	2,075
1978	804	2,038	2,842
1979	947	2,638	3,585

Source: Midland Bank Review, Aug. 1969 and updated.
Bank of England Statiscal Abstract, Nos. 1 & 2 and updated.

(3) acceptances of non-British banks, (4) foreign agency bills, (5) ordinary trade bills, and (6) bills drawn by foreigners on foreigners and payable in London.

THE REVIVAL OF THE COMMERCIAL BILL

In 1958 commercial bills formed only 7% of the discount houses' total assets, but by 1969 this figure had risen to 35%; an increase of some £560 M. in the market's holdings. A number of influences had worked to produce this resurgence, two of which are dominant and prime movers whilst a number of other factors have also contributed. They were:

(1) Successive credit squeezes culminating in resort to methods of finance other than bank overdrafts.

(2) The government's desire to fund the National Debt thereby keeping the Treasury bill issue low over a long period.

(3) The abolition of ad valorem stamp duty in 1961, and the subsequent abolition of all stamp duty in 1971.

(4) A change in the policy of the banks towards commercial bills, and a suspected shift in that of the Bank of England (see 'eligibility' later in the chapter).

(5) Increasing competitiveness in the banking sector stemming from the arrival of foreign banks in London, with a consequent erosion of acceptance commissions.

(6) The increasing financial sophistication of industrial and commercial concerns generally.

The first two factors are considered by many commentators to be the dominant influences.

The fortunes of the London discount market are prone to frequent fluctuations, often violent ones, chiefly because the conditions that determine is profitability or its risk of loss may be powerfully influenced at any given moment by the particular tactics employed by the Bank of England in implementing monetary policy, or technical management of the money markets. This has certainly been true of the commercial bill and the Treasury bill.

Throughout most of the period 1958–68 monetary policy remained active and generally restrictive with the application of both qualitative and quantitative controls to bank lending. Prior to 1965, however, no restrictions were placed on the use of commercial bills and this led to a considerable revival in their use as a substitute for bank overdrafts.

As the deficit in the public sector declined so did the issue of Treasury bills. In 1951 they reached their peak of £5,500 M. and the figure remained high until 1960 when bills issued through the tender declined from £3,480 M. to £2,180 M. in March 1966 and by 1969 the volume had contracted further to only £1,390 M. This dearth of Treasury bills made the market especially receptive to innovations in bill business which might replace the Treasury bill whilst at the same time recurrent credit squeezes had driven businesses, large and small, to obtain bill credit.

The main growth had naturally been in the bills of large public companies with considerable issued capital running into many millions of pounds. This was not to imply that the growth in the use of small trade bills was unimportant, but it is doubtful if more than two discount houses dealt largely in such bills as generally speaking they felt that it would not be economic for them to employ a staff large enough to enquire closely into the creditworthiness of a multitude of small businesses.

The discount houses have not always pursued the business in trade bills with zest and energy. The houses have always had a somewhat unusual historical relationship with the big banks in that they have, until recently, been careful not to encroach on the banker's chief source of profit, the overdraft, by enticing customers into bills or other forms of finance. As a consequence of almost continued credit restrictions the banks were, and remained, fully lent. Thus they were led, by considerations of goodwill, to encourage customers to find new avenues of credit. One course was to discount trade bills in the market. This policy was not so altruistic as it might at first sight appear, since it ultimately created an additional source of liquid asset if a bank chose to buy such bills for its portfolio.

The emergence of more competitive market conditions in many areas of trade, where buyers rather than sellers have had the upper hand, and the introduction of new techniques such as factoring, have brought about changes in the type of trade bill held in the portfolios of the discount houses.

The traditional 'self liquidating' bill, i.e. a bill drawn for the finance of foreign trade and secured by documents of title to goods in transit, which conservative bankers have in the past favoured, has declined as a proportion of the discount market's portfolio, and has been replaced by the pure finance bill. It is difficult to give a precise definition of the term 'finance bill' because experts in the market hold conflicting opinions, e.g. one expert examining a bill will give his opinion that it is a finance bill, while another equally well qualified to judge will argue that it is not. Perhaps the most learned and accurate definition is to be found in Gillett's classic 'it may be said nowadays bills drawn to finance the holding or processing of stocks of raw materials, or to enable the drawer to give credit to his customer by hire purchase or by simple credit terms are frequently but not invariably described as Finance Bills. *

The market therefore buys finance bills of three principal types. First, accommodation bills drawn by finance companies and presented to an acceptance house for acceptance. In this case the bank merely lends its 'name' to the bill. Alternatively the accepting house may be given a charge on the goods underlying the bill;

---

* Gillett, *The Bill on London*, p. 21.

second, where a company raises money by drawing bills against stocks of goods or produce (e.g. cotton wool, etc.) in warehouse; third, where exporters of manufactured goods borrow against a general charge (usually a letter of hypothecation) over goods in transit at any given moment. This is an omnibus arrangement which obviates the necessity of obtaining specific charges against each individual shipment of goods over a period of time. The business surrounding all three types of bills generally utilizes revolving acceptance credits where it is a condition that any portion used by the borrower and repaid to the banker during the period of validity of the credit becomes available again automatically upon such reimbursement. It can be appreciated that the credit sanctions an indefinite amount in total, but nevertheless embodies a stated limit as to the amount of bills that may be outstanding at any one time. Bills are usually drawn in large round amounts, the size of the business frequently being such as to impel a number of merchant banks to group together in a syndicate, and the bills to be accepted in agreed proportions.

The question of 'eligibility'‡ at the Bank of England was of course a major consideration of the discount houses in extending their rediscount business. The term 'eligible bill' has always appeared to have been shrouded in mystery chiefly because the Bank had abstained from giving a precise definition or description. In December 1961* it did, however, lay down certain criteria, firstly, 'to maintain the standards of quality long associated with the London prime bank bill and hence its reputation as a liquid asset of undoubted integrity' and secondly, 'to allow reasonable development of bills of all classes as being useful financial instruments some of which, incidentally, bring in modest net earnings of foreign exchange'. Eligibility then is the extent of a bill's acceptability to the Bank itself either for rediscounting, or, as is more usual today, as collateral. The obtaining of 'last-resort' facilities at the Bank is now virtually obsolete because of the Bank's requirement as to the tenor of the bill. The modern practice is to borrow for a week from the Bank against the security of short-bonds, Treasury bills or eligible paper. This is of crucial importance to the discount houses who would not deal in any volume of bills which would not be eligible. The point is emphasized in the *Quarterly Bulletin*:† The

---

* *Bank of England Quarterly Bulletin*, December 1961, p. 29.
† *Bank of England Quarterly Bulletin*, December 1961, p. 29.
‡ See Appendix III for new arrangements since August 1981.

Bank are the arbiters of the type of bill they will purchase or take as security, and retain the right to vary their practice at any time. The Bank, therefore, are never committed in advance to the purchase of any particular bill'.

The Bank has several methods of influencing acceptance business to ensure that the general criteria (quoted above) are complied with. One way was through prior consultation with the acceptance houses particularly when large credits are involved, thus giving the Bank the opportunity to discourage finance bill business, although Bank policy was much more liberal in 1964 and 1965, and indeed has been since. It is interesting to note that the Bank's policy with regard to finance bills has been somewhat of a 'blow hot—blow cold' nature in that it has had several changes in attitude over the years and has usually shown a distinct preference for the traditional 'self-liquidating' bill.

Prior to the first world war there was a considerable volume of finance bills on the market and whilst there was no discrimination against them it is clear from evidence given by the Bank in 1910 to the National Monetary Commission in the United States of America that finance bills were not regarded with much favour. In 1919 the Bank informed the market that only bills covering the movement of goods could be entitled to fine rates of discount. This restriction continued until 1930 when a change of policy was evidenced by the Bank's willingness to discount a small proportion of finance bills drawn by British companies. The chief reasons for this change of attitude were the shortage of Treasury bills and self-liquidating commercial bills coupled with the growth of hire-purchase finance.

The Bank's policy continued to be relaxed during the second world war but from 1950 until the early 1960s it again sought to restrict their use and in September 1965 it announced that it had reduced from 50% to 35% the proportion of inland finance bills it was prepared to accept in its sampling of prime bills from the market. Today, of course, finance bills are a staple of the discount market.

The process of 'sampling' by the Bank is achieved by buying parcels of bills regularly from the discount houses at a small premium under the bank bill rate, and this enables the discount houses to offer good trade bills to the banks as eligible paper. The Bank has, not, however, bought trade bills since April 1970. It would be as well perhaps at this juncture to give a more specific definition of the term 'eligible paper' than that previously stated in general terms. To be eligible at the Bank a commercial bill must carry two good British names, one of which must be the acceptor. The term 'good British names' is generally interpreted as meaning bills accepted by a limited list of well-known banks, all domiciled in Britain or the Commonwealth. To clarify the position the Bank issued a list of eligible names in 1971.

A further method used by the Bank in its endeavour to ensure that the quality of paper in the market remains high is by the examination of the balance sheets of the accepting houses. Naturally, although there is no compulsion involved, any accepting house which wishes to have eligible status accorded by the Bank to its acceptances is only too happy to co-operate and answer any enquiries as a result of the Bank's sampling of bills coming on the market.

The second influence in growth of commercial bills will, as already indicated, be the subject of the second part of this chapter.

The abolition of ad valorem stamp duty of 1/-% on bills of exchange and its replacement by a flat rate of 2d per bill and eventual abolition has also contributed to the growth in the use of commercial bills. The abolition represented a saving on a three-months bill of ⅕% per annum. Whilst this saving may not appear great, it did effectively reduce the cost of bill finance, particularly at the very 'short' end of the market, thereby stimulating growth and flexibility in this sector. It enabled the discount market to become more profitable in a vital sector of their business where small margins and high turnover were the order of the day.

The shift in attitude of the clearing banks towards commercial bills has certainly been influenced in part by the Bank of England's more liberal interpretation of eligibility. They have however been inevitably forced into commercial bills because of the acute shortage of Treasury bills. This shift in emphasis can be clearly seen from Table 2, which shows the main changes in the assets of the London clearing banks.

An added incentive to participate in this business was the ability of the discount market to offer commercial bills to the banks at an attractive premium. For example, in September 1965 prime banks' acceptances offered a yield a full ⅜% better than Treasury bills – such a wide differential being a very unusual occurrence in bill dealing at that time.

The trade in commercial bill business would probably have grown much faster had it not been for the innate conservatism of the banking community as a whole, and their suspicions that trade bills were akin to a lost overdraft (perhaps the spectre of the ghost of the 1930s walking again?) It is only fair to say however that this reticence to change is now being replaced by the realization that, like it or not, new ideas and policies must be accepted and implemented quickly if banking is to remain competitive.

The market's holdings of commercial bills rose almost five times from 1960 to 1970. This revival in the use of commercial bills commenced in 1959 when the restrictions on the use of such bills for financing trade between overseas residents were removed. It is perhaps strange, therefore, that even in 1961 commentators were still describing the dominant position of the Treasury bill when in fact this long-term trade had already been reversed. However, it is no doubt significant that the growing importance of the commercial bill was well recognized by the discount houses themselves in 1960 This was evidenced by the fact that three houses featured segregated commercial bill holdings in their balance sheets: Union Discount showing £24.5 M., Gillett Brothers £8.7 M, and Gerrard & Reid £5.4 M. Other houses who did not segregate their commercial bill holdings announced increases in turnover of between 13% and 20%.

Even in 1973 a number of houses still failed to separate commercial bills from Treasury bills in their annual accounts, and this makes it impossible to estimate the true extent of the sector's growth. The figures published by the Bank of England are for the market as a whole and only relate to bills detailed in portfolio at the date of the return.

However, as can be seen from Table 1 (*see* p. 20) the size of the market's holdings of commercial bills rose steadily from £249 M. in 1963 to £697 M. in 1970. This represented a increase of 11% from 19% to 30% as a percentage of the market's total assets. The increase was occasioned by the wide use of bills by borrowers as a means of circumventing the continuing severe restrictions on bank advances. Understandably, the authorities decided that the resurgence in the use of commercial bills constituted a threat to the implemention of monetary policy. Subsequently, in May 1965 the Bank of England requested the discount houses and banks to restrict their commercial bill holdings to 5% over the twelve months from end-March. In practice this meant that the market could discount fresh bills only to the extent that bills purchased earlier had matured.

During the 1960s the market was often placed in an untenable position; on the one hand it was exhorted by the authorities to curb

Table 2

MAIN ASSETS OF LONDON CLEARING BANKS

£M. (% of gross deposits in brackets)

End of period	1958	1962	1966	1970	1974	1978
MONEY AT CALL AND SHORT NOTICE TO:						
Money Market	N.A.	590 (7·5)	852 (9·0)	1,225 (11·6)	1,157 (4·5)	N.A.
Other	N.A.	196 (2·5)	319 (3·4)	365 (3·4)	106 (0·4)	N.A.
Total	587 (8·2)	786 (10·0)	1,171 (12·4)	1,590 (15·0)	1,263 (4·9)	1,526 (13·4)
PRIVATE SECTOR						
Advances	2,126 (29·5)	3,506 (44·4)	4,492 (47·3)	5,597 (52·8)	16,047 (63·0)	22,455 (50·6)
Comm. Bills	135 (1·9)	268 (3·4)	474 (5·0)	764 (7·2)	687 (2·7)	742 (1·7)
Total	226 (31·4)	3,774 (47·8)	4,966 (52·3)	6,361 (60·0)	16,734 (65·7)	23,197 (52·3)
PUBLIC SECTOR						
T. Bills	1,185 (16·5)	986 (12·5)	681 (7·2)	406 (3·8)	273 (1·1)	329 (0·7)
Govt. Stocks	1,994 (27·7)	1,204 (15·2)	1,040 (10·9)	873 (8·2)	1,246 (4·9)	1,924 (4·3)
Total	3,179 (44·2)	2,190 (27·7)	1,721 (18·1)	1,279 (12·0)	1,519 (6·0)	2,253 (5·0)
Gross Deposits	7,199	7,903	9,501	10,606	25,511	44,354

Source: Bank of England Statistical Abstract

its commercial bill business, whilst at the same time it was often faced with a shortage of Treasury bills, the supply of which is controlled by these same authorities.

THE COMMERCIAL BILLS POST 1971

One of the prime claims of the Bank's paper 'Competition and Credit Control' was that amongst other things it provided a much more equitable climate in which every sector of the financial markets could operate. Unfortunately, the new framework has created an anomalous situation in the commercial bill market with regard to eligible and ineligible acceptances. The distinction between the two achieved a crucial significance because under the 1972 arrangements only bills which are on the Bank's Official List of Acceptances qualify as reserve assets for the banks whereas, prior to October 1971, the clearing banks could include all bank bills and trade bills in their computation of liquid assets. There is also a further restriction on eligible bills in so far as the banking sector is concerned, since their holdings are limited to 2% of eligible liabilities. Additionally, the discount market's holdings are constrained by their public sector debt requirements, thus these two factors are effectively stifling the growth of the market. This may be precisely the intention of the Bank, in which case it is a somewhat blunt instrument.

The feeling in banking parlours is that the position could readily be rectified without in any way reducing the effectiveness of the Bank's control. This could be achieved by conferring the cachet of eligibility* (as a reserve asset) without extending the privilege of rediscountability at the Bank. The Official List of eligible names has strong historical and traditional ties and includes the clearing banks, the members of the Acceptance House Committee, a few old-established customers of the Bank, and the Commonwealth banks. Amongst the ineligible names are a number of the clearing banks' subsidiaries, the French and American banks, and other foreign banks. A situation now exists where banks of international repute, who finance trade by bills, are having to concede a large premium on their discounts, whereas the bills of a small developer or finance house on an eligible name suffer no such discrimination. The result is that many banks have withdrawn from the market. It would also appear to run contrary to the London market's traditional emphasis on the self-liquidating bill as the present system

---

* Granted in 1981 under new control arrangements.

could be said to encourage accommodation bills to the detriment of the genuine trade bill.

The market's business in trade bills received a boost even before the implementation of the new regulations when the discount houses freed the Fine Bank Bill rate in August 1971. For a time competition was intense and the acceptance credit became fully competitive with the banker's prime overdraft rate, but during 1972 this sector of the bill market declined as companies found other cheaper methods of raising finance. The changing climate in this market merely indicates the differentials that can occur between one sector of the London market and another. One advantage that a discount house has over a bank in the context of trade bills is that when a bank discounts a bill it may be likened to an overdraft, and as such the banker must ensure that his reserve asset position does not deteriorate below the mandatory limit. There is also a marginal advantage for a discount house stemming from the fact that a rate of discount gives a higher yield on a given amount than a rate of interest. Thus the discount house could quote $\frac{5}{8}\%$ for money and $\frac{5}{8}\%$ on bills and obtain a useful turn on the deal.

One area of the bill market which deserves mention is the extension in the use of acceptances to the nationalized industries. In May 1972 the Treasury gave their sanction to the use of bills in payment to suppliers.

As a result of the pressures of the 50% public sector debt ratio and the low demand resulting from the availability of cheaper sources of finance in the form of overdrafts, the amount of commercial bills held by the discount houses fell from £697 M. in 1970 to £586M. in 1971 and £565 M. in 1972. However, with the introduction of the 'undefined asset multiple' in 1973 the trend in commercial bill holdings resumed its upward trend. Discount houses increasingly substituted commercial bills and other private-sector assets for public-sector assets with the result that the undefined asset multiple rose from an initial level of 13·8 times on 15 August 1973 to 19·1 times on 20 March 1974. Since then it has fluctuated between about 16 and 19·5.

Commercial bills were also used, especially during 1976 and 1977, as an alternative to overdrafts, at times when the base rates of the clearing banks have been high relative to money market rates.

Perhaps the most important reason for the continued growth in the use of commercial bills was the so-called 'corset' or Supplementary Special Deposits scheme. This was introduced in 1973 and basically sets limits on the rate of growth of banks' interest bearing eligible liabilities (I.B.E.Ls). If the growth exceeded the permitted limit the offending bank had to place non-interest bearing Supplementary Special Deposits with the Bank of England. The amount rose with the amount of the excess. The result was that banks looked for ways of meeting their customer's borrowing needs without increasing their I.B.E.L.s into the penalty area. One of the most common methods was to encourage customers, and also the subsidiaries of the clearing banks, to borrow by way of bank-accepted commercial bills. These were then sold to others outside the banking system. To such holders, bank bills are as liquid and as safe as a Certificate of Deposit of comparable term, while being a close substitute for bank advances for the borrower. Such 'disintermediation' as it is known, did however have significant advantages as far as the banks were concerned. The alternative was to lend to their customers or subsidiaries by way of overdraft or loan and finance this by issuing a Certificate of Deposit to a non-bank customer. This did however, have the effect of increasing the bank's I.B.E.L.s, thus taking it nearer to the corset limits, as well as putting pressure on its reserve asset ratio. As far as the economy as a whole is concerned, the result is a cosmetic reduction in £M3 with little effect on credit or liquidity.

The corset was abandoned in June 1980 however, and after that time substantial 'reintermediation' occurred, with a resultant decline in the use of commercial bills.

4 The Treasury bill

In this chapter we will be concerning ourselves with an examination of the reasons for the contraction in holdings of Treasury bills by the discount market.

The second world war and the period of inflationary finance which followed it saw a huge expansion of the Treasury bill issue. Table 3 shows the holdings of Treasury bills outside the public sector from the late fifties to 1979. It will be observed that Treasury bill holdings reached a huge level in the later fifties but that the sixties saw a steady decline to a level which left holdings lower than at any time since the war.

Treasury bills issued through the tender fell by nearly a third between 1960 and 1966 from £3,480 M. to £2,190 M. and by 1969 to only £1,390 M. This decline had been the result of a fall in the deficit in the public sector and successive credit restrictions which have called for a reduction in the liquidity of the banking system. The change in government debt policy is clearly illustrated by the fact that the average amount of bills issued at the average weekly tender fell from £232 M. in 1964 to £145 M. in 1968, whilst in the first two months of 1969 it was the only £100 M. (although perhaps not strictly representative because this is the seasonal low point).

The discount market's holdings of Treasury bills has remained fairly constant over the period 1959 to 1969 despite their reduced availability generally. The reason for this apparent paradox can be seen in the syndicate's committal to tendering for all the bills offered when frequently outside competition was reduced owing to a general expectation that interest rates would rise. Consequently, the market has found itself obliged to take up more bills than it would otherwise have done, thus maintaining its holdings. During this period there has been a simultaneous growth in commercial bill holdings which is discussed in Chapter 3.

Table 3

HOLDINGS OF TREASURY BILLS OUTSIDE THE
PUBLIC SECTOR 1955–1979

[£M.] End of	London Clearing Banks	Discount Market	Overseas Official Holdings	Other	Total
1955	1,271	652	961	679	3,563
1956	1,275	523	927	643	3,368
1957	1,403	585	821	579	3,388
1958	1,185	594	891	764	3,434
1959	1,215	635	958	722	3,530
1960	1,017	574	923	975	3,489
1961	1,106	533	1,076	596	3,311
1962	1,067	502	1,023	450	3,042
1963	996	529	1,045	496	3,066
1964	764	453	1,100	374	2,691
1965	784	484	1,027	357	2,652
1966	650	424	1,238	330	2,642
1967	508	548	1,753	347	3,156
1968	518	471	2,466	249	3,704
1969	394	399	1,780	137	2,710
1970	406	876	772	190	2,244
1971	199	871	727	385	2,182
1972	231	475	886	127	1,719
1973	309	321	539	232	1,401
1974	273	721	1,577	372	2,943
1975	912	819	1,069	1,421	4,221
1976	795	563	448	1,245	3,051
1977	710	1,052	334	1,760	3,856
1978	329	845	431	988	2,593
1979	474	709	513	908	2,604

Source: Financial Statistics

The year 1959–60 was a significant one for Lombard Street as it was at this time that the findings of the Radcliffe Committee were published. Perhaps the concern of the market was best summed up by William King* when he commented that 'the Radcliffe enquiry has set at rest some recurrent doubts about the future of the market, has disclosed to the general public some hitherto little known facts about its methods of working, and has provided the first comprehensive official statistics of its operations and of its relationship to other parts of the banking structure'. It is interesting to note that King goes on to express some surprise that the esti-

---

* *The Banker*, August 1960, p. 468. 'New Lights on the Bill Market.'

mates of bill holdings given in his annual series of articles on the discount market were invariably overstated whereas the bond holdings were estimated with reasonable accuracy. The yearly overestimation of bill holdings was in the region of £100 M. The Radcliffe figures also showed that in 1957, for example, at the seasonal low point the market's holdings of Treasury bills fell to as little as £226 M., which was a much smaller figure than had been previously assessed. Other factors which also materially affected the situation were the large seasonal variations in issue and substantial changes in demand which resulted from the banks varying the structure of their money market assets as between call money and bills. A further aspect of the question of estimating bill portfolios which was not readily appreciated at that time, was the large distortions which could and did occur, from an appraisal of balance sheet figures, notably because of the effect on these of 'window dressing' by the banks and the discount market.

Table 4 below reveals the extraordinary effect that the latter has upon the market's bill holdings at the end of the calendar year. In the last two weeks of 1959 the market's aggregate holding of Treasury bills rose by more than 20%; over the same period in 1960 it rose by approximately 25%.

Table 4

DISCOUNT MARKET
TREASURY BILL HOLDINGS
1959 AND 1960

1959	March 18	351
	June 17	341
	September 16	396
	December 16	526
	December 31	635
1960	March 16	446
	June 15	467
	September 21	390
	December 14	458
	December 31	574

Source: Bank of England Quarterly Bulletin. Abstracted from Table 5, p. 32, March 1961, and December 1961, p. 46.

The aggregate tender issue had risen by June 1960 to £3,490 M. – some £500 M. more than a year previously. Despite this increased availability of Treasury bills it is notable that as the result of 'outside' competition at mid-December 1960, which is close to the Treasury's seasonal borrowing peak, the market was actually carrying a smaller portfolio than at mid-June 1960.

The year 1961 was certainly a crisis year for the market chiefly as a result of Bank rate being increased from 5% to 7% (in July) for only the second time in forty years. The discount houses appeared to weather the storm better than on the previous occasions in 1955–6 and 1957, doubtless mainly because the period of stress was of much shorter duration; Bank rate being held at the peak level for only ten weeks as compared with six months in 1957–8.

It is interesting however to chart the changes of the market's bill portfolio over the year. During the first quarter, when the houses' bill holdings usually fall (the 'revenue' quarter) they dropped by £130 M. and it was believed that part of the reduction was the consequence of increased holdings of commercial bills. These increases in holdings of commercial paper were probably associated with sales by overseas banks from which foreign funds were being withdrawn. The external pressures on the pound were mounting and between March and June the total outflow of funds abroad was approximately £200 M. The largest component of this loss was thought to be a withdrawal of funds from Treasury bills. Towards the end of June, however, when the market feeling was that interest rates would rise, to protect the market the discount houses were switching out of bonds into Treasury bills. Bond holdings decreased from £397 M. to £364 M. whilst Treasury bill holdings increased from £328 M. to £345 M.

An additional factor which materially assisted the market in this process was the reluctance of outside tenderers to tender. This is, of course, in marked contrast with the experience when rates are expected to fall. Ultimately the discount houses obtained 66% of the bills on offer.

Not unexpectedly, after the increase in Bank rate there was a rush for bills by the banks and also from overseas buyers which drove the market's holdings down by £48 M. in the quarter to mid-September to £297 M. – the lowest September figure in the twelve years for which figures were then available. This trend was again reversed in the last quarter of the year. Bank rate was lowered to 6½% on October 5 and by a further ½% on November 2. Moreover, there was a widespread conviction in Lombard Street that a further reduction could be expected early in 1962; thus there was a continuing demand for Treasury bills particularly by those houses whose accounting date was end-December. The three largest discount houses publish their accounts early in the year and they were especially concerned to meet the demand for Treasury bills without an extensive fall in their own holdings as they generally wished to show them as roughly equal to or in excess of their bond holdings. Consequently, by mid-December the market's Treasury bill portfolio had risen to £428 M., and to £533 M. by end-December.

The year 1962 continued to be extremely competitive for the discount houses, the outside competition at the tenders hardly abating in the renewed hopes of still lower interest rates. The market's problems in the first quarter were doubtless aggravated by the seasonal decline in the bill issue, and bills allotted at the tenders in the first six months of 1962 averaged only 42% of applications, as against 47% in 1960. Bank rate was reduced to $5\frac{1}{2}$% on March 8 and thereafter in stages to $4\frac{1}{2}$% on April 26. The authorities took full advantage of this downward movement in rates to transfer government finance to marketable securities from floating debt by making substantial funding sales. These operations resulted in significant changes in the composition of the National Debt. There was a decline of nearly £1,100 M. in the total Treasury bill issue, whereas in the previous year there had been an increase of some £680 M. The total of marketable securities, however, rose by £1,200 M. It can therefore be appreciated that the market's difficulties in maintaining an adequate bill portfolio were exacerbated by this reduction in the total available supply. Despite these difficulties the market succeeded in raising its holdings to £502 M. by end-December 1962.

The market's Treasury bill book was largely stabilized by the end of 1963 at £529 M. although the general trend over the preceding ten years had been downwards. It is notable, however, that the scarcity of Treasury bills has seen a counterpart upward trend in bond portfolios (and also commercial paper) as clearly illustrated in Table 5. These movements have altered very considerably the asset structure of the market. Formerly, even when Treasury bill business had been running at a loss or at a minimal profit, the bond book was always smaller than the Treasury bill book.

Although the volume of bills issued through the tenders was still moving downwards, it was much less than in the preceding three years. The total issued in the peak year of 1960 was £14,000 M., falling to £12,000 M. by 1962, and slightly less in 1963. Indeed, it would seem that 1963 marked the discount market's worst point in this respect as several houses commented in their annual state-

Table 5

DISCOUNT MARKET ASSETS

£M. [%]

End of	Government securities £M.	%	Treasury bills £M.	%	Commercial & other sterling bills £M.	%	Local authority securities £M.	%	Sterling Certificates of Deposit £M.	%	Other sterling assets £M.	%	U.S. Dollar Certificates of Deposit £M.	%	Other currency assets £M.	%	Total
1958	321	30·5	594	56·4	70	6·6	—	—	—	—	68	6·5	—	—	—	—	1,053
1963	442	33·9	529	40·5	249	19·0	17	1·3	—	—	68	5·2	—	—	—	—	1,305
1964	438	34·1	453	35·3	302	23·5	39	3·0	—	—	51	4·0	—	—	—	—	1,283
1965	500	34·4	484	33·3	339	23·3	67	4·6	—	—	65	4·5	—	—	—	—	1,455
1966	542	34·6	424	27·1	404	25·8	101	6·5	—	—	94	6·0	—	—	—	—	1,565
1967	544	31·1	548	34·4	437	25·0	115	6·6	—	—	89	5·1	14	0·8	—	—	1,747
1968	306	18·4	471	28·3	560	33·7	148	8·9	56	3·4	83	5·0	39	2·3	—	—	1,663
1969	364	20·0	399	22·0	629	34·6	192	10·6	97	5·3	104	5·7	32	1·7	—	—	1,817
1970	160	6·8	876	37·2	697	29·6	224	9·5	268	11·4	88	3·7	39	1·7	—	—	2,352
1971	391	12·8	871	28·4	586	19·1	478	15·6	457	14·9	175	5·5	108	3·5	—	—	3,066
1972	112	4·3	475	18·1	565	21·6	636	24·3	458	17·5	219	8·4	153	5·8	—	—	2,618
1973	48	1·8	321	12·2	684	26·1	379	14·5	922	35·2	138	5·4	113	4·3	16	0·6	2,621
1974	10	0·3	729	24·1	1,370	45·3	344	11·4	395	13·1	83	2·7	86	2·8	9	0·3	3,026
1975	96	3·4	819	29·1	980	34·8	400	14·2	303	10·8	72	2·6	129	4·6	15	0·5	2,814
1976	261	8·8	563	19·0	1,019	34·5	375	12·7	403	13·6	56	1·9	175	5·9	17	0·6	1,957
1977	557	14·2	1,052	26·8	1,213	30·8	351	8·9	509	12·9	105	2·7	115	2·9	32	0·8	3,934
1978	454	10·5	845	19·6	2,038	47·3	384	8·9	333	7·7	160	3·7	75	1·8	19	0·5	4,308
1979	754	15·4	709	14·4	2,638	53·7	511	10·4	84	1·7	82	1·7	109	2·2	22	0·5	4,909

Source: Bank of England Statistical Abstract, No.2 (1975) and update.

ments on the paucity in the supply of Treasury bills. One house pointed to the fact that its turnover in Treasury bills was the lowest for fourteen years.

The first quarter of 1964 showed an improvement of some £170 M. with total issues at £2,790 M. and by March 31 the amount of all outstanding Treasury bills was £4,418 M. In the second quarter of 1964 the Treasury bills allotted at the tenders were continuing to rise sharply; £2,980 M. was allotted and in the third quarter the figure was as high as £3,230 M. – the highest figure for that quarter since 1961. Fortunately for the market, outside tenders were kept to a minimum by the weakness of sterling which inevitably meant recurrent speculation about a possible increase in Bank rate. Consequently the discount houses were able to increase their share of the allotments until by end-September the market's book totalled £478 M. which was in marked contrast to the small increase in the similar period of 1963.

The final months of 1964 again saw the market struggling to maintain its holdings of Treasury bills. The last quarter of the year is seasonally the Exchequer's borrowing peak and a time when the market's book usually rises. The dominant influence, however, in the day-to-day operation of the market during November and December was the foreign exchange crisis and the upheaval in money rates. The primary effect of this was that the clearing banks found their balances falling as customers switched out of sterling. The discount houses were then called upon to meet the banks' demands for repayment of call money. (The mechanics of this situation with regard to Treasury bills are that as a result of the outflow of money overseas, the Exchequer benefits from the large inflow of sterling into the Exchange Equalization Account in exchange for foreign currencies. The upshot of these transfers is a sharp reduction in the amount of Treasury bills offered weekly at the tender.) These factors then caused a drop in the market's holdings by £25 M. to £453 M. – the lowest end-December figure since 1960.

The market and indeed the banking system generally were again under liquidity pressure early in January 1965 as substantial sums continued to accrue to the Exchequer through the Exchange Equalization Account. In these circumstances the banks and discount houses' holdings of Treasury bills fell by some £550 M. Competition from outside tenderers continued to be strong in the first three months in the persistent hopes of a reduction in Bank rate. Subsequently the shortage of Treasury bills became so acute that the houses found it difficult to maintain a sufficient proportion of

Treasury paper in the security they lodged with banks as security for loans. A further indication of the extent of the shortage was seen to manifest itself when the Bank was sometimes unable to purchase bills of an appropriate maturity when last-resort assistance was required.

Reference to Table 5 shows clearly the changes in the market's asset structure. It will be noticed that after 1958 the decline in the proportion of Treasury bills to all assets became persistent, falling to approximately one-third by the end of 1965 when the total of bonds exceeded that of Treasury bills. The proportion of resources in public sector assets fell below 70% as against 90% ten years before.

The year 1966 saw the introduction of modified arrangements for influencing the discount market when the bank began to lend money to the market overnight at Bank rate and also at current market rates. These new, more flexible techniques assisted the market in its efforts to obtain reasonable allotments at the tenders, but competition remained strong for what were very small offerings. During October and November only £150 M. of bills were offered each week, with maturities frequently in excess of this amount. The offerings at tenders continued to decline because the Exchequer's need for funds diminished and official sales of gilt-edged securities were considerable so that recourse to Treasury bill finance lessened.

The year 1967 opened with a reduction of Bank rate on January 26 from 7% to 6½% as sterling strengthened. The banking sector's holdings of government debt declined considerably by £361 M. and the weekly Treasury bill offer ran at £130 M. in January and was down to £120 M. in February, which was the lowest figure for twenty years. Total bills offered in February were £480 M. as compared with £620 M. for the same period in 1966. Official pressure at this time to keep the discount rate up, together with increased demand from outsiders, resulted in the market's poor allotments from an attenuated bill supply. This continuing downward trend in the total supply of bills was clearly evident since on March 31 tender bills outstanding amounted to only £1,750 M. – a reduction of £430 M. on 31 March 1966. Bank rate was further reduced in two stages, once on March 16 and again on May 4 to 5½% thus making funding sales difficult. At the same time the authorities' own borrowing needs were rising and consequently the amount of Treasury bills offered at tender rose steadily so that by December weekly issues exceeded £200 M. It is interesting to note that from May to

July, when much of the Exchequer's heavy recourse to borrowing took place, the discount market's total assets changed little (they actually showed a small reduction), but within the total the holding of Treasury bills increased sharply from £219 M. to £436 M. Outside the market there were fears that there might be a rise in Bank rate which effectively curbed competition at the tenders, enabling the market to rebuild its portfolio.

Following devaluation in November, the market received considerable assistance from the Bank as the clearing banks called in funds to meet sales of sterling and the market's total assets rose by some £160 M., mainly as a consequence of substantial purchases of short-dated bonds. The year 1968 was the first since 1963 to break the downward trend in holdings of Treasury bills when the market's book stood at £548 M. by end-December.

Mr D. C. G. Jessel, chairman of Jessel, Toynbee & Co., commented in his annual report to shareholders on 31 March 1968 that 'as is often the case in the discount market, circumstances forced us to carry an excessively large number of Treasury bills on rising rates. This is mainly due to the market's agreement to cover the Treasury bill tender each week regardless of the economic outlook. In contrast when rates were falling we have been unable to buy enough bills owing to outside competition', thus highlighting one of the market's perpetual problems, and the year 1968 was no exception. In the first quarter the total assets of the market fell by some £288 M. wholly as the result of low Treasury bills instead of by overnight borrowing in order that cash shortages would not be carried forward day by day.

Reference to Table 5 indicates that the market's Treasury bill portfolio at end-December had risen to £471 M. – admittedly a fall of £77 M. over the previous year but a considerable increase on the holdings at the end of the three previous quarters (all being under £300 M.). The reason for this large increase was the change in the pattern of Exchequer finance and the fact that three of the largest discount houses make up their annual accounts at end-year. The pattern of holdings again showed a substantial fall of £210 M. in the first quarter of 1969 to £261 M. They declined still further to £212 M. by September but increased to £399 M. by end-December. The picture changed dramatically, however, during 1970; after a fall of some £200 M. between December 1969 and March 1970 the houses' portfolio increased in the following quarters by £162 M., £154 M., and a massive £362 M. (in December quarter) totalling a record £876 M. held in the market's book by end-December 1970.

During this same period the discount houses' holdings of gilt-edged securities were reduced from £364 M. (at end-December 1969) to £160 M. by December 1970. Thus, in part, the increase in Treasury bill holdings was to counterbalance the sale of government securities which in turn was influenced by weakness in the gilt-edged market. The position was also affected by redemptions of various government securities, the largest of which were 3% Savings Bonds 1960–70. This stock created a particular problem for the authorities because it had been issued during the war to mainly private holders. Consequently, when a stock is dispersed in this way it is almost impossible for the authorities to spread the impact of redemption over a long period by buying stock well in advance of maturity. Two further factors also influenced the situation: many investors had purchased this stock in 1969 because yields had reached very high levels, but they were unable to sell the stock for twelve months if they wished to avoid payment of short-term capital gains tax. There was, however, a considerable tax advantage to a large number of investors disposing of their stock before July 27. This stemmed from the fact that registered holders of the stock on July 27 would be paid the dividend, whereas sellers before that date received a price which was adjusted to include accrued interest since the date of the previous dividend. The foregoing serves to illustrate the ramifications of debt management which face the authorites and puts the lie to 'simple' solutions to the problems which are sometimes propounded.

Large issues of Treasury bills were made to absorb surplus liquidity and in August and September the offerings at the weekly tender were the largest since September 1967. For example, on August 28 and September 4 offerings were made of £250 M. and £220 M. respectively. It is, of course, well known that the amount of Treasury bills offered at the weekly tender varies with the authorities' desire for flexibility* in the market. Thus they can create shortages of funds from week to week and in so doing achieve a measure of control over short-term rates by deciding how shortages should be relieved. This policy was reflected in the discount houses' record holdings of Treasury bills (£876 M.) in December 1970. The houses received substantial allotments and made very

---

* The methods by which the authorities intervene in the money market are fully described in 'The Management of Money Day by Day', *Bank of England Quarterly Bulletin*, March 1963, pp. 15–19.

few sales chiefly because they would not lower their tender price as this would have meant incurring a loss if any sales had been made. The attraction of this record portfolio would also be influenced by the need for liquidity as the revenue season approached, allied with growing expectations of a reduction in Bank rate. The position at end-March 1971, however, indicated a sharp reduction in the Treasury bill portfolio; the market's holdings falling by an enormous £680 M. to £198 M. The Bank's purchases were made 'on a scale unprecedented on any normal business day' and had arisen as the result of severe cash shortages arising from a concentration of delayed tax payments and government payments.

Treasury bills issued through the tender at end-March 1970 were £1,190 M. and had increased to £1,780 M. by March 1971, thus arresting the declining trend of recent years. (In the year 1968–9 there was a £700 M. reduction and £150 M. in 1969–70).

The market has been faced with a marked shortage of Treasury bills for some years reflecting the run-down of the government's short-term debt. The reasonably stable pattern of holdings in Treasury bills (seasonal swings apart) serves to illustrate perhaps, in the Bank's eyes, the *raison d'être* of the discount market in its ability to regularly take up bills at the weekly tender. For many years now the margins between Treasury bill yields and borrowing costs have been narrow and therefore not very profitable. The amazing consistency of the houses in this sector was shown when their bid at the weekly tender remained unchanged for a period of twenty-one weeks from mid-August until mid-January 1971. Such stability is unprecedented in times of an active monetary policy. The discount markets' portfolio of Treasury bills has fluctuated, as a percentage of total assets, from 40% in 1962 down to 22% in 1969. The exceptionally low figure of 11% was recorded at end-March 1971 and stemmed from large purchases of bills by the Bank to relieve severe cash shortages in the money market. Despite large inflows of funds from overseas and heavy demands for gilt-edged stocks, these flows tended to neutralize one another. Thus the shortages were occasioned by such factors as the postal strike, delayed tax payments, and the disruption of payments generally caused through closure of the banks in preparation for decimalization. In all, the houses' holdings of Treasury bills fell by £680 M. in the quarter ended March 1971. By end-December 1971 the market's holdings of Treasury bills had risen to some 28% of total assets.

TREASURY BILLS POST 1971

One of the most important changes for the discount market brought by Competition and Credit Control was the requirement that at least 50% of funds should be held in public sector debt. What was perhaps more significant was that the Bank stated that the 50% conformed 'closely with the present average practice of the market as a whole'. However, Table 5 shows that the last time holdings of public sector exceeded 50% was in 1967 when they amounted to 62%. Subsequently, in 1968 the proportion dropped to 47%, in 1969 to 42% and 1970 to 44%.

This 50% ratio caused considerable problems for the discount houses. They had been running down their gilt-edged portfolio for many years and had no wish to increase holdings of gilts to maintain the public sector debt ratio. At the same time it was difficult for them to increase holdings of Treasury bills. Government spending was relatively low at this point and was being funded by long-dated stocks, thus issues of Treasury bills were small. The result was a shortage in the supply of Treasury bills. The problems were compounded by the requirement for competitive bidding at the tender by discount houses and the increased demand for Treasury bills by banks trying to build up reserve assets. The result was that Treasury bill rates were forced down to very low levels and, indeed, the yield was below the cost of borrowed money for considerable periods. Discount houses increasingly looked to local authority bills to make up their public sector debt ratio. The new regulations also marked the abandonment of the syndicated bid of the discount houses at the weekly Treasury bill tender. The cartel had its origins in the 1930s when it was agreed that the houses should tender for bills at the same price, and be allocated in proportions based on a formula related to their individual capital resources. The commitment to cover the tender in full still remains, however, and in return the Bank continues to provide the discount houses with exclusive last-resort facilities. From time to time this arrangement has been subject to considerable criticism on the grounds that it contains an element of charade, and certainly the evidence of the Bank to the Radcliffe Committee in 1959 was not accepted. The Bank's claim was that the agreement was necessary to ensure that the financial needs of the central government are met. The flaw in their reasoning is that if there is a shortage of money in the market which prevented the houses taking up the bills at the tender, then the authorities would still have to provide the money to cover the bid. Nevertheless, the system does provide the Bank with control over short-term money rates because they can engineer shortages or surpluses of funds in the market, whichever is appropriate.

October 9 1972 saw the demise of Bank rate and in its place the introduction of the Minimum Lending Rate. The new rate is fixed every Friday and is based on the average rate of discount for Treasury bills at the last tender plus ½% and rounded to the nearest ¼% above. It has been suggested that the abolition of Bank rate and the substitution of the M.L.R. has reduced the authorities' control over the level of the Treasury bill rate, and placed considerable influence in the hands of the discount market. A moment's consideration of the position, however, reveals that the market could only influence the rate in the very short-term. This could be achieved if the amount of bills on offer was small and the discount market were to bid heavily for them, thereby keeping the rate lower than the existing M.L.R. If the Bank had intended the M.L.R. to be increased, the authorities could redress the position by fixing their own buying rate for Treasury bills below the tender rate, thus causing losses for the discount market. On the other hand, if the market were to tender at too low a price and the authorities did not wish to see the M.L.R. rise, then they could tender internally at a higher price, or choose not to allot all the bills. Furthermore, the Bank still reserves the right to change the M.L.R. on Thursdays, as was customary with Bank rate, or at other times to effect a major shift in economic policy following, say, new budgetary measures. As pointed out in the previous section, Bank rate had increasingly become less meaningful, particularly from the mid-1960s, as a means of controlling the level of interest rates in the economy. For example, the pressing needs of the local authorities frequently created an interest arbitrage in London well in excess of Bank rate thereby frustrating the Bank's intentions. More recently, the clearing banks and the finance houses fixed their own deposit rates and base rates for lending, regardless of the level of Bank rate. Finally, in October 1972, Bank rate ceased to be a penal rate for last resort borrowings when the Treasury bill rate moved above it. The abolition of Bank rate also had important connotations both for the domestic economy and for international investment: when Bank rate was moved up or down it was frequently misinterpreted as indicating a significant shift in economic policy rather than a purely technical adjustment in the rate.

The shortage of Treasury bills continued through 1972 and 1973 because of the small amount of bills offered at the weekly tender. Issues fell to as low as £60 M. per week, in particular during the whole of July 1972 and again in February 1973. Despite a large increase in the government's borrowing requirement, sales of debt outside the banking system, special deposits, and heavy currency outflows provided most of the finance. Indeed, Treasury bills were so scarce in 1973 that the Bank of England was forced to make substantial purchases of commercial bills and local authority bills and bonds, and even deposited funds in the short-term local authority market when providing assistance to the discount houses. Traditionally the Bank of England only bought or lent against Treasury bills.

By July 1973 it was recognized that the 50% ratio was causing serious distortions in money market interest rates. Discount houses were bidding strongly for Treasury bills, thereby forcing down the discount rate (and consequently Minimum Lending Rate). At the same time they were reluctant to buy private sector assets such as commercial bills which pushed these rates up.

The public sector debt ratio was therefore abolished in July 1973. In its place was substituted a rule that private sector assets could be held up to a maximum of twenty times capital plus reserves. This reduced the need for discount houses to bid so strongly for Treasury bills and restored the traditional differentials in money market rates, however, in November 1973 the formula linking Minimum Lending Rate to the average rate of discount at the tender was abandoned.

During 1974 and 1975 the amount of Treasury bills issued increased substantially in view of the large P.S.B.R. and difficulties in selling gilts. Similarly, because of their obligation to cover the tender, holdings of Treasury bills by discount houses increased substantially – there is in fact a direct relationship between the amount of Treasury bills issued and discount houses' holdings since they tend to be residual holders while the demand by other holders tends to be relatively stable. The result was that the Bank of England was again able to provide most of the lender of last resort assistance needed by purchasing Treasury bills and local authority bills.

A growing demand for Treasury bills from outside the banking system is evident from Table 3, during 1975, and in order to meet this demand Treasury bills with a denomination of £1 M. were made available from November 1975 – previously the largest denomination had been £250,000.

Table 6 shows the discount market's holdings of Treasury bills since 1973. It is particularly noticeable that average holdings since 1975, have been significantly higher than in preceding years. This can be partly explained by the fact that, because of the economic recession in this country, there was for a time some falling off in the use made of commercial bills as a source of finance for industrial and commercial companies. This has obliged the discount houses to hold a higher proportion of Treasury paper. In addition, the average size of the Treasury bill issue has increased greatly in the last few years. In 1973, it was £100 M., in 1975, £268 M., and in 1976 it was £460 M. These large issues have been the result of the authorities' intermittent difficulties in selling gilt-edged stock to the public, consequently the Bank of England has been forced to rely upon short-term residual financing through increasingly large issues of Treasury bills.

Table 6

DISCOUNT MARKET HOLDINGS OF U.K. AND NORTHERN IRELAND
TREASURY BILLS 1973–9

			£M				*£M*
1973	21	March	300	1977	16	March	844
	20	June	261		15	June	1,245
	19	September	206		21	September	917
	12	December	269		14	December	1,052
1974	20	March	209	1978	15	March	800
	19	June	213		21	June	505
	18	September	574		20	September	707
	11	December	535		18	December	845
1975	19	March	412	1979	21	March	643
	18	June	728		20	June	507
	17	September	996		19	September	442
	10	December	829		12	December	709
1976	17	March	1,203				
	16	June	803				
	15	September	1,284				
	8	December	563				

The discount houses were obliged to take up these issues during a period of uncertainty and fears that interest rates would rise. They were anxious to keep their portfolios small, but they were still obliged to tender for all the Treasury bills issued each Friday. In the circumstances it became increasingly difficult to find enough buyers of Treasury bills amongst traditional holders, and consequently the houses began to seek customers for the paper outside the banking system. They approached companies all over the country in an attempt to interest them in using the discount market as a means of gaining access to the attractive yields available on money market assets. The houses have already met great success in their search for new markets, primarily because industrial companies are currently holding large liquid reserves in anticipation of more favourable trading conditions in the future and the consequent need for investment. However, an unfortunate result of this success is that major companies are now tendering through their banks on their own behalf, thereby cutting supplies of bills to the market. This can be most undesirable when the issue is low, as it was during the boom in gilt-edged stock (from 10 December to 4 March 1977 the weekly issue was as low as £300 M.), since Treasury bills are a vital element in the asset structure of the discount houses.

5 The short-bond market

It is perhaps as well to ask at the outset of this chapter why the discount houses operate in the short-bond market, and also to define the term 'short-bond'.

After the second world war the growth of the government's funded debt showed the clear necessity for market facilities on a larger scale than could be provided by Stock Exchange jobbers alone, and it also gave encouragement to the discount market's responsibility in this sphere. Official recognition of the help that the market could afford in developing a wider and more effective bond market came from the Bank when the discount houses were given jobbers' facilities for government bonds having a final maturity date of not longer than five years.* Furthermore, it was made clear to them that the authorities would approve of the market's holding a reasonable amount of such securities, and that such bonds would be eligible security at the Bank if the need to borrow were to arise.

The term 'short' now perhaps has a slightly wider meaning than the purely technical definition, as all stocks automatically become 'shorts' as they approach maturity. Thus the market frequently purchases long-dated securities which are due to mature shortly, mainly from the institutional investors who are seeking a higher return on their money. By 1967, £50 M. of securities were in fact held by the discount market which were outside the traditional five-year range.

It was at one time widely believed that by operating in the short-bond market, the discount houses provided a great shock-absorbing cushion. But, as the acknowledged expert W. T. C. King pointed out, this function was frequently overrated. The discount houses certainly at times, when small quantities of bonds are

---

* Namely the quick registration facilities at the Bank of England known as Z Accounts.

offered on the market, perform an equalizing function whilst the
larger houses often operate as jobbers. The true shock-absorbing
system is, however, provided by the issue department of the Bank
of England which stands behind the market. Clearly, as a professional dealer in short-bonds (and also longer-dated stocks which
are near maturity) the market has greater need for flexibility in the
maturity structure of its holdings. This brings a great advantage to
the Treasury and the Bank of England in conducting the management of the National Debt because they will know where they can
find the near-maturities in the various stocks. This is the important
function rather than the shock-absorbing function.

It is noteworthy that Professor Sayers* stated when discussing
the bond market generally, and jobbing in particular, 'In 1957 experience was particularly harsh, and there was an abrupt further
change of attitude; since that date it cannot be pretended that the
discount houses serve any substantial jobbing function in this
market'. This comment is in sharp contrast to an opinion expressed
by Bernard Wesson in 1969 when it was thought that jobbing was
likely to become more pronounced as a direct result of the authorities' new policy of allowing bond prices to find their own level.
The two statements are not in fact as conflicting as they might
appear as they merely reflect the constantly changing mood of
market approach to bond dealing, stemming from discount houses'
harsh experiences in 1957 and 1964 when heavy losses were
incurred on bond portfolios. Bond holdings reached a new peak in
March 1967 when bond books reached £678 M. after a brief period
of optimism about falling interest rates; by March 1969 holdings
had fallen by well over half to £254 M. Comment will be made on
these figures later in the chapter when the position of the bond
portfolio of the market is looked at for the whole period from 1959
to 1969.

So far we have been discussing the reasons for the discount
market's participation in the short-bond market; it is now pertinent
to ask to what extent the houses are able to operate in this market
and what, if any, are the houses' limitations. Quite obviously there
are very definite limits to the extent to which a discount house can
invest in bonds; firstly, it is limited by its total resources, and
secondly by the multiplier, that is the ratio of published resources
to investments. There may be a big disparity between the multi-
pliers of different houses, but a generally accepted figure is ap-

* R. S. Sayers, *Modern Banking*, seventh edition, p. 61. *See also* Eric Chalmers,
The Gilt-Edged Market, August 1967, pp. 167–8.

proximately eight to one. Variations from house to house will also depend on the size of inner reserves and the pattern of its book. For example, it is safer to hold £120 M. bonds with twelve months to maturity than to have £60 M. due in five years' time. A fall of 10% in some cases, as was experienced in 1955, on a multiplier of ten could mean the immediate loss of one's resources.

The practical significance of this to a discount house is that whilst apparently only a paper loss will have been incurred, it is customary for it to provide immediately out of its reserve portfolio an additional 5% margin* of security to compensate for the fall in bond prices. It is readily apparent then that any change in Bank rate could cause grievous losses or, alternatively, bring welcome relief depending on whether the movement be up or down. Any upward movement has a concomitant to higher interest rates which bring not only running losses, but also realized losses on bills and bonds. Moreover, as money rates rise immediately, yields on bonds already in portfolio are fixed and cannot be changed and the discount houses face considerable running losses. To ease this kind of situation the market endeavours to keep its book as 'short' as possible but for the house holding bonds with a relatively long life, a heavy loss is inescapable. A depreciation of 3% in bond values to a house having a ratio of bonds to capital resources of say, eight to one, would mean an immediate paper loss of 24% of such resources. Furthermore, it would still have to find extra collateral (as mentioned above) to maintain its margin of 5% on borrowed money. Thus the importance of a house keeping its multiplier carefully within the limit of its resources cannot be too greatly stressed; a recent example of imprudence in this connection is evidenced by the National Discount which got into serious difficulties but fortunately was rescued by a merger with the smaller but stronger Gerrard & Reid in June 1969.

Before embarking on a yearly analysis of the short-bond market let us examine the general trends since 1958. Reference to Table 5 on p. 36 clearly shows the dramatic fall in size of government securities (and Treasury bills) as a percentage of total discount market assets. In 1958 bond holdings of £321 M. accounted for 30% of total assets but by 1968 the book had fallen to only 18% or £306 M. The basic reason for this large percentage fall is, of course, the now cau-

---

* H. F. Goodson, *The Functioning of the London Discount Houses*, pp. 29–30. The formula being:

$$\frac{100 \ (\text{amoung of loan} + 5\%)}{\text{Market value of the bonds}}$$

tious attitude of the market to this aspect of its business, coupled
with an ever-increasing tendency for interest rates to rise. (Bank
rate was 4% in 1958 and reached 8% in 1968.) As is well known
increases in Bank rate put pressure on the market and it was in 1955
that even with its increased resources, it first felt the real strain.

The depression in the gilt-edged market caused some bonds to
fall by as much as 10% with heavy losses being incurred by the
market. Indeed, no less than five of the twelve houses showed uncovered depreciation on bond portfolios.

Probably the most adverse year during the 1960s was (November) 1964 when Bank rate was raised by 3%. Fortunately, between
March and September 1964 the market reduced its gilt-edged portfolio from £437 M. to £288 M., once more demonstrating its agility
and foresight in minimizing possible losses. This is by no means the
whole picture, however; the dominating feature of bond portfolios
is their short-term fluctuations, especially in the five years from
1965 to 1969, indicating the extent of the houses' rethinking as they
have changed their views about the future course of interest rates.
In the six months to end-September 1964, the portfolio fell by
£149 M. to £288 M., which was the lowest published figure since
September 1958; in the next nine months to end-June 1965 it rose
by £283 M. to £571 M. and then fell back in the ensuing year by
£156 M. to £415 M. By March 1967, further buying had carried it to
a new peak of £678 M. Later in that year it was brought down in anticipation of the autumn crisis; at the end of September 1967, bond
holdings stood at £452 M. and may have been reduced still further
before the storm broke. Thus by 1968 it became evident that the
discount houses attached great importance to the relationship
between interest rates and the composition of the market's book to
total resources. Formerly, the houses had considered that their
bond portfolio could be as high as either times true capital resources, but in later years a more conservative and prudent view
has rightly manifested itself. This is shown by the higher proportion
of relatively short-dated bonds held by the market. Holdings of
government securities with more than five years to run to maturity
have never been substantial. In March 1967, for example, they
accounted for only £51 M. of peak holdings of government stocks
of £678 M. By March 1969 they had fallen to a mere £2 M. The
discount market has always had to exist by its wits and this serves as
a fine indication of its flexibility of approach to current problems.

In 1967 the market's purchases and sales of bonds totalled
£6,115 M. which represented more than one-third of all trans-

actions at the short end of the market – roughly, ten to twelve times the average level of the market's bond holdings. In 1968 the rate of turnover fell to less than nine times total holdings or one-quarter of total dealings.

During 1968, despite the substantial fall in turnover, the market's agility in adjusting its portfolio was even more manifest, with reductions of £195 M. and £215 M. in the second and fourth quarters punctuated by a rise of £143 M. in the third quarter. Fluctuations of that order were the result of a general reappraisal of bond-dealing policy stemming from the heavy losses suffered in 1955. Subsequently, even with interest yields at their existing high levels, there has been no comparable fall in prices, mainly because subsequent issues of government stocks have carried higher coupons.

The proportion of gilts held by the market in 1962 was 39% and fell to 7% by December 1970. From 1963 to 1967 the market's holdings remained fairly steady at about 30%–33%, when the bond portfolio peaked at £678 M. (early in 1967) after a brief period of optimism about the outlook for interest rates. The next two years saw a sharp diminution of the market's holdings from 31% at end-December 1967 to 20% in 1969, thus effecting a fall of more than one-third in their book. Clearly, the bond market is the most delicate of all the major sectors of operations since when gilts rise the houses make big profits, but unfortunately the underlying trend had been downwards for some years. Understandably then severe losses were made on bonds during these two years and one house, National Discount, was even forced into a merger with Gerrard & Reid to save itself.

BOND-DEALING IN THE DISCOUNT MARKET 1959–79

The market had built up a strong position in the year 1958–9 as Bank rate came steadily down from 7% to 4% and gave the discount houses an automatic profit attributable to the lag of earnings yields behind the rates they pay on borrowed money. During 1959 Bank rate remained unchanged and there were therefore no similar gains of this kind but it was nevertheless an excellent year for profits. Despite this the houses were still led astray by the vagaries of official tactics. A dominant influence in the gilt-edged market since autumn 1958 was the unprecedented weight of selling by the clearing banks, but until the end of 1959 the Bank purchased excess stock on terms that involved only a small net fall in short-bond prices. The authorities' support tactics were, however, dramatically reversed on February 24 and the decline in prices gathered pace. Needless to say there was much confusion in the City when no official explanation was then given, but the next week a government spokesman stated in the House of Lords, 'The Government does not believe that the market ought to be insulated by official action from the effects of decisions by holders of gilt-edged stock to buy or sell, though at times it may be desirable to assist in maintaining orderly market conditions...' and in a further statement '...the Government broker who accordingly marked down the price by one point, because he felt it undesirable that an artificially high price should be maintained....' Presumably the object of discontinuing support of the market was to curtail further sales of stock in an endeavour to exert a restraining influence on bank lending.

Table 7

DISCOUNT HOUSES SHORT BONDS 1960

	High	Low	June 28
Funding 2½% 1956–61	98$\frac{29}{32}$ (June 30)	97$\frac{13}{16}$ (March 4)	98$\frac{1}{32}$
Conversion 4½% 1962	100$\frac{29}{32}$ (January 4)	97$\frac{11}{16}$ (June 28)	97$\frac{11}{16}$
Exchequer 3% 1962–3	96$\frac{5}{32}$ (January 5)	92$\frac{7}{8}$ (June 28)	92$\frac{7}{8}$
Conversion 4¾% 1963	101$\frac{5}{32}$ (January 4)	96$\frac{11}{16}$ (June 28)	96$\frac{11}{16}$

Source: The Banker, Aug. 1965, p. 546.

On the eve of the 1% Bank rate rise in June prices were effectively at their lowest since the 7% Bank rate in 1957–8 with the shortest bonds showing a depreciation of over 2% since end-1959 and 2⅜% from their peak earlier in that year. At the other end of the scale the longest bonds held showed a loss of 3¼ to 3$\frac{11}{16}$% over the period. Immediately after the rise in Bank rate to 6%, 4½% Conversion Stock fell by almost a further 2% (see Table 7). Although the market made moderate profits on current trading, they were by no means sufficient to offset the capital depreciation on bonds.

The fall in the gilt-edged market thus effectively caused some decline in the true capital resources of the discount market. At end-1959 they had climbed to a peak of £55 M. and to approximately £60 M. in mid-1960, but after the rise in Bank rate (to 6%) they fell again to approximately £55 M. The strain was heightened by the size of the market's holdings which were some £321 M. at end-1958 and had been further built up during 1959 and early 1960.

A further tactic of the authorities earlier in the year (after the rise of Bank rate to 5% in January) was also to mislead the market – there was an immediate demand for 4½% Conversion Stock 1964 but for several days the Bank delayed the release of further supplies of stock during which time the price continued to rise. Then, when the new tranche was brought out it was offered at 99¼ to the bewilderment of the market, because this represented a yield more appropriate to a 4½% Bank rate than to 5%. This action, not unreasonably, led the market to believe that the higher Bank rate was to be only short-lived and on this misplaced hypothesis it again began purchasing bonds, only to realize its error when the official support prices were lowered on February 24. The market's holdings were estimated still to be in the region of £375 M. in mid-June, and after this salutary experience some of the smaller houses decided to cut their losses by selling bonds. There is little doubt that mere size of resources in this market is a mixed blessing as the larger houses invariably find it almost impossible to substantially reduce their holdings in difficult markets. This point was emphasized at the Bank Rate Tribunal* in 1957 when the manager of one of the leading houses said in evidence, 'I have a large book. I am supposed to be a large dealer and it is practically impossible for me to deal largely enough to be effective.'

The continuing upward trend in bond portfolios in the early 1960s considerably altered the assets structure of the market. Formerly, the bond book had always been much smaller than the Treasury bill book. The proportion of bonds to total securities held had risen from one-third in 1958 to nearly half in 1962. The market's average total holdings of securities (bills and bonds combined) had, chiefly as a result of the expansion in bonds, reached record levels of almost £1,000 M. for the four quarters to March 1963 compared with £930 M. in 1961 and £830 M. in 1959. The prosperous trading of the early 1960s substantially increased the market's bond-carrying capacity and Wilfrid King estimated that by mid-1962 the market's capital resources were in excess of £60 M.

---

* Bank Rate Tribunal, 18 December 1957, Question 8978.

and by August 1963 were capital perhaps as high as £70 M.

The authorities took an unusual step on 21 August 1963 when they announced that for the first time since the end of the second world war, a new stock issue, £400 M. 5% Exchequer Loan 1976–8, could be held in bearer form. Presumably the object of this move was to widen the attraction of such stocks by adding the virtue of negotiability to them.

During the year 1963–4 it became obvious to the market that the exceptional profits earned in 1962–3, especially from bond business, following the steady decline in money rates from the high levels of 1961, could not continue, and in fact by the end of 1963 running margins on bond portfolios were reduced as bond prices fell from their peaks. These margins were cut significantly in February 1964 when Bank rate was increased from 4% to 5%.

Most houses generally foresaw the changing climate and bond holdings were steeply reduced in the first quarter of 1963 from their then all-time peak of £488 M. to £428 M. The significant factor about the period (1963–4) certainly prior to the 2% increase in Bank rate in November, had been the gradual erosion of unusually high running margins. These resulted from redemptions and the transference of bond books to a lower yield basis on the one hand, and the upward trend of money rate on the other, rather than from a violent movement in capital values of the kind which occurred in 1955 or 1959. Furthermore, since 1963 there was also a tendency to shorten the life of bonds held in portfolio. According to published accounts the average life of bond books appeared to vary from eighteen to twenty-eight months, thus placing the market as a whole in a strong position to withstand the stresses that any further rise in interest rates might bring.

The true capital resources of the market in 1964 remained at a similar level to 1963 – that is approximately £70 M., giving a bond portfolio to total resources ratio of six to one which was very modest compared with previous years when the figure was generally approximately eight to one.

The market's bond portfolio dropped from £437 M. at end-March to no more than £288 M. in September. Thus there was a fall of almost £150 M. in six months and it was probably carried significantly further during early October. Unhappily, after the election on October 15 events were to induce the discount houses into a serious miscalculation of government policy. There was a general atmosphere of confidence in the City and the gilt-edged market remained firm. The then new government's first policy statement imposed an import surcharge, which seemed to imply that it intended to deal with the balance of payments deficit by restraining imports rather than by the use of monetary policy. Some sections of the market then began repurchasing operations in the gilt-edged market thinking that interest rates would be left untouched for the time being at least. This view was reinforced by remarks made by the then Foreign Minister, Mr Gordon Walker, when he was widely reported as saying that the government had no intention of raising Bank rate and had indeed deliberately chosen not to do so. Consequently, the market was seduced into continuous purchases of gilts. Quite obviously they did not wish to miss the opportunity of buying bonds with Bank rate at 7%. From end-December 1964 to end-March 1965 the market's aggregate bond portfolio rose by £83 M. to £521 M.

It must be appreciated that the period was one of extreme difficulty for the discount houses because of the strong political overtones. The Labour Government's capital gains tax announced in November caused much apprehension in the City, and the uncertainty generated by this announcement later gave way to dismay when the Chancellor of the Exchequer made it clear that gilt-edged stocks would be subject to the new tax. Clearly the market was in a vulnerable state with instability of prices providing a salutary tactical lesson for the future.

The chief reasons for the market's difficulties during this phase of development are manifest. Bank rate was increased from 4% to 7% in the short space of only nine months and was then maintained at that level for over six months. During the previous crises in 1961 and 1957 the periods of stress had been of shorter duration and Bank rate had not been below 5% for over a year before the 7% level was reached. The situation was further compounded by the Labour government's stringent fiscal measures and imposition of capital gains tax which resulted in profound disillusionment in the gilt-edged market with yields reaching unprecedented high levels. Thus the houses' asset structure was placed under pressure from the resultant depreciation of its bond book coupled with severe running losses on bonds. These distortions stemmed from the fact that the market had purchased the bulk of its bond portfolio prior to the upswing in interest rates. Further exacerbating the discount houses' position was the shortage of Treasury bills. Finally, the high level of Bank rate did not stimulate the expected reflux of funds into London.

One result of raising Bank rate to 7% was that the yields on gilt-edged securities throughout the range of maturities became un-usually bunched; among short bonds the yield on 5% Exchequer Stock 1967 prior to the Bank rate increase was 5½% but by the end of the year it had reached 6½% and was even higher by end-March 1965.

In the undated stocks the yield on 3½% War Loan rose from about 6% in January 1964 to almost 6½% by the end of the year.

It is significant that despite the prosperous years of 1962 and 1963 not all houses demonstrated a similar degree of prudence in providing for contingencies and only had themselves to blame for the unusual severity of the strains they had to bear. Their first miscalculation was to assume that a Labour government would not press home with the use of monetary policy and then, after the event, they then presumed that future experience would follow previous precedents – notwithstanding the changed economic en-vironment and international finance influences. Inevitably, this was a bad year for market profits and this is clearly illustrated in Table 8. Nevertheless all twelve houses succeeded in writing down the book values of their bonds to the then current market values; National Discount, however, found their inner reserves were insuf-ficient for this purpose and had to supplement them by drawing £430,000 from previous profit.

Table 8

NET PROFIT AND EQUITY DIVIDENDS— FOUR SELECTED HOUSES

	1962–3	1963–4	1964–5
Union Discount	754,203	885,481	718,823
December 31	12½%	12½%	12½%
National Discount	676,105	817,308	382,496
December 31	12½%	16%	12½
Alexanders Discount	307,655	343,112	240,092
December 31	12½%	12½%	12½%
Gillett Bros. Discount	404,046	451,075	149,149
January 31	15%	15%	15%

Source: *The Banker*, Aug. 1966, p. 560

They were also obliged to cut their dividend distribution from 15% to 12½% – the only one of the twelve members of the Discount Houses' Association to do so. The profits of the members had declined considerably over previous years; ranging from 1%

(by King & Shaxson), 12% by Smith St Aubyn to 18% or more for the other companies.

A significant example of the general mistrust within the City concerning the gilt-edged market manifested itself when Hambros' deposits increased by £38 M. thus raising total deposits to £187 M., representing an increase of approximately 25% over the previous year. With both advances and commercial bill holdings controlled by the Bank of England, the traditional outlet for funds was therefore limited. Nevertheless, Hambros sold its entire portfolio of government securities in November 1965 and still held none in March 1966. The funds were in fact invested in the local authority market. Not unnaturally these continuing doubts about the market were reflected in the figures for turnover: £938 M. in April, £458 M. in May, £407 M. in June, and by August it had dropped to a then all-time monthly low of £289 M. The authorities were again obliged to make purchases to steady the market and restrain prices from falling further.

Although the market had partially discounted the 1% Bank rate rise in advance, it seems that the other measures announced – the 105% ceiling on lendings to remain, special deposits increased from 1% to 2% etc. – added to the psychological impact. Table 9 includes the figures for July 13 and 15, the day before and the day after Bank rate change. It shows that between the end of May and July 15 yields on gilt-edged securities rose approximately ½%. slightly less on the long-term stocks and rather more on the short. Yields had been fluctuating up and down for several months in the first quarter of the year so that by end-March an apparently anomalous situation had arisen, in that yields throughout the whole range of gilt-edged were substantially higher than they had been twelve months earlier when Bank rate was 1% lower. Bank rate normally tended to have a dominant effect on short-term money rates in contrast to its more moderate influence on long-term rates.

The year 1966 saw changes in the Bank's techniques for overnight borrowing (fully discussed in the previous chapter) and there had also been much discussion and criticism of the Bank's official support tactics in the gilt-edged market. The Bank of England's main aim in its open market operations was originally set out in the *Quarterly Bulletin*:* 'It is to maintain market conditions that will maximize, both now and in the future, the desire of investors at home and abroad to hold British Government debt'. The auth-

---

* *Bank of England Quarterly Bulletin*, June 1966, pp. 141–8, for a full description.

Table 9

YIELDS AND INTEREST RATES

	1965 July 30	1966 May 27	1966 June	1966 July 13	1966 July 15
Bank Rate	6	6	6	6	7
Treasury Bills	5·63	5·66	5·73	5·81	6·68
Government Securities*					
Maturing					
1969	6·95	6·75	7·00	7·33	7·38
1974	6·81	6·73	6·95	7·23	7·35
1988	6·69	6·78	6·90	7·10	7·13
Undated	6·66	6·71	6·90	7·10	7·13

* Gross redemption yields.

Source: Banker's Magazine, August 1966, p. 141. Abstracted from 'Interest Rates and Yields'.

orities' apparent lack of concern about the strength of the gilt-edged market in recent years probably, in part, reflected the lack of need to borrow from the public through the sale of marketable stocks. From 1963 to 1965 the government was a net purchaser of its own securities to the extent of £29 M. Practically all new stocks created during the period were absorbed by the government departments, a major factor of this being the growing sterling content of the Exchange Equalization Account as a consequence of the balance of payments deficit. It became clear by 1969–70 that although there may not have been a change of policy there had been a discernible change in tactics. Formerly it had been the policy of the Bank to allow the broad level of prices to be determined by purchases and sales of investors, but intervening from time to time to keep movements steady and regular. Thus it did not try to stop downward movements, but bid on successively lower levels so as to secure a drop in market prices of broadly the dimensions thought desirable. In times of crisis the Bank would, of course, have to act more decisively to ensure the long-term health of the market, otherwise the authorities' future ability to borrow would be seriously curtailed. In the *Quarterly Bulletin** the Bank

* *Bank of England Quarterly Bulletin*, March 1969, pp. 15 and 16. See also 'Radcliffe – ten years after', paper prepared by Bank of England in consultation with the Treasury.

stated, when referring to the period November 1968 to February 1969, that 'the authorities readily allowed this (selling of stock) to have its effects on yields' indicating some modification of previous practices. At the time of the international currency crisis in November (1968) the Bank then modified its tactics* by 'reverting to a policy of allowing any weakness to be fully reflected in prices'. The use of these modified practices has subsequently continued and has brought strong criticism from some quarters:† 'the Bank has ditched its traditional role . . . and is posing a threat to some of the basic functions of the City', but nevertheless a government spokesman stated in the House of Commons that the Bank's official policy in relation to the market had not changed. Notwithstanding this denial, however, the *Bulletin** stated that 'changes in the surrounding circumstances led to adjustments in the authorities' tactics regarding the prices at which they were prepared to deal'.

It would appear that certainly by mid-1969 the authorities were significantly less willing to intervene in the market as buyers than they would have been in similar circumstances previously and generally showed much more flexibility in their handling of the market.

Turnover figures in short-dated gilt-edged stocks varied substantially between October 1966 and January 1967 reflecting the continued market doubts and subsequent changes of tactic. By November the figure had fallen to £857 M. from the previous peak in October of £2,166 M., reducing to £750 M. in December. In January it had expanded to £1,867 M. in a more confident market. The quarter ended March 1967 saw the market's bond portfolio reach an all-time peak of £678 M. when there had been a brief period of optimism about the outlook for interest rates. During the second quarter a number of factors were instrumental in causing the market's holdings of bonds to fall by almost £300 M. to £498 M. The poor April trade figures provoked substantial sales and it was noteworthy* that this was an occasion when the authorities invoked their new support tactics. Secondly, although the reduction in Bank rate to $5\frac{1}{2}\%$ on May 4 brought a temporary rise in prices they soon started to ease because there was a growing belief amongst investors that, for the time being, there would be no further decline in interest rates and this led to some profit taking. Furthermore, an announcement was made on April 27 of a vesting

---

* *Bank of England Quarterly Bulletin*, September 1967, p. 227.

† *Sunday Times Business News* (Graham Sergeant, James Poole and Peter Kellner), 13 September 1970.

date for steel securities with the result that institutional investors started large-scale switching from gilts to these securities.*

Subsequently, the authorities had to step in to steady the market; their buying being in marked contrast to the substantial selling which they had had to make in the previous six months. The discount houses were again sellers of gilts in the quarter ended September and more again was sold in October in anticipation of the rise in Bank rate to 6%. By end-October the yield on short-dated stocks was about ¼% higher than three months earlier. Such was market activity in bonds during 1967 that purchases plus sales totalled £6,098 M. or more than one-third of all transactions at the short end of the market.

In the final quarter the discount market's total assets rose by about £160 M. to £1,747 M., the highest ever figure up to that time.

The period just after devaluation (November 18) was a hectic one for the market. Official sales of gilt-edged were very large for a week or so as investors seized the opportunity of obtaining yields associated with an 8% Bank rate. The money market generally experienced an extreme shortage of funds for three days after devaluation, followed by two days of large surpluses thus reflecting the intense activity in the foreign exchange market and gilt-edged markets. The discount houses' holdings of short bonds increased substantially from £452 M. in September to £544 M. at end-December reflecting their heavy buying after the increase in Bank rate to 8%.

For much of the year 1968 the gilt-edged market was weak and only in the third quarter were the authorities consistently able to sell stock. In spite of a substantial fall in turnover, the market's agility in adjusting its bond portfolio was still more manifest than in 1967 with reductions of £195 M. and £215 M. in the second and fourth quarters punctuated by a rise of £145 M. in the third quarter thus indicating the extent of the market's re-thinking as a result of continued balance of payment problems and the behaviour of sterling. It is significant that by March 1969 the bond portfolio had fallen to little more than one-third of the end-March 1967 total.

Probably the most notable feature of 1968 and 1969 was the ever-changing tactics employed by the Bank of England in the gilt-edged

---

* The attraction of switching lay in the 'franked' income which could be obtained, i.e. dividend income derived by one company from another. Such income has already been subject to both corporation and income tax and is not taxed again. The income tax which has been paid can be set off against the receiving company's income tax liability on its own dividends.

market. When referring to the position during the last quarter,* 'Thereafter the market became increasingly depressed; the authorities began to be offered stock and ... purchases became very heavy. ... Until then the market's sales had been allowed to have their effect on yields, but the situation became very heavy. ... Until then the market's sales had been allowed to have their effect on yields, but the situation became so disturbed that ... the authorities stepped in to steady the market', and then when 'a rise in United Kingdom interest rates was deemed both appropriate and tolerable ... the authorities reverted to a policy of allowing any weakness to be fully reflected in prices'. Not unnaturally, these tactics, coupled with a historically high Bank rate of 8%, produced the highest yields in short- and long-term gilts since the Bank was founded in 1694.

Subsequently, comment continued on this somewhat contentious topic and many writers have pointed out some of the pitfalls of the Bank's revised policies. The arguments centre around the economic thesis that the authorities have the choice of either controlling the level of interest rates or controlling the money supply, but cannot do both. Many critics have forecast that if the Bank's support policy were abandoned the authorities would be unable to sell long-term stock and also preserve an orderly market, thereby causing grave disruption of the financial structure. Two developments in the late 1960s were major factors in enabling the Bank to pursue a more flexible policy, however. The first was the movement of the government's financial position into a surplus of £287 M. in 1968–9, followed by a further improvement in 1969–70. This was the first time since 1962–3 that central government had repaid debt thus creating a more favourable climate in which to operate monetary policy. The second was the letter of intent to the I.M.F. in 1967, in which the authorities undertook that their borrowing requirement for the year 1968–9 would be financed 'as far as possible by the sale of debt to the non-bank public', and that this would be achieved through interest rate policy. A subsequent letter of intent in 1969 specified targets for domestic credit expansion.

The authorities have endeavoured to meet this undertaking by emphasizing the level of interest rates and control of the money supply as the important determinants of official policy, rather than the maximization of sales of gilt-edged stocks.

Throughout 1969 the market's bond portfolio remained rela-

* Bank of England. Report for the year ended 28 February 1969, p. 31.

tively constant varying between £254 M. and £259 M. until end-September. In the final quarter, however, the houses bought £110 M. gilt-edged, pushing total bond holdings to £364 M. by end-December. The reductions in Bank rate (1% on February 27 1969 and March 25 1970) understandably gave the market bumper profits from bond holdings and permitted it to rebuild badly depleted inner reserves.

The year 1970 saw a drop of some £200 M. in the discount market's holdings of government securities, from £364 M. (at end-December 1969) to £160 M. by end-December 1970. The major part of this reduction occurred between the March and June quarters when the portfolio fell by £134 M. Indeed, the sales of the banking sector as a whole for the six months to end-June amounted to £280 M. of stock and involved the authorities in purchases of a similar amount. This massive selling was attributable to a number of factors which disturbed the market such as the Middle East situation, the June general election, and fears of a dock strike. In such an unsettled climate the market (and the clearing banks) probably decided to take their profits from bonds held in portfolio, reaping the benefits of two reductions in Bank rate early in the year. The heavy selling was accompanied by a steep rise in yields which attracted domestic investors who purchased some £260 M. of stock. The market also no doubt had well in mind that they could probably repurchase stocks at a later date, at much lower prices. This view would certainly seem to be confirmed by the rise in the market's holdings of gilts of approximately £218 M. (to £378 M.) by March 1971.

During May 1971 the Bank announced its proposals for reforming the structure of the banking system. The new arrangements were formally implemented in September after discussions with the banks, discount houses, and finance houses and have had far-reaching consequences for the discount market. The houses were initially required to maintain a minimum of 50% of their assets in the form of public sector debt* which is defined as Treasury bills, government and local authority stocks, and government-guaranteed stocks with not more than five years to run. Also included are local authority bills and bonds.

Possibly the most significant element of Competition and Credit Control for the discount market lay in the treatment of the gilt-edged market. This sector was at one time the houses' largest single

---

* Subsequently changed in July 1973 to a 20 times capital and reserves multiple in 'undefined assets'.

asset and, during periods of falling interest rates, certainly its most profitable. The modified arrangements for dealing in gilts are as follows:

(1) The Bank is no longer prepared to respond to requests to buy stock outright except in the case of stock with one year or less to run to maturity.
(2) It reserves the right to make outright purchases of stock with more than a year to run solely at its discretion and initiative.
(3) It will be prepared to undertake, at prices of its own choosing, exchanges of stock with the market except those which unduly shorten the life of the debt.
(4) It will be prepared to respond to the bids for the sale of 'tap' stocks and such other stocks held by it as it may wish to sell.
(5) Stocks with less than one year to run to maturity are eligible reserve assets for the banking system.

In the past the Bank had sought to exercise control of the general level of interest rates through bank rate policy and support of the gilt-edged market. The underlying aim of the policy was '. . . to ensure as far as possible that suitable finance is available, and will continue to be available in the future, so that there need be no excessive recourse to short-term borrowing from the banks on Treasury bills and accompanying increase in the money supply'.* It follows then, that previous Bank policy in gilt-edged was to maintain a fairly stable long-term rate and facilitate funding of debt. The emphasis for the future has moved more towards increased control of the money supply with consequent greater fluctuations in interest rates. This tactical change by the authorities has had some far-reaching effects on the discount houses and may have perverse effects in the future on Bank monetary policy. In particular, from the standpoint of the houses they are no longer prepared to purchase large quantities of such stocks in the knowledge that on a falling market they would lose substantial sums of money.

During the year to April 1972 the gilt-edged market remained reasonably buoyant, no doubt assisted by the reductions in Bank rate, a continuing influx of overseas funds and a healthy balance of payments, all of which enabled the Bank to make substantial funding sales as the opportunity arose. The position after April was less satisfactory, however. The FT index of government security prices fell from over 80 in April 1972 to around 71 in the middle of

* *Bank of England Quarterly Bulletin*, 'Official Transactions in the Gilt-edged Market', June 1966.

June, and after stabilizing for a short time, fell to 69 in March 1973. A number of factors served to depress the gilt-edged market around this time. First, the government seemed unable to curb wages and price inflation and a large visible trade deficit has now reappeared. Secondly, the banks sold substantial amounts of gilts to enable them to finance the rise in advances. Thirdly, the discount houses suffered the withdrawal of some £249 M. of call money and other borrowed funds. Fourthly, there was an acute shortage of funds in June 1972 following the outflow of over £1,000 M. in the week prior to the floating of sterling on the foreign exchange market. The Bank of England support of the discount houses was enormous with many houses taking large loans for over seven days. Consequently, the authorities were forced to make available to the banks temporary sale and repurchase facilities of short-dated gilts to the extent of some £360 M. The object of this support operation was obviously to avoid violent fluctuations in interest rates, but the significant point is that it marked the first breach of the Bank's new policies only ten months after their inception. Critics of the new measures immediately pointed out that they had fallen at their first hurdle even though the Bank had made provision for such emergency support in its policy directive. The more balanced view is to regard the June crisis as exceptional and therefore justifying the Bank's action rather than as a total failure of the current tactics. The help arose from the prudent desire to ensure that an exceptional event did not have too disruptive an effect.

The discount houses suffered heavy losses on bond dealing in the 1950s and 1960s, and their experience in 1972 only served to make them take an even more cautious attitude to the gilt-edged market. Such caution is predictable and prudent in view of the market's small capital resources relative to the aggregate of both holdings and turnover. At times, when the gilt-edged market is depressed, the houses' participation is likely to be limited to dealing transactions rather than obtaining running profits by holding gilts as investments. Again, during July 1973, due to a fall in gilt-edged prices, the discount houses virtually moved out of gilts. On 20 June 1973, the discount market held £313 M. of British Government stocks, but by 19 September this figure had fallen to £31 M. The discount houses feared capital losses on bonds as this is traditionally the most sensitive part of their portfolio, although there was ample scope to make profits as a trader, and this was the direction in which the houses turned. A shortening of books and an emphasis

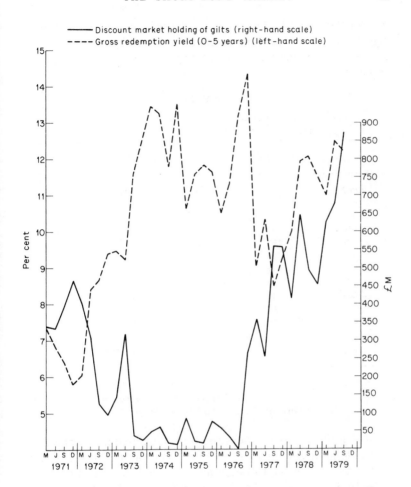

Discount market holding of gilts (right-hand scale)
Gross redemption yield (0-5 years) (left-hand scale)

Graph 1 shows the relationship between holdings of gilts by the discount market and the gross redemption yield on short-dated gilts. It is clear that there is an inverse relationship between yield and holdings – i.e. when the yield is low, holdings are high. Since there is also an inverse relationship between yield and price of fixed coupon stocks this means that gilt holdings are lowest when gilt prices are depressed. The market's inhibitions are fully reflected by the figures for gilts held in portfolio during the year ended December 1972. In January holdings were £404 M. falling to £275 M. in July, £131 M. in October and £112 M. in December.

on trading was the pattern that was established by 1975. On this basis, the discount houses were again able to make good profits. This trend towards trading rather than investing in gilts is evident from an examination of Table 10 where it can be seen that the turn-

over of short-dated gilts has become very high in relation to holdings; while this has to some extent been a traditional characteristic
of the discount market, it is clear that it has become especially
apparent from 1972 onwards.

Table 10

HOLDINGS AND TURNOVER OF SHORT-DATES GILT-EDGED
SECURITIES BY THE DISCOUNT MARKET (0–5 YEARS)

(£M.) (%)	HOLDINGS	%	TURNOVER	%
1967	627	10	6,115	37
1968	556	8	5,671	39
1969	252	4	4,492	39
1970	282	5	5,170	40
1971	253	4	N/A	N/A
1972	410	6	6,495	41
1973	135	2	7,602	37
1974	39	1	5,663	28
1975	33	1	9,577	23
1976	65	1	13,863	29
1977	321	2	22,017	34
1978	417	2	22,408	36
1979	668		N/A	N/A

Notes: Holdings as at 31 March
        Percentages = discounts Market's share of total holdings and turnover.
Source: *Bank of England Quarterly Bulletin,* various issues.

During the periods of depression in the gilt-edged market, the
houses tend to deal on an 'in and out' basis within 24 hours. This is
greatly assisted by the fact that they enjoy 'jobbing facilities' in the
gilt-edged market (they have 'Z' accounts at the Bank of England)
which means that ownership of the stock can be transferred within
the same day. These facilities have been available for many years
on stocks with up to five years to redemption. This was extended to
seven years on 11 February 1972.

A boom developed in the gilt-edged market towards the end of
1975, but, up to December, very few houses were investing in the
gilt-edged market. The discount markets' holding did increase
sharply, however, in January 1978 when £300 M. of stocks were on
their books. During a year of changing fortunes in the gilt-edged
market in 1976, holdings fell steadily to only £2 M. in September,
but subsequently rose to £261 M. in December. During the year the
discount market strongly favoured stock which matured in one to

five years but tended only to hold readily marketable stock for short periods, largely because the cost of borrowing money often exceeded the profits to be made from the investment.

The upward trend in holdings which was evident in the latter part of 1976 resulted from the boom in the gilt-edged market. This movement continued into 1977 and in January holdings amounted to £439 M. which is significantly higher than their holding in June 1973, shortly before the houses sold the bulk of their gilts. The reason for this renewed interest in gilts is the high coupon on some of the stocks which were issued (for example, Treasury 14% 1982). Due to taxation and the volatility of the market, the houses are far more interested in high interest yields than they are in capital appreciation.

VARIABLE COUPON GILT-EDGED STOCK

During recent years, it has been suggested that the authorities should introduce a new type of gilt-edged security with a variable or floating coupon to render the gilt-edged market more attractive to the potential investor in times of uncertainty about the future course of interest rates and inflation.

At times when interest rates are expected to rise, the demand for conventional fixed interest gilts is poor as holders would face a capital loss. Variable rate gilts would not, however, suffer such a fall in price, thus enabling the government to continue funding its borrowing requirement outside the banking system even at times of interest rate uncertainty.

Variable coupon gilts also have the attraction that, should the general level of interest rates fall the government would not have to continue to service such stocks at the high level prevailing at the time of issue.

Subsequently two short-dated variable coupon gilts were issued in 1977: £400 M. of Treasury Variable 1981 and £400 M. Treasury Variable 1982. The coupon is linked to the average allotment rate of Treasury bills over the previous six months. These two stocks have not proved attractive to investors however because they were introduced during a period when the minimum lending rate fell dramatically from a historically high level of 15% to 5%. Neither has the operation been successful from the point of view of the Bank of England's control of the money supply because the stock has not proved to be a 'true gilt stock' in so far as the principal holders are the clearing banks, the discount market, and the Building Societies. It was originally hoped that it would be held by non-bank private investors and therefore assist in monetary control.

These stocks would appear to be more attractive than traditional gilts to the discount houses, in view of their relative price stability. Naturally, in avoiding the risk of making heavy capital losses, investors in variable rate stocks also forfeit the chance of capital gains, but because their yield is linked to market rates they do yield a satisfactory running profit to discount houses.

At the time of their evidence to the Wilson Committee the discount houses appeared unconvinced as to the value of variables, but since then their attitude appears to have changed somewhat and certainly at the end of 1979 the gilt portfolio of Union Discount was comprised solely of variable rate stocks.

Part III

The Complementary Markets

This part of the book describes the emergence and development of the seven complementary markets which have evolved in London since the late 1950s. Chapters 6 to 13 inclusive provide a detailed examination of these markets and show the extent of the discount market's participation in them.

The importance of the evolution of these markets, particularly the local authorities' and Euro-dollar markets, are analysed in detail.

6 Local authority market

This chapter is to be devoted to a rigorous account of short-term local authority borrowing in the London money market and other sources. Fundamentally it is probably true to say that it is not so much the story of local authority borrowing as of continual official attempts to secure and maintain orderliness in public debt arrangements, particularly the gilt-edged market. Throughout the postwar period local authority capital financing has been governed by major shifts in official policy. For some years after the war the only source from which local authorities were permitted to borrow was the Public Works Loan Board (from now on to be referred to as the P.W.L.B.) which in turn received its resources from the Exchequer. Then in 1955 the role of the P.W.L.B. was relegated virtually to that of a lender of the last resort; the local authorities were only allowed to borrow from the board if they were unable to meet their requirements through the open market. The reasons for this *volte-face* – from all P.W.L.B. to practically no P.W.L.B. – lay in the financial difficulties of central government who were concerned to reduce demand throughout the economy. Having undertaken a high level of current expenditure as well as heavy capital commitments – the largest being the P.W.L.B. – the Exchequer was running at an overall deficit which was exacerbating other inflationary tendencies in the economy. Furthermore large capital sums were being raised by nationalized industries by issues of government-guaranteed stocks, which were virtually gilt-edged, and affected the gilt-edged market accordingly. As events have subsequently proved, both these positions were essentially false because government cannot avoid ultimate responsibility for local authority investment since it decides the ends and must therefore be ready to provide the means. The underlying arguments for each extreme were well stated in the *Bank of England Quarterly* in 1966:

It can be argued that as a large part of local authority expenditure is effectively made on behalf of the central government, or in pursuance of central government policies, their finance should be provided entirely by the Exchequer at rates at which the central government themselves can borrow. Such co-ordination of public sector borrowing might not only reduce the cost of local authorities' money but might also give central authorities more control over the financial markets. On the other hand, an increase in the amount of finance needed by the Exchequer would raise its own problems. If the Exchequer attracted all funds from the general public which would otherwise have been lent to local authorities, the result would merely be a switch from one sort of public debt to another and there would be little or no monetary effect; but to the extent that the general public were unwilling to take up all the extra government debt, at rates of interest the Exchequer was prepared to pay in the forms in which it was offered, the Exchequer would be forced to borrow the balance from the banking system. Bank deposits and bank liquidity would rise and this would affect the monetary authorities' control over the banking system.

By 1963 a point had been reached at which total temporary debt ranged from NIL to 60% of total debt. When total borrowing, which varied from nought to two-thirds of total individual debts, was creeping up towards 20% of all local authority debt, the Treasury's growing concern (because over half of this short-term debt was repayable within seven days) at the disturbance of the short-term money market turned to action. Subsequently, as the result of a meeting between the Treasury and local government officials, a White Paper was produced which attempted to devise a reasonable way of bringing order to the situation. Briefly, the agreement reached was as follows:

A maximum temporary debt commitment for each authority of 20% of the current year's total debt was fixed, of which not more than 15% of the debt could be for three months or under, the remaining 5% being from three months to 364 days. In addition, access to the P.W.L.B. was extended with the intention that by 1968 local authorities could meet up to 50% of requirements from this source. In fact this ratio was never reached and the present arrangement is that local authorities can borrow from the P.W.L.B. as follows:

(a) by quota loans – up to a maximum of $3\frac{1}{2}$% of debt outstanding plus 30% of gross borrowing requirements,

(b) by non-quota A loans – this is a last resort facility charged at a higher rate than on quota loans and only available if the local authority can show that it is unable to raise long-term capital on the open market
(c) by non-quota B loans – this provides virtually unlimited access to the P.W.L.B. at a rate of 1% over the cost of non-quota A loans.

LAYFIELD COMMITTEE

The issue of centralizing local authority borrowing was again considered by the Layfield Committee on Local Government Financing but it was rejected. The Committee advocated a continuation of the existing arrangements whereby the local authorities are able to borrow a certain amount of their requirements from the P.W.L.B. but are also dependent on the money and capital markets for a significant percentage.

If borrowing were centralized the Committee suggested that the results would be:

(1) increased problems for debt management due to the increased P.S.B.R;
(2) the loss of investors in local authority tap bonds who would not invest in other forms of government debt;
(3) an increase in the cost of government debt and consequently only small savings in debt service costs.

VOLUNTARY BORROWING CODE

During 1976 the Treasury became increasingly worried by the shortening maturity of aggregate local authority debt. This had occurred despite the 20% limit on short-term borrowing because the long-term loans were being raised with maturities of only 2 or 3 years so as to avoid a commitment to high interest rates for long periods, and a large amount of long-term debt was maturing. By the end of March 1977 as much as £14 billion of the total outstanding debt of £31 billion fell due within one year and a further £6 billion in the next two years. The Treasury was concerned that local authorities might have difficulties raising finance should a crisis arise and also wished to reduce their exposure to interest rate changes.

The result was a voluntary code of practice which came into effect in August 1977 and which requires the authorities to gradually extend the average maturity of their new long-term borrowing. The code requires that the average period to maturity on new long-term borrowings will be:

in the financial year ending in March 1978 not less than 4 years,
in the financial year ending in March 1979 not less than 5 years,
in the financial year ending in March 1980 not less than 6 years,
in the financial year ending in March 1981 and thereafter 7 years.

It should be noted that these provisions relate only to the 80% of capital finance which must be raised by long-term loans; the 20% limit on temporary borrowing remains unchanged.

AREA OF STUDY

This section is not concerned with the scale of local authority capital expenditure but rather with how it is financed through the money market and other sources. Local authorities generally only meet a small part of their capital expenditure out of revenue and a further small amount by capital grants from the central government. The rest has to be financed by borrowing – either from central government or from the capital and money markets. We shall therefore be concerning ourselves with this debt; special reference being made to the short-term or 'temporary' aspect of it and the changes in the composition of local authority debt that have taken place.

The term 'short-term' is to be defined as up to two years and occasionally five years. This distinction is made because the Chartered Institute of Public Finance and Accountancy in their returns to the Treasury define short-term or temporary borrowing in two forms only: (1) debt repayable in not more than three months, and (2) debt repayable in more than three months but less than one year. All other borrowing is defined as long-term. Long-term borrowing for the purposes of this chapter will however be described as 'anything over five years' and will only be referred to in the context of the relationship of one form of debt to another as this emerges from the discussion of general developments.

SOURCES OF FUNDS

STOCK ISSUES

This is a long-term method of raising funds with periods generally ranging from seven to ten years. All issues must have a maturity of at least five years. The timing of issues is strictly controlled by the Bank of England and the terms fixed subject to the Bank's approval. Issues of less than £3 M. are not allowed with the average being in the region of £12 M., consequently the marketability of such stocks is somewhat restricted by the narrowness of the market. They appeal mostly to investors seeking a secure long-term outlet for funds, such as pension funds, insurance companies and trustee savings banks, etc.

Because of the similarity of local authority stocks with gilt-edged securities the Bank maintains tight control of this sector to preserve orderliness in the gilt-edged market.

Table 11

LOCAL AUTHORITY STOCKS (£M.)
AS AT 1 MAY 1980

Final Maturity Date	Amounts in Issue		
	Fixed Rate	Variable Rate	Total
1980	148	–	148
1981	208	–	208
1982	215	118	333
1983	202	87	289
1984	151	5	156
1985	177	50	227
1986–90	195	–	195
1991 and after	107	–	107
TOTAL	1,403	260	1,663

Source: Phillips & Drew.

Table 11 gives a breakdown of fixed and variable rate stock issues as at 1 May 1980. 79% (in value) of all variable rate issues were due to mature in under three years, while 84% or £1,403 M. or total outstandings were fixed rate issues.

The ability and willingness of local authorities to raise finance by stock issues is especially subject to the state of general financial conditions and interest rate expectations. Thus in 1974 only £6 M. of local authority stocks were issued while in 1978 £232 M. was raised by stock issues.

In 1977 local authorities were permitted to issue variable rate stocks. The first issue of these new stocks was made on 11 August 1977 by Bristol Corporation for £10 M. By December 1977 approximately ten other authorities had availed themselves of the new vehicle for borrowing with total issues amounting to over £120 M. The new stocks follow the pattern recently established in the gilt-edged market and are advantageous to local authorities in smoothing their long-term funding operations. The variable rate stocks impart greater flexibility to Treasurers in their debt management and are cheaper to issue than traditional fixed rate stock.

The rate of interest is determined by taking the six months' LIBOR rate (London Inter-Bank Offered Rate) plus a margin which is determined by the market. The margin agreed for most of the initial issues towards the end of 1977 was $\frac{3}{4}\%$ over LIBOR but clearly this will fluctuate with the overall movement in the level of market rates. Interest will be payable half yearly in arrears. The market price of the stocks will depend upon three factors: (1) the redemption date; (2) the dividend date to the extent that interest rates may have moved up or down since that date and (3) the margin over LIBOR.

The advantage of such issues is that local authorities can borrow for long periods but pay short-term interest rates.

MORTGAGES AND BONDS

These are usually considered by local authorities to be a method of raising long-term finance. Terms vary widely from one year to twenty years but the most common period lies in the two- to five-year range. Today the mortgage is a somewhat outmoded method of raising money because of the complications of issue which arise from the fact that it is a legal document under seal drawn up by the authorities' legal department. Since 1964, however, mortgages have largely been replaced by an all-purpose bond, often referred to as the 'local tap bond' or 'over the counter bond'. Its registration and transfer are simple and it can quite literally be issued over the counter with little formality.

An interesting distinction may be drawn not between bonds and mortgages but between the two separate types of borrowing which apply to each of these instruments. Lenders on mortgage were found by advertising in the local press or by circular; the loans usually having a minimum subscription of £500 thus ensuring that administrative costs were covered when sold in 'mortgage' format and carrying an interest rate of about ½% lower than offered to institutions for larger amounts. It is believed that considerable funds were (and still are) attracted to the public sector in this way which might otherwise have been placed with building societies or the commercial banks. For larger loans, however, the local authorities had to rely on money brokers in London to find them lenders. The terms and amount of these loans are agreed individually between lenders and the local authority with periods varying from one to seven years and amounts not usually less than £100,000. Yields vary, but approximate between ¼% and 1% higher than on the equivalent gilt-edged stocks. On rare occasions the local authorities have had to offer rates on a par with industrial debentures. The restrictions placed on temporary debt by the government made permanent reliance on short-term borrowing impossible. Consequently, as stock and marketable bond issues are regulated by the Bank, and P.W.L.B. finance by a formula, and because the smaller loans by their nature were unable to provide the necessary residual finance, the local authorities had to look to the money market to meet their needs.

MARKETABLE OR NEGOTIABLE BONDS

The local Government (Financial Provisions) Act 1963 provided that local authorities might issue bonds for periods of not less than one year, in denominations of £5 in multiples thereof. The title 'yearling bonds' is often used to describe these bonds although, in fact, they have a life of between one and four years.

Local authority bonds are attractive to the discount market on a number of counts. First, there are few other assets with a maturity between the three months of a Treasury bill and the shortest-dated Government security. Negotiable bonds also have 'same-day transferability', which increases their marketability. While these bonds are not 'eligible' security at the Bank they are 'defined' assets for the discount houses and so are excluded from the twenty-times capital ratio. More than 90% of all bonds in issue are held by the discount houses and whilst this provides an element of stability to their public sector debt portfolios, it severely restricts the liquidity of bonds as the only prospective purchasers would be other discount houses. This particular difficulty has only manifested itself since October 1971 because the banking sector is now much less willing to hold bonds as they do not count as reserve assets.

Issues are made either through the Stock Exchange or direct to the discount market. The Bank of England requires a minimum issue of £250,000 and also controls the timing and terms of the issues so as to maintain an orderly market. Limits are also imposed on issues of bonds in relation to local authorities total debt. Authorities with loan debt not exceeding £40 M. may only issue £1½ M. of bonds and when loan debt exceeds £400 M. the limit is £15 M.

Local authorities are now also able to issue variable rate negotiable bonds. The bonds were first issued on Tuesday, 22 November 1977 and this day and each subsequent Tuesday thereafter was designated as a 'Rate Fixing Day.'

The Reference Rate is computed from the average LIBOR rate for six month deposits in the same way as the stock issues. In all other respects the terms and conditions of issue are identical with fixed rate negotiable bonds.

The outstanding features of the distribution of negotiable bonds as between fixed rate and variable rate and maturity structure is illustrated in Table 12. Total fixed rate issues as at 1 May 1980 amounted to £872 M. (89% of issue) whilst variable rate issues stood at £106 M. or 11% of the total.

An examination of the maturity structure shows that 86% of fixed rate issues were due in less than twelve months, whereas only 6% of outstanding variable rate issues were due to mature within the same period demonstrating the reluctance of Treasurers to borrow longer at times of high interest rates.

TEMPORARY DEBT

Temporary debt is defined as debt with an initial maturity of less than one year. Local authorities are permitted to hold not more than 20% of total outstanding loan debt in the form of temporary debt and not more than 15% of total debt may be for three months or less.

Table 13 analyses the sources and maturity structure of temporary debt. It is clear that a large proportion of temporary borrowing is by way of short-term deposits repayable in up to seven days time. In 1969 temporary borrowing for up to seven days amounted to 72% of temporary debt, although since 1974 this proportion has declined somewhat and currently stands at about 57%.

Sources of temporary money come under three headings:
(1) Bank overdrafts
(2) Loans through money brokers
(3) Bill finance.

Table 12

LOCAL AUTHORITY NEGOTIABLE BONDS (£M.)
AS AT 1 MAY 1980

Maturing within (months)	Amounts in Issue		
	Fixed Rate	Variable Rate	Total
1	63	–	63
2	57	–	57
3	82	–	82
4–6	177	–	177
7–9	145	4	149
10–12	224	2	226
13–18	42	1	43
19–24	31	6	37
25–36	40	45	85
37–48	8	44	52
49–60	3	4	7
TOTAL	872	106	978

Source: Phillips & Drew.

(1) *Bank overdrafts*

Bank borrowings are not significant in total borrowings of local authorities and are looked upon as a means of smoothing overnight fluctuations in cash positions. The use of overdrafts has been reduced even more since 1974, as is clear from Table 13 by the imposition of limits on overdraft facilities by central government. These are designed to prevent 'soft arbitrage' by local authorities (i.e. switching between overdrafts and short-term money market finance depending on which is cheaper).

(2) *Loans through money brokers*

The acquisition of short-term deposits, for periods of two days to twelve months, but usually for less than a week, comprises the main form of temporary borrowing. The market is run by London money brokers (and some stock brokers) and funds are obtained from banks, financial institutions, industrial and commercial companies and overseas holders of sterling. As Table 13 shows, the most important source of deposits are the banks and other financial

Table 13

LOCAL AUTHORITY TEMPORARY DEBT OUTSTANDING

(£M.) 31 March	By type of debt									By term to repayment			
	Total	Revenue Bills (1)	Overdraft (2)	Other loans	Other financial institutions	Industrial and commercial companies	Personal sector	Other	Inter-authority	Total	Up to 7 days	Over 7 days up to 3 months	Over 3 months up to 12 months
1969	2,023		133	501	438	312	330	245	64	2,023	1,467	211	345
1970	2,013		163	442	470	274	336	251	77	2,013	1,450	240	323
1971	2,013	108	129	449	563	217	300	153	94	2,013	1,396	277	340
1972	2,115	187	43	429	571	276	267	237	105	2,115	1,401	320	394
1973	2,762	229	152	385	681	395	343	421	156	2,762	1,982	387	393
1974	3,562	277	265	306	1,069	519	329	588	209	3,562	2,468	524	570
1975	3,983	401	54	371	1,510	424	244	662	317	3,983	2,116	855	1,012
1976	3,909	407	23	368	1,462	443	210	616	380	3,909	2,019	921	969
1977	4,693	429	68	402	1,703	477	264	904	446	4,693	2,549	1,000	1,144
1978	4,358	455	37	751	1,489	280	207	730	419	4,358	2,428	998	932
1979	5,170	515	99	645	2,000	446	250	770	445	5,170	2,960	1,175	1,035

Notes: (1) before 1971 revenue bills were classified according to the sector taking them up.
(2) before 1973 bank overdrafts were measured net (i.e. credit balances were deducted from overdrafts).

Source: Financial Statistics, various issues.

institutions which deposit their excess resources in a reasonably liquid asset that offers a good return. A significant part of these deposits also represent on-lending of overseas funds held on deposit in sterling and foreign currencies. Indeed the local authority deposit rate is now the principal arbitrage rate. This market therefore has strong links with both the Euro-currency and sterling inter-bank markets in London.

Loans are generally in units of £100,000 to £1 M. although the larger authorities deal in larger figures. The instrument of borrowing is the deposit receipt and deals are arranged by telephone. The deposit receipt is simply an acknowledgement of the debt and is not negotiable. Therefore the deposit has to be held until maturity and cannot be traded on a secondary market.

Local authority deposit rates are closely correlated with inter-bank rates for similar maturities and are generally $\frac{1}{4}$ to $\frac{1}{2}\%$ above inter-bank rates. If rates move from the normal differential arbitrage flows between the markets will soon restore the balance.

(3) *Bill finance*

Since 1972 all local authorities have been permitted to issue revenue bills in anticipation of the receipt of revenues provided gross income from rates exceeds £3 M. Authorities may borrow up to one-fifth of such income by bills. Bills are usually issued in multiples of £25,000 and generally have a tenor of ninety-one days. The maximum theoretical life of a bill is twelve months, but in practice they are never issued for more than six months. This is because bills with a maturity not exceeding six months are eligible for rediscount at the Bank of England, as well as qualifying as reserve assets for banks and as 'defined assets' for discount houses.

The prices bid at the tender for local authority bills are largely a product of the size of the Treasury bill issue, the current level of short-term interest rates, and the likely future trend of interest rates. Thus, for example, when the volume of Treasury bills in issue is small there will be a keen demand for local authority bills. This is compounded by the fact that most local authority tenders occur on Friday afternoons after the results of the Treasury bill tender are known. Thus discount houses, which require public sector assets and were unsuccessful at the Treasury bill tender, compete in the local authority bill tender, forcing rates down. On occasions the local authority bill rate has in fact fallen below Treasury bill rate. In addition to being eligible for rediscount at the

Bank, local authority bills also have the attraction to discount houses that they are short-term instruments and thus less vulnerable to price movements at times of unstable interest rates than other public sector assets such as gilts and negotiable bonds.

Table 14 gives an analysis of bill portfolio of the banks and discount houses. Between them they hold approximately 50% of total issues although there have been wide fluctuations from time to time. Local authority revenue bills are classified as reserve assets and consequently there is competition between the banks and discount houses for these bills. During the last quarter of 1979 and the first quarter of 1980 the banks increased the share substantially from 25% to 39% of issues. Unfortunately it is not possible to ascertain from the published data which banks are holding the bills or indeed what proportion of issues are held by the Building Societies, although the latter were thought to be about £50 M. in 1979.

Table 14

REVENUE BILLS

	Total in issue (end quarter) £M.	Banks in UK (last make-up day in quarter)		Discount Houses (last make-up day in quarter)	
		Holding (£M.)	% of total	Holding (£M.)	% of total
1978 4	499	148	30	48	10
1979 1	515	87	17	230	45
2	541	169	31	140	26
3	565	172	30	140	25
4	599	152	25	64	11
1980 1	624	241	39	83	13
2					

Source: Phillips & Drew.

THE LOCAL AUTHORITY LOANS BUREAU

Inter-authority loans are by no means a new or recent innovation as is often supposed. The basic concept of self-help between local authorities was originated by the Treasurer of Wallasey before the First World War but interest in the scheme waned for a variety of reasons, until the mid-1950s when access by the P.W.L.B. was severely curtailed. The number of bureaux throughout the country has varied considerably over the years; at one time there were as many as sixteen reducing to five in 1968 and two by April 1970.

In an effort to simplify and streamline operations further, the Institute of Municipal Treasurers and Accountants* established a loans bureau as from 1 April 1971, which is managed by a loans bureau executive. There were two branches, one in the north at Nelson, and one in the south at Westminster. But now the northern office is closed and all operations are carried out in London.

Originally the intention was to channel funds from one local authority to another, but now the bureau will raise funds from or lend funds to public sector bodies or anyone in the private sector in competition with the London money brokers. The bureau has made large inroads into the brokers' business, especially as its commission rates can be lower (though the basis for charging is different). It is however handicapped to some extent by the limited contact with the Euro-currency and inter-bank markets – links which the money brokers have fostered for many years. Formally set up to facilitate the movement of funds between local authorities, the loans bureau has developed into a competitive and full-blooded money market operation. This is generally done by telephone at any time of day up to 4.30 p.m. from Monday to Friday. The bureau advises the potential borrowing authority of funds available and transfer of the loan is made against receipt at the London office of the borrowing authority's bank, or in accordance with the lender's instructions. The expenses incurred in operating the bureau are met from an annual subscription based on the rateable value of the local authority, and there is also an additional fee per transaction. The annual subscriptions are based on a sliding scale. The bureau is also used extensively as a source of information as to market conditions, etc., and by this procedure does make some contribution towards establishing a common rate of interest.

The present size and scope of the loans bureaux operations are shown in Table 15.

The number of loans granted has almost doubled since 1972 to 11,986 at the end of 1979 whilst sources of funds increased 600% from £963 M. to £6,857 M. It is clear that although there were substantial increases in funds between 1972 and 1974 the spectacular

---

* Now Chartered Institute of Public Finance and Accountancy.

Table 15

SOURCES OF FUNDS

Year ended 31 December	No. of Loans	Local Authority £M.	Other Sources £M.	Total £M.
1972	6,039	459·0	504·4	963·4
1973	8,481	566·6	1,415·0	1,981·6
1974	9,120	975·8	2,638·3	3,614·1
		PUBLIC SECTOR £M.	PRIVATE SECTOR £M.	
1975	11,962	3,072·3	1,925·6	4,997·9
1976	13,133	3,465·5	1,987·0	5,452·5
1977	12,937	3,571·4	2,261·7	5,833·1
1978	12,781	3,037·0	3,352·2	6,389·2
1979	11,986	2,372·7	4,485·0	6,857·7
9 Months ended 30.09.80	8,069	1,805·1	3,690·7	5,495·8

growth took place during 1975 and after. The chief reason for the growth lies in the fact that prior to 1974 only funds from local authorities and other private sector funds were included, but from 1975 onwards the nationalized industries and other public sector institutions lent funds to the bureau. During 1978 and 1979 the private sector sources also increased markedly from £2,261 M. in 1977 to £4,485 M. in 1979 as the bureau was successful in attracting additional funds from building societies, banks and commercial companies.

Another factor, which appears to distort the pattern of growth in the number of loans, occurs between 1977, 1978 and 1979 when the total number of loans fell by 156 and 797 respectively. This was probably due to the introduction of Loan Syndication techniques by the bureau where a lead manager (a major bank) places a loan with usually eight or nine other participants. The average size of syndicated loans is approximately £10 M.

THE SAFETY OF LOCAL AUTHORITY DEBT

The 1970s have witnessed a number of damaging financial crises which have tended to erode confidence in various markets.

The local authorities market is no exception and has been adversely affected by a number of events, quite unrelated in time and indeed in geographical location.

During 1975 the financial crisis in the city of New York emerged, revealing that the city was virtually bankrupt. The New York difficulties arose because of a rapidly falling tax base caused by a steadily declining population as people moved elsewhere. Consequently, the city council was borrowing to pay the wages of policemen and other municipal workers and to meet interest payments on funds already borrowed. The crisis undoubtedly caused international investment managers to reassess the safety of municipal debt. So even though this was not a British concern, international money markets are highly sensitive places, and the ripple effects were felt in London.

In addition, from time to time in recent years both central and local government politicians in the U.K. have made statements, however inadvertently, which have caused considerable difficulty for local authority treasurers in endeavouring to fund their borrowing needs. The net result has been a trend amongst investors which attempts to place local authorities in a ranking order.

Throughout 1979 and 1980 there has been a wide ranging debate about the size of public spending and local authority borrowing in particular. While few would quarrel, at least in essence, with the commendable efforts of the government to cut the level of public spending, there is no doubt that certain action taken by the authorities in 1980 reduced confidence in local authority investments. Clearly this was not the intention of the government but the scene was set when it was announced that the Rate Support Grant Settlement was to be abandoned in favour of a Block Grant, based on the government's view of each individual authority assessed spending need. Certain local authorities were named as over-spenders and thus authorities were being categorized on some scale of ranking by investors. The immediate result was that on 20 October 1980, the Japanese banks participating in the money market, withdrew from the local authority segment of the market. It can be seen therefore, that what originated in a sensible policy decision by Government to reduce its own expenditure, had unforseen and adverse secondary effects not only on the local authorities but also on London as a financial centre.

The point must be emphasized that U.K. local authorities debt is quite undoubted and therefore, that a two-tier local authority market is illogical for a number of reasons. First, all local authorities have lender of last resort facilities through the P.W.L.B. Secondly, all investments are secured and rank equally against the authorities revenues. All loans have equal rights i.e. there are no preferential rankings. Thirdly, U.K. local authorities can only borrow for capital purposes when a government loan sanction exists. Moreover, borrowing for revenue purposes can only be done against known revenue in that year. This last point in particular differentiates the British situation from New York. Finally, most local authorities debt is held against assets (e.g. council houses valued at cost not current value) the value of which far exceeds the particular authority's total debt.

CHANGES IN THE COMPOSITION OF
LOCAL AUTHORITY BORROWING

The Radcliffe Committee gave the total amount of temporary borrowing (that is, due within twelve months) in March 1958 as £512 M. out of a total indebtedness of £5,859 M. Thus temporary money had increased from £170 M. in 1955, or approximately three and a half times in only three years, and, more significantly, over 50% of the £512 M. was callable within seven days. This posed the question of whether or not local councils should finance their permanent investment in housing, roads, etc., by short-term borrowing. Radcliffe said that they should not be allowed to do so, but its objections were not because it thought short-term borrowing was unsound, but because it was 'clean contrary' to the funding policy of the government. It was ironic that the central government's own policies had caused this changing emphasis in local authorities' borrowing techniques. In 1955 the government had hoped, by forcing local authorities into the general capital market, that central government's control of the monetary and credit position would be improved, but in fact, after September 1957 local authorities felt that interest rates were (then) abnormally high and consequently borrowed extensively on short-term in the expectation of being able to finance these borrowings more cheaply at a later date. This then set the pattern of events until 1963 when the government introduced new measures to combat the trend. As a percentage of total borrowing, funds repayable within twelve months increased from 3¼% in 1955 to over 25% by 1963. Not surprisingly the London market for local authority short-term loans expanded at a spectacular rate during this period and by 1963 was a major sector in the London money market. This development of what was in effect a second and parallel money market complicated the Treasury's control of monetary policy and had significant and powerful implications for the balance of payments. Statistical information regarding the proportion of overseas funds which are invested in the local authority market tend at best to be 'guesstimates' and are only useful in giving some indication of general trends. In 1963 it was believed that a figure of £200 M.–£300 M. was reasonable. Quite obviously any sudden repatriation of funds of this order by overseas investors could cause serious embarrassment because in the final analysis had there been a withdrawal and had the local authorities been unable to meet it, the central government would have had to step in. It is, of course, inconceivable that the local authorities would, under any circumstances, be allowed to default but nevertheless paradoxical that this factor probably influenced foreign lenders by attracting additional 'hot money' into the country. An example of the difficulties that can arise occurred in 1962 when Bank rate was reduced, chiefly to discourage 'hot money' from coming in. However, the local authorities who were still in need of funds continued to attract foreign deposits by offering higher rates, thereby to that extent nullifying official policy. This method of attracting deposits can also be a means of circumventing a credit squeeze since the cost of money from any particular source is unlikely to have much effect on local authorities' total borrowing except over a long period, because most of their spending is determined by considerations of long-term policy. Local authority borrowing from the market, rather than from the P.W.L.B., rose dramatically between 1958 and 1961. During this period the overseas and foreign banks provided an important and, until the second quarter of 1961, an increasing share of short-term finance. At 31 March 1961 their loans totalled £121 M. This represented about 15% of total local authority borrowing at that date. The main lenders during the period (1957–61) were the 'other foreign banks' whose loans rose from £2 M. in December 1957 to £85 M. in March 1961 whilst British overseas banks' loans rose from £4 M. to £30 M. in the same period. The total loans by the overseas and foreign banks to local authorities fell from £121 M. to £93 M. during the second quarter of 1961 and this was probably associated with the outflow of foreign money which occurred at that time.

The Radcliffe Committee commented in 1958 on the lack of information concerning local authority outstanding debt. At the

Committee's request special surveys were made for 1955 and 1958 and subsequently these have been continued each year. The figures supplied in the original surveys were not completely accurate since some 110 authorities failed to make returns in 1960 (there was then no compulsion on local councils to render returns), but notwithstanding these omissions the general trend in the composition of local authority debt towards short-term borrowing was, even at this early stage, becoming evident. Borrowing from the P.W.L.B. fell by 18% in the five years to 1960. Meanwhile, temporary borrowing had increased from 4% to 12% and other mortgages had more than doubled to provide 22% of the debt.

With the escalation in the growth of short-term debt the local authorities were confronted with new problems. Firstly, the process sets up a need to borrow further, not only to finance new developments, but also to repay maturing advances. In 1960 over £370 M. or about 6% of total borrowing was repayable in seven days or less – some of it to overseas investors. Secondly, it was thought that the development might lead to a conflict with government monetary policy.

Towards the end of 1963 the government announced the terms of its revised arrangements for local authorities which we discussed earlier. Briefly, temporary borrowing was restricted to 20% of total debt and quotas were set for borrowing from the P.W.L.B. In one sense the White Paper was a contradiction in terms in that it created a paradoxical situation whereby a 'permanent' amount of temporary borrowing had been sanctified and moreover treasurers and money brokers soon realized that the new provisions were easily circumvented by borrowing for periods slightly in excess of one year. So, in fact, in 1964 there was little sign of a readjustment in temporary borrowing and a sharp increase in demands on the P.W.L.B. precipitated chiefly by the two increases in Bank rate. Local authority short-term debt (that is up to one year) increased by some £250 M. of which £185 M. was repayable within seven days. Furthermore, after the Bank rate increase in November with no change in the P.W.L.B. 'quota' rates, drawings escalated, and less was borrowed in the mortgage market where rates had risen appreciably. The rates for loans in excess of quotas were raised in concert with Bank rate. The government had estimated that additional borrowings from the P.W.L.B. would initially be approximately £200 M. rising to nearer £500 M. by 1968. By 31 March 1966, however, the local authorities had borrowed £535 M.

A further event which influenced the local authorities to borrow extensively from the P.W.L.B. and which also brought into prominence the risks of short-term borrowing, occurred at the end of 1964 when the drain on sterling sharply reduced the loans to local authorities by the overseas banks and accepting houses by £124 M., thus highlighting the government's concern. The year 1964 also saw the emergence of a new development in this market which only served to aggravate the government's fears regarding the short-term money market – this was the issue of local – or short-term bonds. Formerly, only two authorities – Manchester and Berkshire – had been empowered by Private Acts to issue bonds for general purposes. The Local Government (Financial Provisions) Act 1963 gave powers to all local authorities to issue bonds. In June four issues were made totalling £3 M. by placement with the discount houses. It soon became evident that a very large number of local councils were anxious to place substantial amounts of them because the bonds were easily transferable, a more attractive investment and thus a cheaper form of borrowing than mortgages of comparable maturity. Consequently the issue of bonds was strictly controlled by the Bank and furthermore such paper was not to be 'eligible' security at the Bank for loans to the discount market. It was feared that the effects of the measures introduced in April 1964 to curb the growth ot the short-term money market might be negated by allowing the local authorities to issue negotiable bonds.

If a substantial flow of the new bonds had been placed with the discount houses or the Stock Exchange, the Bank feared that their control over the short-term money market might be undermined. Therefore the authorities restricted the market for the bonds by informal hints and requests. The clearing banks were advised not to accept substantial amounts of the bonds as security for loans to the discount market and it was intimated to the merchant banks that they must not try to avoid the restrictions by issuing large quantities of 365-day paper in substitution for the existing 364-day obligations. The Bank's concern was that if substantial amounts of this new short-term paper were 'monetized' by the discount market (by obtaining loans against bonds from the clearing banks) it would have an expansionary effect on liquidity. By the end of 1964 local authority temporary debt stood some £359 M. higher than at the end of 1963. During the crisis caused by the withdrawal of foreign funds (in quarter ended 31 December 1964) the local authorities, by bidding high enough and by extensive use of domestic bank overdraft facilities, were able to raise their temporary debt from

£1,650 M. to £1,708 M. As a further extension of the new borrowing arrangements, during the financial year 1965–6, local authorities were allowed to draw 30% of their capital requirements from the P.W.L.B., as compared with 20% for the previous year with the exception that authorities in the 'less prosperous areas' were allowed to apply for 50% of their long-term requirements. Drawings on the board were so heavy that by July many authorities had already exceeded more than half their year's quota. In fact, by end-June £180 M. h.⸱d been drawn which was half the amount budgeted for the whole ⸱⸱ar. Subsequently, in August the government decided that local au ⸱⸱orities would only be able to draw the balance of their quota for th⸱ year by phased instalments with the proviso that authorities which had already drawn more than one half of their year's quota by late July would not be allowed any further drawings before October. Despite these restrictions, however, consolidated fund loans to local authorities during 1965–6 totalled £525 M. which exceeded the budget estimate by £165 M. At the same time considerable sums were raised by the issue of short-term bonds and stocks – £80 M. and £119 M. respectively, thus easing the pressure on the short-term money market.

In 1965 a significant development took place as City treasurers endeavoured to widen the scope of local authority borrowing albeit at the short end of the market. Manchester Corporation issued £3 M. of ninety-day bills in anticipation of revenue. The bills were very similar in nature to the Treasury bill, being readily negotiable and rediscountable at the Bank – thus making them very attractive to the discount market. Prior to this issue many local authorities had power, under local Acts, to issue bills but only for capital purposes; Treasury consent, which was required under the Control of Borrowing Order 1958, was not usually forthcoming. Under the Manchester Corporation Act 1965, Manchester's powers were extended to cover issues for revenue purposes up to a limit of £3 M. The Bank was not too concerned about the effects on liquidity of the new paper, despite its 'eligibility', because they stipulated that for sixty days of the year there must be no bills on issue. Furthermore, the local bills were (unlike the Treasury bill) self-liquidating when the revenue matured. Drawings from the P.W.L.B. in 1966–7 continued on a massive scale particularly during the March quarter because many authorities' quotas had been underestimated stemming from the extent to which temporary borrowing was being replaced by longer-term debt. In all approximately £170 M. was borrowed from the board during the three months. Not unnaturally, the government felt unable to follow the White Paper (of 1963) and a further 10% increase in the proportion of long-term debt which could be obtained from the P.W.L.B. was not sanctioned. Instead the 1965–6 quotas were applied but long-term borrowing was redefined more narrowly to exclude the refinancing of debt that had been included in the previous financial year as part of an authority's long-term borrowing in the calculation of its quota. The object of this restriction was to exclude from quotas the renewal of the growing number of one-year bonds and short-dated mortgages in the market.

Mention was made earlier of the difficulty in obtaining reliable figures to show the extent that local authorities have relied on overseas funds. The chief difficulty arises in identifying the sources of funds which are received by local authorities through various intermediaries in this country. For example, in March 1966 direct overseas holdings totalled £215 M., £172 M. in temporary debt, £29 M. in mortgages and £14 M. in stocks. In addition, however, a considerable proportion of the £556 M. held by banks and accepting houses represented reinvestments by these organizations of funds from abroad. Of this total it was estimated that about £370 M. of foreign funds were invested in local authority temporary loans. At the same time the sterling inter-bank market was estimated to have liabilities in the region of £400 M.–£1,000 M. It becomes obvious that there can be no claim to precision in the figures and the best that can be said for them is that they show an ever-growing market for foreign investment, direct or indirect, in London. What does become clear, however, is the danger to sterling because the great bulk of funds lent to the London discount market, local authorities and in the inter-bank market are very short-term funds, short-term here being defined as call to seven days. The significance of these very short-term funds was not fully appreciated in the early and middle 1960s because the key covered arbitrage margin was considered to be the one covering swaps of three-month Euro-dollar deposits against local authority loans. At times when confidence in sterling is low it is the volatile uncovered deposits for seven days or less which are pulled out of London and, conversely, flood back in again (once more uncovered), when confidence in the pound returns. Three-month's money is, of course, almost invariably never switched without foreign exchange cover and so long as the cost of such cover is taken into account, an interest incentive could continue to attract funds even when confidence in sterling is low. Therefore, at times when sterling is under pressure, it is pertinent to concentrate on the covered margin on three-months' Euro-dollar and local authority loans as the vital indicator to the flows of sterling, but when sterling is not under pressure it is the combination of this margin plus the uncovered margin on very short-term funds which will be the deciding factor as to whether or not the London money market is attracting foreign money.

During the financial year 1967–8 changes were made to the criteria for access to the P.W.L.B. Authorities were to be allowed to borrow up to 34% of their capital expenditure, that is actual capital payments during the year less capital receipts and central government grants and loans. Formerly, the basis for calculating access to the P.W.L.B. had been a variable percentage of their gross long-term borrowing requirements. The purpose of the new formula was primarily to bring actual local authority drawings on the board more into line with budget estimates since capital expenditure can be more easily estimated than the gross amount of long-term borrowing. The limit on temporary debt remained at 20% of all outstanding borrowing but authorities with proportions in excess of this were allowed to borrow up to 30% of the amount of funding which it carries out in reducing its temporary debt to the 20% limit. The time limit which was set in 1964, whereby local authorities were required to reduce their temporary debt to not more than 20% of total debt in 1968, was extended a further year until 31 March 1969. The arrangements for smaller authorities were continued as before and the board was to remain as a lender of the last resort for those authorities who were unable to meet their requirements in the market. The net borrowing of local authorities from central government during 1967–8 in fact fell, and was only £347 M. against a budget estimate of £480 M. The chief reason for this decline was attributable to the high rates of interest particularly early in 1968, when $9\frac{1}{4}$% was quoted in March for seven-day money (the rate had only been 8% in February). In May 1967 the government altered the rate structure of the P.W.L.B. when all the board's loan rates, both within or outside quotas, reflected the appropriate government lending rates. Previously, the rates had carried an element of subsidy; quota borrowing rates had been unchanged since August 1964, ranging between $5\frac{3}{4}$% to $6\frac{1}{8}$%. These rates were gradually increased to $7\frac{5}{8}$%. The local authorities not surprisingly continued to borrow short and this was fully reflected in the banking sector's figures for advances to local authorities – total advances rose from £657 M. in December 1966 to £1,017 M. in December 1967. The accepting houses and overseas banks increased their lending by £269 M. to £796 M. while domestic bank advances jumped by £91 M. to £217 M. – a figure only subsequently exceeded in March 1968 when advances rose to £237 M. The year 1968–9 saw an increase of about one-third in net borrowings from central government to a total of some £469 M., the rise illustrating the local authorities' efforts to fund under the new formula. This trend did not continue, however, in the following financial year when only £56 M. was borrowed bringing the total net borrowing to £525 M. The local authorities also continued to raise funds in the new capital issues market although borrowings from this source fell for the third consecutive year in 1968 to £159 M. from £192 M. in 1967.

By 31 March 1968 the local authorities had, in aggregate, achieved the target set in 1964 of reducing their temporary borrowing to 20% of total debt, but notwithstanding this it was estimated that some 300 authorities were still in excess and that about £250 M. of funding would still be necessary to bring them into line. However, local authorities continued to rely heavily on temporary borrowing; in 1966 approximately 70% was repayable within seven days and by 1973 the proportion remained substantially the same. If we compare the 'other loans' figure of £527 M. with the quoted lendings to local authorities by the overseas banks and accepting houses of £1,307 M. (as at end-June 1969) it would appear to suggest that much of the authorities' borrowing from these banks was for periods of *more* than one year.

Table 16

LOCAL AUTHORITY NET EXTERNAL BORROWINGS* (£M.)

	Total Net Borrowings	Net Temporary Borrowings	Net Long-Term Borrowings
1974/75	3,185	189	2,996
1975/76	2,443	−143	2,576
1976/77	1,971	696	1,275
1977/78	1,442	−325	1,767
1978/79	1,206	717	489
1979/80	2,830	1,256	1,574
TOTAL	13,067	2,390	10,677

Sources: CSO Financial Statistics.
* Excluding Inter-Authority Debt.

Table 16 shows the movements in net external borrowings by
local authorities since 1974 and these show a continuing decline
from 1974/5 to £489 M. in 1978/9 and a substantial increase in 1979/
80 to £1,574 M. For 1980/81 it is estimated that the total will rise to
some £2,100 M.

A more revealing change which is however highlighted in the
table, is the switch to short-term borrowing which has taken place
in 1978/9 and 1979/80. Thus in 1974/5 94% of local authority borrowing was long-term but by 1978/79 and 1979/80 the figures were
41% and 56% respectively. The major factors underlying this
change have been the general high level of interest rates and the
impact of the General Consent under the Control of Borrowing
Order, the Voluntary Borrowing Code and the availability of interest rates charged on P.W.L.B. funds.

Table 17

LOCAL AUTHORITY BORROWINGS FROM THE PWLB

	Net Borrowings		Gross Borrowings		
	Amount (£M.)	As % of net long-term borrowings by local authorities	Amount (£M)	As % of estimated quota available	Average rates of Interest on new borrowings (%)
1974/75	1,121	37·4	1,834	113	12½
1975/76	1,149	44·6	2,113	101	11½
1976/77	613	48·1	1,679	65	12¼
1977/78	1,060	60·0	2,273	95	10⅛
1978/79	337	68·6	1,670	64	12
1979/80	797	50·6	2,361	94	12⅞

Sources: CSO Financial Statistics and P.W.L.B. Reports.

Borrowings from the P.W.L.B. are analysed in Table 17 and this
shows how successful the local authorities have been in borrowing
for longer periods. In 1976/77 advances repayable over 10 years
were only 6·2% of the total, in 1977/78 they had risen to 10·6%,
reaching 16·9% in 1978/79.

An examination of gross borrowings shows the proportion of the amounts the Government estimated could be drawn from the P.W.L.B. In 1974/5 and 1975/76 drawings actually exceeded originally estimated quotas but by 1978/9 drawings amounted to only 64% of quota. Drawings in 1979/80 represented 94% of quota at an average rate of $12\frac{7}{8}\%$. The largest net drawings occurred in 1975/76 and 1977/78 when long-term interest rates were at relatively low levels. These two periods were when long-term borrowings were exceptionally heavy and there was a net reduction in temporary debt.

MONEY MARKET FUNDING

The term 'money market' is defined as borrowings from the Personal sector, Public Corporations and other government sources other than the P.W.L.B. Table 18 shows the extent of the use of money market funds and especially the impact of changes in the relative rates charged by the P.W.L.B. compared to the money market. It is particularly noticeable in 1977/78 when P.W.L.B. rates were very low in anticipation of a reduced rate of inflation. Yields on gilt-edged securities govern the rates charged by the P.W.L.B. which fell to $10\frac{1}{8}\%$ in 1977/78. At all other times during the six year period net borrowings by the local authorities never fell below 44·9% and were usually 60% or over.

Table 18

LOCAL AUTHORITY BORROWINGS THROUGH
THE MONEY MARKETS (%)

| | As percentage of total net borrowings | | |
	Long Term	Short term	Total
1974/75	55·1	5·7	60·8
1975/76	50·8	−5·9	44·9
1976/77	28·3	34·9	63·2
1977/78	36·9	−22·2	14·7
1978/79	8·3	56·2	64·5
1979/80	30·9	42·7	73·6

Source: CSO Financial Statistics.

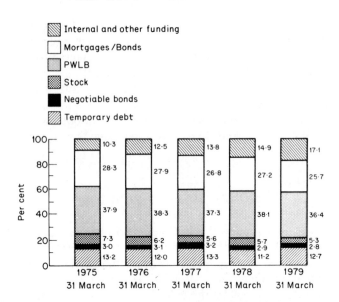

Graph 2 shows the various sources of local authority borrowing as percentages of outstanding debt. Despite the variations in funding patterns over the period, the proportions remain surprisingly consistent. No fund source has varied by more than 2% of the total, except for internal sources which rose 6.8% over the period.

Source: Phillips & Drew.

AN ANALYSIS OF MONEY MARKET
AND OFFICIAL SOURCES OF FUNDS

A significant feature of Table 19 is the steep upward trend in the percentage of funds, both temporary and longer term, which the banks are providing to local authorities (i.e. *excluding* official debt). This has risen from 42% in 1975 to 43·7% in 1977, and then a steep rise of 11% in 1978 (in temporary borrowing) to 55·5%. Market debt currently stands at 61% (in mid-1980). This increasing level of funding by the banking system stems from the declining liquidity of other lenders and the continuing development of London as a financial centre. Before turning to a more detailed analysis of the figures there are a number of definitional problems which need explanation.

First, the Trustee Savings Banks are not included in the 'banks' sector but listed among 'Other Financial Institutions'. The banking tables in Financial Statistics include a heading 'market loans to local authorities' and this includes not only temporary loans but

Table 19

OFFICIAL AND MONEY MARKET DEBT (£M.)

| | OFFICIAL | | MONEY MARKET | | | | | |
| | *Central Govt & Public* | | *Banks* | | | *Other Financial Institu- tions* | | |
	P.W.L.B.	*Corpns*	*O/D*	*Temp*	*L/T*		*Rest*	*TOTAL*
1975	10,044	143	54	371	2357	4227	3947	21,143
1976	11,193	265	23	368	2,856	4,872	3,811	23,388
1977	11,806	530	68	402	3,030	5,209	4,216	25,261
1978	12,866	417	37	751	3,200	5,436	3,828	26,535
1979	13,203	412	99	645	3,897	5,639	3,800	27,697*
1980	14,000	768	166	904	4,681	6,094	4,045	30,660*

*Minor discrepancies caused by roundings.

MONEY MARKET DEBT
Banks as a Proportion of the Total

31 March	Temporary %	Longer Term %
1975	11·8	30·2
1976	12·8	31·6
1977	12·0	31·7
1978	23·8	31·7
1979	16·5	38·3
1980	18·9	42·1

Source: Phillips & Drew.

also rollovers and other loans and mortgages with a life of less than five years, and loans negotiated through brokers. This distinction is noted because *direct* loans in these categories are included under 'public sector advances'. Stocks, bonds, longer loans, and mortgages are listed under other investments.

The simplest way round these statistical inconsistencies is to compare market loans and public sector advances and relate them to inter-bank loans. The comparisons in Table 20 shows the prominent position of the clearing banks in the inter-bank market and contrasts their relatively low involvement in local authority financing. The important feature of the accepting houses however, is that

Table 20

BANKS IN THE U.K.

Sterling Assets (other than reserve Assets) – 19 March 1980

No. of Institutions in category 1 Jan 1980		A. Market Loans to UK Local Authorities £M.	B. Advances to UK Public Sector £M.	C. Market Loans to Banks in UK and Discount Market £M.	A + B as proportion of C %
6	London Clearing Banks	364	247	6,401	9·5
3	Scottish Clearing Banks	21	88	508	21·5
4	N Ireland Banks	59	17	138	55·1
35	Accepting Houses	548	143	1,063	65·0
70	British Banks – other	1,132	108	6,412	19·3
62	Overseas Banks – American	376	270	1.587	40·7
22	– Japanese	7	157	293	56·0
129	– Other	514	351	2.429	35·6
29	Consortium Banks	141	158	362	82·6
360	TOTAL	3,162	1,540*	19,192*	24·5

*Minor discrepancies caused by rounding.

Source: Phillips & Drew

they provide over 17% of market loans to local authorities but less than 6% of market loans to banks. The American banks participation in both market loans and public sector is also greater than the clearing banks as are the figures for 'other overseas banks'. 'Other British banks' are the largest operators in the inter-bank market but are proportionally smaller in the local authority sector. The consortium banks are the most heavily committed with some 82% of their inter-bank business carried out through market loans to local authorities and public sector advances.

The debt holdings of 'other financial institutions' totalled some £6 bn. now exceed the total of all the banks in aggregate and a breakdown of the investments is shown in Table 21. The close financial ties between the local authorities and the building societies are evidenced by the 39% of short-term assets, and 31% of long-term investments held in local authority debt.

Table 21

OTHER FINANCIAL INSTITUTIONS
Local Authority Exposure

		Amount £M.	%
Building Societies	– short	964	39
	– long	1,783	31
TSB	– short	102	4
	– long	1,163	31
NSB	– Investments	257	21
Insurance Companies	– short	310	11
	– long (est)	2,000	5
Superannuation Funds	– short	433	30
	– long (est)	420	1

Source: Phillips & Drew

The Trustee Savings Bank held only £102 M. in local authority short-term debt because at present most of their short-term funds are held as balances of the National Debt Office and Central Trustee Savings Bank. Their holdings of longer-term investments amounts to 31% of Trustee Savings Bank longer maturities. The breakdown of National Savings Banks investments (not shown in the table) is 5% of temporary local authority debt (£61 M.) and 16% in longer investments (£196 M.). Perhaps of more significance for both Trustee Savings Banks and National Savings Banks is their high level of market purchases and sales, in the latter case the annual turnover in 1979 was some nine times the average holding.

As might be envisaged the insurance companies held a much lower proportion of short-term debt (11%) than the banks and Building Societies together. Their longer term local authority investments although substantial at £2,000 M. is dwarfed by their total investments of £44,000 M. Similarly the Superannuation Funds total of £853 M. in all local authority debt must be kept in perspective against total investments of £29,584 M.

7 The sterling inter-bank market

ITS NATURE AND ORIGINS

It is not too difficult to pinpoint the emergence of the inter-bank market, at least in embryo, in the late 1950s. The first significant moves were made in 1955 when the government effectively closed the Public Works Loan Board to local authorities, forcing them to bid for funds in the open market. At about that time the Euro-dollar market was in the early stages of its development, and there is little doubt that the latter market inspired the close identity of methods and techniques now existing in the inter-bank market. Indeed, there are many similarities between the inter-bank and Euro-dollar markets – most importantly they are both essentially systems of 'matched deposit'* banking whereby loans are negotiated between banks in large round amounts on an unsecured basis. Most of the inherent faults of the Euro-dollar system (discussed in Chapter 8) exist in the inter-bank market – such problems as 'double' counting and the difficulties of control.

Initially, the sterling inter-bank market was little more than an adjunct of the local authority market enabling the non-clearing banks to borrow from each other and on-lend the funds to local authorities. Subsequently, specialist money brokers entered the field acting as intermediaries between them. The market has developed virtually into a sterling equivalent of the Euro-currency markets. In 1955 the London money market was a relatively simple mechanism with the discount houses borrowing mostly overnight from the clearing banks to finance their holdings of government short-term paper. The Bank of England thus had a moderately responsive method of credit control and effective control of short-

---

* J. R. S. Revell, 'Changes in British Banking – The Growth of a Secondary Banking System', Hill Samuel Occasional Paper No. 3, February 1968, p. 25.

term interest rates through the media of open-market operations and the syndicated bid of the discount houses at the weekly Treasury bill tender. The advent of the local authorities' market, the lifting of lending restrictions on banks and finance houses, the removal of official restrictions on the flows of short-term funds, both nationally and internationally, created a climate of competition for funds. While subsequent official restriction hampered growth in the primary market, the maintenance by the clearing banks of rigid long-established cartel agreements on interest rates (until September 1971) left many opportunities which the new markets have exploited to the full. The vital element in the parallel markets is the competition in interest rates. The genesis of the new monetary developments was the return of a flexible Bank rate policy in the early 1950s. A system existed therefore where the local authorities, finance houses, and other borrowers compete for funds with the discount market: the inter-bank market is now a general purpose money market, which allowed the non-clearing banks to bypass the discount market thereby diminishing the Bank of England's control over credit and, more significantly, over short-term rates. Since the implementation of the Bank's measures in September 1971, the non-clearing banks have, of course, once more increased the quantity of their funds placed in the discount market following the more competitive rates offered and the fact that call money with the discount market is now a reserve asset.

Such a brief introduction serves only to indicate the *raison d'être* of the sterling inter-bank market. At this point, however, the area of study undertaken in this chapter must be defined more precisely. It is not intended to review in detail the complete range of assets and liabilities of the non-clearing banks and their business. The analysis will be confined to the sterling deposit liabilities of these banks, held by other United Kingdom banks, and their counterparts on the opposite side of the balance sheet, the liquid assets, comprising balances with other United Kingdom banks and loans to local authorities. These are the items which reflect the growth of the sterling inter-bank market.

THE OPERATORS IN THE MARKET

Since the sterling inter-bank market is the key link between all the other sectors of the London money market it is hardly surprising that the operators in this market consist of an amalgam comprising almost every branch of finance in the city. The main lenders of funds are the merchant banks (or accepting houses), the overseas and foreign banks in London, the clearing banks' subsidiaries and affiliates, central banks, and 'supra-national' institutions and (since 1971) the clearing banks themselves. Many non-bank lenders with surplus funds are also involved including pension funds, large commercial and industrial companies, insurance companies, finance companies, savings banks, and even the discount houses. In addition, acting as intermediaries are the six main sterling money brokers: Butler Till, Martins, Kirkland-Whittaker, Marshalls, Fulton Packshaw and Astley-Pearce, and some fourteen members of the Foreign Exchange and Currency Deposit Brokers' Association. It has been estimated that approximately 300 institutions take part in the inter-bank market, rendering it an impossible task to trace the course of transactions. As with the Euro-currency market, the original lender of funds, which might be a bank or a non-bank institution, has no control over or knowledge of the identify of the final user. Moreover, even if all lenders and subsequent borrowers could be identified, a complete picture would still not be obtained since funds may change hands several times, thereby constructing a complicated chain of borrowers and lenders.

REASONS FOR GROWTH

We must now be more specific and discuss the reasons for the development of the sterling inter-bank market. As a concomitant of this we must also examine the significance of inter-bank deposits which in essence are a breach of English deposit banking tradition, and therefore fundamental to a discussion of this sector of the money market. As with most other facets of the money market, the reasons underlying the growth of the inter-bank market are complex and not always easily identified. There are, however, three factors which may be singled out as being of particular importance: a substantial rise in demand for relatively cheap short-term bank and other finance; the increased sophistication and complexity of the financial system in meeting the diverse requirements of the economy, and the ability of the secondary banks to make optimum use of their financial resources in the absence of restrictions on interest rates, creating increasing competition among them. As noted in the first part of the chapter, the most significant reason underlying these factors has been the massive requirements of the local authorities and the increasing sophistication of corporate treasurers. Looked at from the standpoint of the non-clearing banks, the complementary markets had, prior to the introduction of the Bank's new policies in 1971, two crucial advantages.

First, they enabled the secondary banker to meet his liquidity requirements with not nearly so great a sacrifice of yield as the conventional discount market imposed on the deposit banker. The interest rates in parallel markets fluctuate with supply and demand for short-term funds and the markets were outside the direct control of the authorities. Despite considerable variations in the relative levels of interest rates between the different complementary markets, yields were substantially higher than the traditional discount market would offer on Treasury bills, call money, and commercial bills. Since September 1971, however, there has been a much closer identity of rates throughout the money market as competition from the discount houses was increasingly felt. The effects of this competition can be seen from the fact that in 1970 over 60% of the discount market's borrowed funds came from the clearing banks, but by the end of 1971 the proportion had dropped to 42%. The secondary banks increased their proportion from 23% to over 35% during the same period. Secondly, the newer markets offered a much wider variety of paper and maturities than the discount market. American influence in the sterling inter-bank market has been very strong, stemming from the very large contingent of banks owned or controlled by U.S. parent organizations. These banks were attracted to London by the necessity of operating in the Euro-dollar market. Furthermore, a London address would, in American eyes, have tremendous prestige in the United States, especially in view of the large number of American companies operating in Great Britain. It is also significant to the institutional arrangements which exist in the inter-bank market, that the American banks already operate in the Federal Funds' Market where techniques are substantially similar. Since almost a quarter of the foreign banks operating in London are American it is hardly surprising that many of the techniques and innovations emanate from this source. The following are among the more important of the developments which they pioneered:

(1) Stemming from their reliance on bought money, American banks gave the initial impetus to the growth of the inter-bank

market, thus maximizing the use of available short-term funds.
(2) The sterling and dollar Certificates of Deposit.
(3) The introduction of lending rates geared to the cost of money rather than Bank rate, a feature now common to all British banks.
(4) Special savings accounts.
(5) Cash flow credit analysis and the term or 'roll-over' loan.

Table 22 shows that the movement out of discount market assets since 1966 has continued unabated. The somewhat depressing situation for the discount houses is that in each of the four groups of banks the percentage of discount market assets held has fallen. Furthermore, it is also noticeable that the deterioration continued after the Bank's new arrangements for competition were put into force. The trends shown by Table 22 must mean a large loss of business for the discount market as a whole and may have been attributed to a certain distaste, in the early days of the new markets at least, by the more traditional sections of the City, for the perhaps revolutionary business methods utilized in the complementary markets. Undboutedly, the discount houses and many others in the City completely miscalculated the extent to which the local authority market in particular would grow, coupled with grave doubts concerning the viability and safety of a sterling market carrying substantial unsecured loans.

The other significant trend shown in the table is the enormous growth in parallel market assets for all groups of banks. This shows the general trend of banks away from public sector paper towards private sector instruments such as certificates of deposit and acceptances.

THE SIGNIFICANCE OF MATCHED DEPOSIT BANKING

It is now a matter of historical record that the deposit banks did not borrow funds from other banks within the system, whether it be another deposit bank or the Bank of England – it was a convention that was never broken. It would perhaps be more realistic to say that the banks did not borrow direct from each other, but in practice they did so through the medium of the discount market by either advancing or withdrawing call money. Thus the emergence of the inter-bank sterling market represents a significant breach in tradition. The genesis of this innovation undoubtedly came from

Table 22

LIQUID ASSETS AS A PERCENTAGE OF
STERLING DEPOSITS

(%) December make-up date	Discount Market*						Parallel Market†					
	1958	1966	1970	1972	1976	1979	1958	1966	1970	1972	1976	1979
London Clearing banks	26·5	24·5	26·0	12·7	8·7	8·1	–	–	–	11·2	14·0	20·9
Accepting Houses	45·1	15·3	21·2	10·0	12·6	10·4	15·8	43·0	59·5	60·4	51·4	53·6
American Banks	41·0	8·7	9·7	9·6	10·6	8·1	9·0	23·1	50·5	54·6	34·6	35·0
Other foreign and Consortium Banks	43·2	16·9	12·6	11·6	12·7	9·4	13·6	35·4	60·6	59·2	35·6	50·0

* Defined to include: call money and sterling bills discounted.
† Defined to include: sterling loans to other U.K. banks, loans to U.K. local authorities and sterling Certificates of Deposit.

Note: (1) It is only possible to obtain figures for total deposits (sterling and foreign currency) for the year 1958 and for the London Clearing Banks prior to 1971 therefore the figures are not strictly comparable. However, the foreign currency activities of the banks concerned during these periods were very small.

Source: Bank of England Statistical Abstract and update.

the Euro-dollar market with its strong American influence. The nature of the business undertaken by the deposit banks in Great Britain until 1971 at least is well known: it is predominantly domestic in character with the majority of deposits held on current account. Advances are generally in the form of overdrafts, which are subject to annual review and renewal, or cancellation. There are considerable numbers of small accounts. When examining the non-clearing bank deposit liabilities, however, it can be seen that nearly all deposits (and loans) are for a fixed term and bear interest, which fluctuates with market conditions. Normally, rates were lower than the rates paid by local authorities for deposits of a similar maturity, the usual range extended between Bank rate and 1% below Bank rate.* The other principal feature of both deposits and advances is that units are large, with minimum sums of £50,000 or £100,000 being the norm. Deposit banks are, of course, distinctive in that they also provide a money transmission service which, in the main, the non-clearing banks do not provide.

Since 1971 of course, there have been significant changes in the nature of the clearing banks' activities and the distinction between clearing and non-clearing banks is no longer so clear. The clearing banks are making increasing use of term loans and wholesale deposits. By 1974 44% of total sterling deposits came from the money markets, although this proportion has subsequently declined. Similarly, in 1976 contractual term loans amounted to 40% of total advances to U.K. non-personal borrowers.

In order to complete the contrast between the two types of banker, there is one other factor, which must be examined in some detail, and that is the question of liquidity. The make-up of the clearing banker's balance sheet is totally different from that of the secondary banker and, indeed, there are also considerable contrasts between the individual groups of non-clearing banks.

The reasons underlying these variations are not easily identified by the outside observer but exist because of the differences in the institutional organization of the groups. For instance, the British banks with overseas branch networks are obliged to maintain a higher degree of liquidity than the foreign banks, because they may be called upon to act as a lender of the last resort in addition to providing normal liquidity requirements dictated by the level of business in London. The foreign banks, however, are in the happy position of being able to call upon their head office or parent

---

* Now Minimum Lending Rate.

abroad if for some reason money becomes tight and produces sudden demands on their liquid resources. There is one drawback in relying on the parent office, however, which manifests itself in times of crises. If the foreign bank is in a particularly illiquid position it may be forced to bring in funds from abroad in disadvantageous conditions deriving from unfavourable interest rates or arbitrage costs. Generally, of course, they endeavour to avoid such situations by judicious liquidity control in the light of experience. Now that the British banking system is subject to a universal reserve ratio, the question of liquidity of the non-clearing banks does not have quite its former importance. Under the old methods of control the secondary banker was virtually outside Bank of England jurisdiction and consequently certain liquid assets, such as call money with the discount market, were kept to a minimum. Under the present arrangements approximately 50% of their reserve ratio is made up by call money with the discount market. Such funds must, of course, be secured and at call or at least 'callable' to qualify as reserve assets. To this extent only, then, the non-clearing banks' operations in the inter-bank sterling market are less at risk. In no way does it affect the dangers, which are ever present in this market and which could arise from a bank overextending itself, or from the dangers, which stem from the lending banker being unaware of the identify of the ultimate borrower, or the purpose for which the funds were borrowed. Money lent in the traditional market is generally utilized for sound self-liquidating purposes.

The controlling of the maturity and currency structure of a banker's balance sheet is known as 'matching'; one banker's loan is another banker's deposit. Thus the main function of inter-bank deposits is that of filling gaps in the maturity structure on each side of the balance sheet. The non-clearing banker can therefore control the liquidity of his balance sheet in two important ways: currency and maturity. He must be in a position to do so because of the exceptionally large units of account in which he deals. There are two important reasons for the need for this liquidity:

(1) Deposits are generally short-term in nature and must, therefore, be covered by assets of a similar short maturity.
(2) The Bank of England maintains a close scrutiny of the asset structure of London banks and in particular the adequacy of their liquid position.*

At this juncture the assets and liabilities which, in the main, comprise the non-clearing banker's liquidity, must be examined. On the liability side of the balance sheet the principal items are deposits with other United Kingdom banks and, since 1968, sterling Certificates of Deposit; this latter instrument amounted to some 26% of the secondary bank's gross sterling deposits by October 1972. During the same period balances with other U.K. banks rose from 26% to 36% of gross sterling deposits indicating the ever-increasing activity in the market. When Certificates of Deposit were introduced in 1968 many observers questioned the usefulness of the new instrument and the viability of a substantial market arising in them. Any such doubts have now been dispelled and although the Certificate of Deposit market is dwarfed in size by the inter-bank market it still attracts a considerable volume of funds.

Of the assets, apart from balances with other United Kingdom banks (the counterpart of deposits on the liabilities side of the balance sheet), the loans to local authorities comprise the other main component of liquid assets. It is, of course, impossible to determine the true liquidity of local authority borrowings without a close examination of each bank's portfolio, but such an examination would undoubtedly reveal a wide range of maturities. The loans amounted to approximately £2,000 M. by the end of 1972. It is often said that the market provides a cushion of liquidity for the other complementary markets. Whilst this is undoubtedly true it should be pointed out that the market is not a source of liquidity for the banking sector as a whole because each claim is matched by a liability elsewhere in the system.

Before leaving this vital question of liquidity, it is important to discuss one further factor, which has a strong influence in the inter-bank market. The Bank will stand behind the traditional market by acting as a lender of the last resort; the inter-bank market has no such safeguard. There is always the possibility, when tight money conditions arise, that a bank might not be able to borrow the funds it requires to meet its commitments for short maturities, however solvent it might prove in the long run. Such a situation did in fact arise in 1973/74 with the 'fringe banking crisis'. Following the collapse of London and County Securities there was an acute loss of

---

* During 1980 the Bank of England introduced proposals for capital adequacy measurement which were formalised in September 1980. Proposals for liquidity measurement and control were also discussed but remain still to be agreed with the Clearing and other banks (October 1980).

confidence in many 'fringe' banks as well as in some of the listed banks such as United Dominions Trust. The result was that many non-clearing banks suffered a rapid withdrawal of deposits, which they were unable to replace from the money markets, and were left with insufficient liquid resources to meet their commitments.

In the event few of these banks were allowed to fail as the Bank of England launched a 'lifeboat operation' by which the clearing banks recycled the deposits back to the fringe banks in order to provide them with the required liquidity. Thus it is clear that the Bank of England is in fact willing to act as a lender of last resort in the inter-bank market if this is necessary to avert a major banking crisis.

Although all banks in the market generally place limits on the total amount in which they will deal with any other bank, the methods used for determining any individual are many and varied. Most of the banks operating in this market also operate in the Euro-dollar market, and consequently most names are fairly well known. For example, the names of affiliates of the clearing banks or banks controlled by clearing banks are taken for very substnatial amounts. The limits set for the many American and foreign banks in London are based upon the standing of the parent institution abroad. Special relationships between banks are taken into consideration so that banks owned by a number of banks of various nationalities are also usually given substantial limits. Balance sheets may be examined and limits fixed on the basis of a percentage of the bank's capital resources. This may vary as much as from 10% to 30% of resources. Sometimes limits are determined as a fixed proportion of total or liquid assets. Other banks may assess the position by examination of the balance sheet as a whole or pay particular attention, as in the case of foreign banks, to the size of their sterling or foreign currency commitments. There is always a danger of onerous exchange control regulations being imposed by other countries.

Whatever limits are fixed they are not generally a permanent feature; this stems from the fact that this market is so active and volatile that the extent and nature of a bank's operations will influence its credit rating. If a bank wishes its name to retain a first-class rating in the market it must be seen to be a borrower as well as a lender. Thus any bank which became an unduly large and persistent borrower would soon have its limits lowered by the banks in the market. It is one of the main criticisms of this market that there is no 'clearing house' for, or pooling of, information regarding the creditworthiness of the many operators. The bulk of the business done is, however, transacted through brokers who are therefore in the best position to know if a particular bank is over-borrowing Indeed, it is known to be the policy of many banks to place up to 50% of their total deposits into the market and then borrow it back again to ensure that their name remains first-class. Admittedly, this percentage is high and is not necessarily representative of the market as a whole but it is an established practice. The brokers are not, of course, allowed to divulge information they may have concerning an individual bank over-borrowing but they are in a position not to conduct any further business with that particular bank until the position has improved. Whatever precautions may be taken by the banks in this market and however strictly limits are observed, no one bank (or broker) can ever know the true extent of a particular bank's total aggregate borrowing in the market as a whole. It is this unknown quantity that renders the lack of last-resort facilities of such importance and which has caused misgivings from time to time about the true strength of the market.

THE GROWTH OF THE MARKET

Table 23 sets out some important indicators in the growth of the sterling inter-bank market. It must be emphasized, however, that because of certain discontinuities which occur in the Bank of England's statistical material, particularly in 1967 and in 1971 when the deposit banks were included, and the problems of double counting, the conclusions to be drawn can therefore only be general ones and show the order of magnitude of resources and development in the market. The inter-bank market in sterling with its facilities for very short-term borrowing at rates of interest, certainly until September 1971, usually considerably higher than the traditional discount market, created a ready supply of funds from the secondary banking system. Table 23 clearly shows the extent of this growth, which has been supplemented by the participation of the clearing banks, and other banks in the United Kingdom have increased sevenfold in the eight years from end-December 1963 to December 1970 from £228 M. to £1,598 M. As a percentage of gross sterling deposits these balances rose from 11% in 1963 to 25% in 1970 and this figure was perhaps the most significant benchmark of the use being made of the market. Between 1969 and 1970

Table 23

SIZE OF STERLING INTER-BANK MARKET
(£M.) DECEMBER

	Inter-bank deposits*	As a % of total sterling deposits
1963	228	10·9
1964	266	11·3
1965	365	13·2
1966	484	16·7
1967	736	21·1
1968	1,059	25·9
1969	1,483	31·8
1970	1,598	25·1 +
1971	2,200	10·0
1972	4,573	14·9
1973	7,694	18·7
1974	8,582	19·6
1975	7,415	16·9
1976	8,605	17·7
1977	11,497	20·3
1978	13,424	21·4
1979	19,317	25·1

Notes * Measured from the liabilities side of the balance sheet – 'liabilities to U.K. banks in sterling'. It can also be measured from the assets side of the balance sheet (i.e. balances with other U.K. banks). This should give the same figure but in fact there are always slight differences.

† Pre-1971 figures exclude deposit banks.

Source: Bank of England Statistical Abstract.

it appears that the position remained static at approximately one-third of the total sterling deposits. It is likely that this was the result of an increased commitment to the local authority market by the secondary banks at the expense of inter-bank deposits. Certainly, this view was confirmed by the Bank, in the case of the American banks, when it pointed to their increased investment in local authorities at the expense of inter-bank lending. See also the comment in Chapter 6.

Since 1971 the market has grown considerably, in particular as a result of the entry of the clearing banks. Clearly after 1971 inter-bank deposits have constituted a much lower proportion of total sterling deposits than before since the figure for total deposits includes a large amount of retail deposits of the clearing banks. Nevertheless inter-bank deposits have still continued to grow as a percentage of total deposits.

THE INTER-BANK MARKET POST-1971

Since 1971 the management of the balance sheets of U.K. banks has undergone a profound change as the banking system began to practise 'liability management' on a far larger scale than had been envisaged at the time Competition and Credit Control was being devised. Liability management involves the banks in bidding competitively for deposits in the wholesale money markets (i.e. the inter-bank and Certificate of Deposit markets) to meet loan demands, rather than operating with a fixed level of deposits and managing the asset side of their balance sheet. Thus in response to a shortage of reserve assets produced by a call for Special Deposits, banks have tended to bid for funds in the interbank market, thus increasing their liabilities and using this to purchase reserve assets, rather than reducing total assets in the way predicted by the traditional bank credit multiplier approach. This led to serious distortions in the structure of interest rates in 1972–3. In bidding for funds the inter-bank and Certificate of Deposit rates would be pushed up relative to other rates thus attracting private sector funds. At the same time Treasury bill rates were depressed by the increased demand for reserve assets, which in turn reduced Minimum Lending Rate since this was linked by a formula to the Treasury bill rate. The result was that bank lending rates were kept below money market rates, producing opportunities for 'round tripping'; namely borrowing on overdraft to re-lend at higher interest rates on the money markets. This produced distortions in the money supply figures which confuses the task of monetary control.

The corset was introduced in December 1973 as a way of restraining bank liability management, by setting limits on the rate of growth of interest bearing deposits, and as a way of removing the distortions in money market interest rates and in $£M_3$. While the corset was successful in eliminating 'round tripping', the existence of the inter-bank market has continued to cause problems. For instance banks can in certain circumstances 'create' reserve assets. If banks have a shortage of reserve assets but are below their corset limit they can withdraw deposits from the inter-bank market and place it at call with a discount house. This should cause interest rates in the inter-bank market to rise relative to call money rates and induce the discount houses to lend the extra call money in the inter-bank market. Thus the effect will have been that banks have lent call money to the discount houses which is immediately lent back to the banks. The result is that both reserve assets (i.e. call money) and eligible liabilities will be increased, and the shortage of reserve assets relieved.

The reverse operation – i.e. withdrawing call money from the discount market and depositing it in the inter-bank market – can have the effect of relieving the pressure of the corset, provided banks are holding excess reserve assets. This has meant that the authorities have been forced to control the amount of reserve assets in existence to a far greater extent than was envisaged in 1971. The corset controls were subsequently abandoned in 1980 pending the introduction of a new system of monetary control.

THE OPERATIONS AND TECHNIQUES
OF THE MARKET

In the early days of the market, deals were largely arranged by direct deals between various secondary banks or by direct deals between a bank and a local authority. As the size and scope of the market grew it became advantageous for the banks and local authorities to make use of the specialist money brokers who were rapidly emerging to cope with the greatly increasing scale of operations. Today most dealing in the market is carried out through the money brokers, although banks and discount houses do also have direct dealing lines. There are now fourteen foreign exchange and currency deposit brokers operating in the market, the bulk of the business being carried out by the six firms mentioned on p. 103. In addition it is believed that there are over thirty other firms, including stockbrokers who also act as brokers on a small scale.

The methods and techniques used show a close identity with those of the Euro-dollar market, and both of these markets in turn have similarities with the American Federal Funds market. The creation of a market with such strong American influence is hardly surprising, since the largest operators in the Euro-dollar market are the U.S. banks who imported their native methods of working. Many deals represent a series of movements between several of the markets; for example, funds may have been placed in the Euro-dollar market from overseas, switched into sterling and placed in the inter-bank market, and then placed in the local authorities' or C.D. markets.

The money brokers are in regular contact by telephone with each other and also the bank's money market departments. Active dealing may commence as early as 8.15 a.m. and continues until approximately 3.15 p.m. although many transactions are arranged up to 5.30 p.m., but these are on a 'value tomorrow' basis. Transactions are binding immediately, that is within a few moments of a quotation being made, and the whole operation may be likened to a bank's telephone dealings with a stockbroker when purchases or sales of securities are made.

The majority of transactions are for up to three months and a large proportion is on an overnight basis, although no detailed figures for this are published by the Bank of England. For deposits over three months a Certificate of Deposit is usually used. The range of maturities varies widely from bank to bank and can be affected by seasonal and unusual tendencies in the interest-rate structure. Termination of a transaction may be brought about by negotiation with the book concerned. Deposits taken for over one month usually require notice of one month to be given. Deals are usually for a minimum of £500,000 and normally range from £5 M. to £20 M.

The rates of interest obtained in the sterling inter-bank market are particularly volatile and may show wide fluctuations from day to day depending largely on the demand for and supply of funds in the market. Thus, for instance, during the sterling crisis of 1972 overnight rates went as high as 500%.

Naturally, interest rates in the traditional market influenced the position in the sterling inter-bank market, and until 1966 or thereabouts it was possible to indicate a fairly typical pattern of interest rates in the parallel markets which was linked to the level of Bank rate. By 1969 and since, however, such a pattern had become tenuous in the extreme and was virtually impossible to trace. Many influences affect interest rates in the London markets, some of which manifest themselves on a weekly or monthly basis and others are seasonal or annual. A technical influence, which emerges weekly and monthly, is the requirement by the Bank of England that all banks must render returns of their cash positions, and similarly at the year end when widespread adjustments are made for window dressing purposes. Other less predictable influences are the fluctuations that occur on the gilt-edged market and the Stock Exchange, and the capital market's demands for funds created by new issues of stock. Changes in expectations as to future trends in the movement of interest rates in general and speculative trends on the foreign exchange markets can also, at times, dominate the interest rate structure. Forward transactions and arbitrage arising between the numerous other short-term money markets also cause unpredictable changes in interest rate levels. The whole question of the structure of interest rates within both the traditional discount market and the newer complementary markets will be fully examined in Chapter 15.

THE CONTINUING DIVERSIFICATION OF BUSINESS

SYNDICATED LENDING

This innovation arose from co-operation with local authorities in 1977 when the first syndicated loans worth over £500 M. were transacted by Butler Till. The loans are in substance local authority bonds which have no secondary market with maturities up to 4, 5, 6 or 7 years. Stimulus was given to the market at a time when there was a general lack of demand for term lending from banks by industrial and commercial companies.

Syndication fees for placing loans or bonds amongst clients range from $\frac{3}{8}\%$ to $\frac{7}{8}\%$ front-end commission. The loan agreements are drawn similarly to commercial bank loan forms with 'roll-over' arrangements built in as required. The loans can be repaid at any time as the debt is not assignable. The scheme has been further refined by the development of split-rate syndicated loans giving a better return over the first three years or so.

The underlying safety of the transactions is underpinned by the P.W.L.B. which acts as lender of last resort to local authorities.

The market has from time to time caused a problem for local treasurers because short-term funds in the sterling inter-bank market have been channelled into syndicated loans causing rates to harden at the short end of the market.

GROWTH OF LINKS WITH INDUSTRIAL & COMMERCIAL COMPANIES

Money brokers have considerable long-term links with large multinational and other companies. But there now also exist strong links with substantial numbers of second rank public companies and private companies who have surplus funds to invest. These relationships subsequently led to the disposal of money broking subsidiaries by the discount houses. The money broking firms have also established themselves in other overseas financial centres such as New York, Japan, the Middle East and others to enable them to offer a completely international money broking service.

LEASE BROKING

This arm of the brokers' business has evolved with the ever-increasing size of the leasing market and their natural link with industrial and commercial companies and local authorities who are major users of leased equipment.

8 The Euro-Dollar Market I

Before embarking on a discussion of this sector of the London money markets, it will be as well to identify some of the problems inherent in such a review.

First, the name 'Euro-dollar' is something of a misnomer because it seems to imply that the market is exclusively in dollars and is based only in Europe. The 'dollar' aspect of the market is in fact only one segment of the development of a foreign currency market in London dealing in many other currencies such as Deutschemarks, guilders, Swiss and French francs, etc. The term 'Euro-dollar' is therefore frequently (and incorrectly) used to describe what should properly be called the Euro-currency market. 78% of total Euro-currency deposits are denominated in dollars however. The next largest currency is the Euro Deutsche mark with 12% while the Euro-Swiss franc market accounts for less than 5%. A rapid growth in the Euro-Japanese yen market has occurred since restrictions on the use of yens were lifted. All Euro-currencies are dealt in London with the exception of Euro-sterling, the market for which is dominated by Paris.

As is evident from Table 24 other countries outside Europe have in recent years captured a growing share of the market. In particular in 'offshore' markets in the Bahamas and Cayman Islands, Bahrain and the so-called 'Asian dollar' market located in Hong Kong and Singapore are becoming increasingly important. Other European centres have also increased their share of the market; notably Paris for Euro-sterling and Luxembourg for Euro-Deutsche marks. Nevertheless, London still remains by far the most important centre and with a market share of about 33%, it is still larger than the next two largest centres combined.

Secondly, the use of the word 'market' is ambiguous when used in this context because it may be misleading to speak of the whole system of transactions involved with Euro-dollars as a market,

Table 24

MAJOR EURO-CURRENCY MARKETS

Commercial banks external foreign currency liabilities U.S. $ billion (%)

End Year	1971		1973		1975		1976		1977		1978	
	$b	%	$b	%	$b	%	$b	%	$b	%	$b	%
U.K.	45·7	41·4	90·7	36·7	128·2	36·1	148·6	34·8	171·4	33·2	213·4	32·6
Belgium/ Luxembourg	10·5	9·5	23·8	9·6	37·9	10·7	47·5	11·1	65·5	12·7	88·0	13·5
France	13·9	12·6	27·4	11·1	38·1	10·7	48·7	11·4	63·0	12·2	78·8	12·1
Germany	3·1	2·8	6·6	2·7	9·3	2·6	13·7	3·2	15·2	2·9	18·9	2·9
Italy	12·4	11·2	23·9	9·7	15·0	4·2	15·0	3·5	21·5	4·2	27·8	4·3
Netherlands	4·9	4·4	9·6	3·9	16·4	4·6	19·6	4·6	25·5	4·9	35·5	5·4
Switzerland	6·5	5·9	9·2	3·7	12·0	3·4	15·3	3·6	18·0	3·5	26·9	4·1
Sweden	0·6	0·5	0·9	0·4	1·8	0·5	2·3	0·5	3·4	0·7	4·5	0·7
Japan	6·6	6·0	12·8	5·2	25·2	7·1	27·2	6·4	24·5	4·7	30·3	4·6
Canada	6·3	5·7	11·5	4·6	12·1	3·4	14·6	3·4	16·7	3·2	22·4	3·4
Caribbean*	N/A	—	25·0	10·1	47·5 }	13·4	74·1	17·4	91·7	17·8	107·5	16·4
Far East*	N/A	—	5·9	2·4	12·0 }	3·4						
Total	110·5	100·0	247·3	100·0	355·0	100·0	426·6	100·0	516·4	100·0	654·0	100·0

Note: Caribbean and Far East relate to branches of U.S. banks only.
Source: Bank for International Settlements, Annual reports.

since the market aspects of it are only part of the picture. Market aspects in regard to Euro-dollars are defined by Machlup* as new offers of, and bids for, credit in Euro-dollars, the new loans contracted during a market day and the re-negotiations of old loans'. Non-market features of the system are defined as 'loans outstanding, assets held, deposit liabilities owed, the creation, turnover, conversion and cancellation of international money...', Machlup's point being that there is a fundamental distinction between flow concepts and stock concepts. In the past few years statistical information on the Euro-dollar market has been improved considerably. The main sources of information are the Bank for International Settlements, the World Bank and Morgan Guaranty Trust Company (Euro-currency lending) and the Bank of England. Since our concern in this book is with the London money markets we shall concentrate on data provided by the Bank of England in its *Quarterly Bulletin*.

The most useful series published by the Bank of England shows the external liabilities and claims of banks in the United Kingdom and therefore provides a reasonably accurate measure of growth in the London market. These figures will be used as the basis for discussion throughout this chapter on the development of the London market.

The first part of this chapter will be concerned with a brief description of the nature and origins of the Euro-dollar system. The remainder will be split into six sections: sources of funds, employment of funds, maturity of funds, structure of the market, interest rates, and international implications.

NATURE AND ORIGINS OF THE MARKET

Undoubtedly the most discussed money market today is the Euro-dollar market. Much has been written on it and a great deal of the literature has contained uncertainties and controversy as to the true nature of the Euro-dollar, and which transactions conducted by banks outside the United States constitute Euro-dollar operations and which do not. Clendenning* possibly gives the best defi-

---

* Fritz Machlup, 'Euro-Dollar Creation: A Mystery Story', *Banca Nazionale Del Lavoro Quarterly Review,* September 1970, p. 221.

* W. Clendenning, *The Euro-Dollar Market*, p. 16. See also Bank of International Settlement definition, 'a dollar that has been acquired by a bank outside the U.S. and used directly, or after conversion into another currency, for lending to a non-bank customer, perhaps after one or more redeposits from one bank to another'.

nition available and, at the same time, differentiates between Euro-dollar and ordinary United States dollar operations conducted by banks outside the United States. Euro-dollars are essentially deposits of United States dollars with commercial banks outside the United States of America. A Euro-dollar transaction is 'any transaction in United States dollars undertaken by a commercial bank operating outside the United States of America (including the foreign branches of United States banks) at Euro-dollar rates. This definition emphasizes the distinctive feature of the Euro-dollar system which is the formation of an international interest-rate structure that is distinct from national interest rates.

The market is a wholesale one in the sense that it deals only in large amounts. Transactions are usually for amount of $1 million or more and banks in the market lend on the strength of the 'name' of the banks or companies with which they deal. It is important to appreciate that one of the vital functions of the London banks was to act as a guarantor not merely to act as a clearing centre.

All transactions are done on an unsecured basis and in order to limit their risks the banks set limits on the amount they will lend to any one bank in any one country. However, since borrowers can obtain funds from many different sources, it is impossible for any one bank to establish these limits and to know whether or not they are realistic. The difficulty in quantifying risks has led many banks to create a second line of defence in the form of standby credit arrangements, thus compounding the risk in so far as they may be exposing themselves both to a direct and an indirect risk.

The major factors influencing the development of the market have been well documented by numerous writers, but it is still a common misconception that markets in funds deposited by overseas residents and re-lent abroad are a new phenomenon. This of course is not so as there was an active business in sterling and dollar deposits in Berlin and Vienna in the 1920s and up until the financial crisis of 1931. The foreign exchange markets in London were re-opened in 1951, but it was not until 1957 that the total of overseas borrowing and lending began to expand when a number of coincident forces provided the impetus for the market's birth.

The main reasons which explain the birth of the market are:

(i) The greater freedom which banks were allowed in the conduct of their foreign exchange operations as a result of external convertibility in Western Europe at the end of 1958 (the ability to arbitrage funds between dollars and European currencies is an integral part of Euro-dollar activities).

(ii) The relaxation of exchange controls in West European countries, which gave commercial banks and business firms greater freedom to conduct foreign capital operations.

(iii) The restriction of the use of sterling to finance third party trade imposed in 1957 which encouraged banks to use dollars to finance such activities.

(iv) The tendency of East European Countries to hold dollars through West European intermediaries rather than in the United States.

GROWTH AND SIZE OF THE MARKET

Table 25 shows the growth of the Euro-dollar market in London, as measured by the size of external claims and liabilities of banks. It is clear that the general trend in the size of the Euro-dollar market has been steadily upwards although there are certain periods which have shown particularly rapid growth. Before we discuss particular periods in the growth of the market a word of warning should be given concerning the data given in the above table. This is shown in sterling while most external liabilities and claims are denominated in dollars. The result is that the growth trend will be distorted by changes in the sterling dollar exchange rate. To give just one example, when measured in sterling the market grew by only 3% in 1977, while in terms of dollars it grew by 15%; the difference being accounted for by the appreciation of sterling over the period.

There has been much discussion as to which factor has been the most significant in the development of the market. Probably the major reasons favouring its initial growth were the rigidities in the United States banking system that allowed international and national interest-rate differentials to persist and the fact that European banks participated, notwithstanding the fact that they had to operate on relatively narrow profit margins. Perhaps most important among the rigidities in the United States banking system was Regulation Q, which limited the rate of interest that U.S. banks may pay on deposits. In addition, beginning in 1965 the United States imposed a series of measures designed to restrict capital outflows and so improve the balance of payments position. The Foreign Direct Investment Regulations prevented U.S. multinationals from financing overseas operations with funds borrowed in the United States.

Table 25

GROWTH OF THE EURO-DOLLAR MARKET IN LONDON

External liabilities and claims of banks in the U.K.
in non-sterling currencies 1957–79

(£M)

End of Period	% Change in Total (annual % growth)	LIABILITIES Total	% of Total	U.S. $ Total	Other	CLAIMS Total	U.S. $	Other
1957		65	86	56	9	102	71	31
1958	92	125	83	104	21	135	89	46
1959	111	264	88	232	32	296	248	48
1960	140	633	88	560	73	604	504	100
1961	18	749	88	663	86	733	589	144
1962	39	1,038	85	884	154	1,010	803	207
1963	23	1,280	84	1,072	208	1,268	1,024	244
1964	39	1,786	88	1,566	220	1,626	1,312	314
1965	19	2,122	89	1,893	229	1,980	1,624	356
1966	41	3,002	91	2,727	275	3,020	2,611	409
1967	46	4,384	92	4,038	346	4,376	3,837	539
1968	63	7,139	90	6,404	735	7,117	6,245	872
1969	68	11,994	89	10,728	1,266	12,006	10,514	1,492
1970	26	15,153	86	13,086	2,067	14,691	12,189	2,502
1971	16	17,610	80	14,172	3,438	16,720	13,104	3,616
1972	45	25,460	81	20,539	4,921	24,019	19,422	4,597
1973	53	39,017	76	29,770	9,247	36,274	28,174	8,100
1974	21	47,287	80	37,661	9,626	43,762	35,289	8,473
1975	34	63,368	81	51,488	11,880	58,440	47,914	10,526
1976	38	87,319	82	71,958	15,361	81,076	66,139	14,937
1977	3	89,516	80	71,969	17,547	82,997	66,178	16,819
1978	17	104,601	78	81,979	22,622	99,496	76,978	22,518
1979*	21	126,726	78	98,871	27,855	121,351	95,174	26,177

* 1979 figures converted from U.S.$ at rate of 2·225.

Source: Bank of England Quarterly Bulletin, various issues.

The Voluntary Foreign Credit Restraint Program restricted U.S. bank foreign lending and the Interest Equalization Tax discouraged foreign borrowers from raising funds in the United States through securities issues. All of these measures had the effect of forcing borrowers to the Euro-dollar market rather than the domestic dollar market. At the same time, however, it should be pointed out that these restrictions were not crucial for the growth or survival of the Euro-dollar market as it has continued its rapid growth after the controls were removed in January 1974.

Another important factor for the growth of the market had undoubtedly been its competitiveness. As can be seen from Graph 3 the Euro-dollar market has a much narrower spread between deposit and lending rates than exists in the domestic dollar market and can therefore squeeze in between domestic deposit and lending rates, thus offering an incentive to both depositors and borrowers to use the Euro-dollar market. This is the result of the lower transaction costs that prevail in the Euro-dollar market. Banks are not subject to official reserve requirements or deposit insurance costs, and, since it is a wholesale market, banks avoid the cost of a retail branch network. It is this competitiveness that has ensured the continued growth of the Euro-dollar market despite the removal of some of the artificial barriers.

It is sometimes suggested that the existence of a balance of payments deficit in the United States has been important for the growth of the Euro-dollar market, since it provides the rest of the world, and especially Western Europe with increased holdings of dollars. In fact a United States balance of payments deficit is not a necessary condition for the growth of the Euro-dollar market. Indeed the market has grown fastest at times when the deficit has been very small. The reason is of course, that exporters to the United States may not want to hold the dollars they receive, or even if they do, they may not be deposited in the Euro-dollar market. Firm evidence to support the view that a balance of payments deficit is not a necessary condition for the growth of the Euro-currency market may be drawn from the case of Germany. The Euro-deutschemark market has grown rapidly despite a persistent balance of payments surplus.

In addition to these general observations it is also possible to point to certain specific factors, which have assisted in the growth of the Euro-dollar market.

The years of greatest growth have generally been those when credit restrictions have been most severe in the United States.

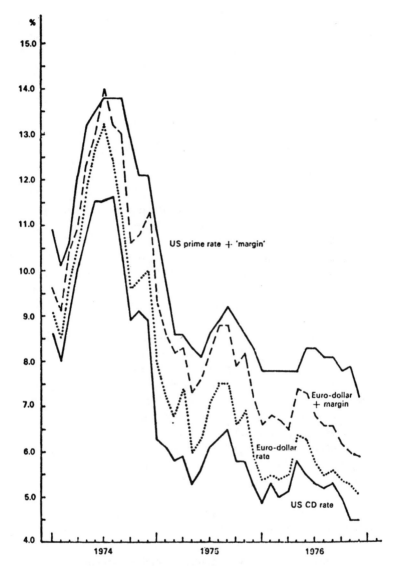

Graph 3. Domestic and Euro-dollar borrowing and lending rates, 1974–6.
Source: S. Frowen, *A Framework of International Banking*, 1977.

Restrictive monetary policy in the United States in 1966 and especially in 1969 forced interest rates on U.S. Treasury bills about the maximum rates allowed on Certificates of Deposit under Regulation Q. American investors therefore liquidated their Certificates of Deposit and invested in Treasury bills, while American banks sought to make up their lost deposits by borrowing from their foreign branches, which in turn raised the funds on the Euro-dollar market. In 1966 there was a 25% increase in United Kingdom banks' gross foreign currency liabilities whilst in 1968 the rate of increase jumped to 50% and to 75% in 1969.

Secondly, until 1971 central banks in many European countries deposited their substantial dollar reserves in the Euro-dollar market. This practice was, however, stopped in 1971 when it was recognized that it might be facilitating a multiple expansion in the Euro-dollar market – companies were borrowing Euro-dollars and switching them into say, sterling. Since central banks were pledged to support their exchange rates under the Bretton Woods agreement they therefore had to supply sterling in return for the dollars which they then re-deposited in the Euro-dollar market, thus allowing the cycle to start again.

Thirdly, the commodity price boom in the early 1970s, and in particular the quintupling of oil prices by OPEC countries in 1973 provided these countries with supplies of dollars far in excess of their investment requirements. A large proportion of these dollars were deposited in the Euro-dollar market.

1974 saw the only real interruption in the growth of the Euro-dollar market, although even this was a temporary phenomenon. It came as a result of loss of confidence in the market due in particular to the collapse of Bankhaus Herstatt which forced a reappraisal of attitudes to the riskiness of inter-bank transactions. Further concern was also expressed about the soundness of lending to less developed countries and about the capital inadequacy and increased maturity mismatching of banks operating in the Euro-dollar market. Since 1974 the market has continued to expand although its growth now appears to be more dependent on the trend of the world economy. Thus growth slowed in the 1974–5 recession, speeded up in 1976 and then flagged again.

There has been much controversy over the years as to whether or not the market was (or presently is!) to be a permanent feature of the international monetary system. Some surprising statements have been made: in 1962 Sir Charles Hambro (who significantly was a director of the Bank of England) described the market as 'likely to be a temporary phenomenon'. This view seemed to be also held in 1969 by Dr Schweitzer, chairman of the Swiss Banking Corporation, when he was quoted as saying he did not think that the Euro-dollar market was a permanent feature of international finance. More optimistic about the market's future, and probably more realistic in the light of events, were several other well-known commentators: in 1962 Sir George Bolton, chairman of the Bank of London and South America, spoke out in defence of the market saying 'if the Euro-dollar market does complicate problems of monetary control (national or international) the right solution is not to suppress it, but rather to develop official techniques as may be necessary to vitiate the adverse side-effects of an otherwise useful market'. He subsequently reaffirmed his view in 1968 when he said that he did not believe the market was a 'transient phenomena'. Similarly, Paul Einzig and Mr Alfred Hayes, president of the Federal Reserve Bank of New York, expressed the view that the market is here to stay.

The removal of capital controls in the United States in January 1974 has had no noticeable effect on the growth of the market, despite predictions to the contrary at the time, and while the end of these controls enabled foreigners to borrow in the United States domestic market instead of the Euro-dollar market it should be remembered that this also facilitated the flow of funds *into* the Euro-dollar market. Moreover the Euro-dollar still retains a competitive advantage since banks in the United States are not permitted to pay interest on deposits of less than 30 days and they have to hold reserve assets, unlike Eurobanks.

Perhaps the greatest threat to the future of the Euro-dollar market lies in the possibility of creating a free banking zone in New York where banks would be exempt from reserve requirements and Regulation Q. While this might slow down the growth of the Euro-dollar market it is unlikely that it would prove fatal to its survival as undoubtedly many borrowers and depositors will still find it advantageous to conduct business with banks in London rather than in New York.

SOURCES OF FUNDS

The primary suppliers of funds to the Euro-dollar market may be divided into three groups:

(i) Official institutions – including overseas central banks, international monetary organizations, and governments.

(ii) Commercial banks.

(iii) Non-financial institutions – consisting of business concerns and individual investors.

In attempting to rank the three types of institutions according to their importance as suppliers of Euro-dollars, it was held in the early years that central banks were the largest contributors. In 1963 it was estimated that at least two-thirds of the funds in European markets had emanated from central banks. However, non-bank sources were also considered of great importance, and in its 1963–4 annual report the Bank for International Settlements observed that of all the sources they listed that have helped to supply the Euro-dollar market since 1961, there was a shift of emphasis from central-bank to non-bank sources.

This view was confirmed by the Bank of England in 1964 when it noted that in previous years various central banks such as the Deutsche Bundesbank, Banca d'Italia and the Swiss National Bank had made deposits, either directly by placings of their own or by channelling dollars to commercial banks which were provided with a 'swap' back into their own currency, so that the central bank remained the beneficial owner of the foreign exchange. Instead, this source of funds declined and business concerns and commercial banks were thought to be the primary suppliers to the market. Dominant in this field were the large American non-financial corporations with important foreign operations who wished to gain the benefits afforded by short-term investment in Euro-dollars.

In 1968 the Bank for International Settlements published estimates of central bank participation for the period 1964–7 (admittedly worldwide figures from eight countries – but since the London market transacts 80% of the business the figures are a reasonable guide), from which it appeared that although central banks had been substantial contributors, the dominant suppliers were now the non-banks. The Bank for International Settlements' estimates are year-end figures and therefore tend to overstate the contribution of international monetary institutions because they include an element of window dressing when central bank funds are substituted for private funds until the commercial banks reverse their year-end Euro-dollar operations.

Since 1971 central banks in the Group of Ten countries have agreed not to deposit reserves in the Euro-dollar market. Their place has, however, been taken by monetary institutions in OPEC countries. Thus the place of official institutions in the supply of funds is likely to be large.

A second important source of funds is from other commercial banks. Indeed, the Euro-dollar market is, when measured on a 'gross' basis, to a very large extent an inter-bank market. Frequently banks receive dollar deposits from non-bank customers and are unable to find non-bank customers who require a similar amount for a similar maturity. These funds will therefore be lent to a second Eurobank at a marginally higher rate and so on until the funds ultimately reach the end users of the funds such as companies or governments.

This is why when measuring the size of the Euro-dollar market, it is common to 'net' out inter-bank transactions so that all that is included is the ultimate liability to a non-bank depositor or the claim on the non-bank borrower.

Table 26 gives a geographical analysis of deposits from overseas (this is a new series published by the Bank of England in March 1970) and indicates the sources from which United Kingdom banks have received funds. This does not, however, necessarily reveal the country of beneficial ownership – for example an East European country might deposit dollars with a bank on the Continent which in turn re-deposits them with a London bank; they would then appear in the United Kingdom figures as a liability to a West European country, thus underlining the danger of placing too much reliance on the figures for individual countries.

There was comparatively little change in the supply pattern from 1963 to 1969 notwithstanding the fact that deposits grew from £652 M. to £6,709 M. There was a startling increase of some £2,800 M. in West European countries' deposits during 1969 which was mainly attributable to the record levels to which interest rates rose, reflecting the desire of the commercial banks in the various countries to employ their liquid funds more profitably. Switzerland was the largest source of funds since it largely operates as an entrepôt centre for funds from elsewhere. The figures include deposits by the Bank for International Settlements, which puts funds in the market, for example, over the end of the year to counter the effects of sudden withdrawals for 'window-dressing' purposes. The deposits from the Netherlands more than doubled, whilst Italy showed an increase of one-third and France a rise of approximately 80%. These increases were perhaps all the more surprising in view of the fact that many countries adopted measures to discourage or even reverse the outflow of funds following a tightening of monetary policy during the year. Deposits from the overseas sterling area countries also showed a remarkable increase from £41 M. to £994 M. which was attributable in the main to the funds placed by the West Indies and Persian Gulf territories. As a proportion of total deposits these countries' holdings rose from 3% to 8%.

Table 26

GEOGRAPHICAL ANALYSIS OF EXTERNAL LIABILITIES OF U.K. BANKS IN FOREIGN CURRENCIES

(£M) End of Period

U.K. Liabilities	Total	West. Europe E.E.C.	West. Europe Other	North America U.S.A.	North America Canada	Oil Exporting	Offshore Banking Centres	Non-oil Developing Countries	Other*
1963	1,280		652	153	133		342		
1966	3,002		1,692	349	200		761		
1967	4,384		2,413	588	324		1,059		
1968	7,139		3,917	1,119	505		1,598		
1969	11,994		6,709	1,270	1,087		2,928		
1970	15,153		9,045	1,280	1,277		3,551		
1971	17,610		10,457	1,291	1,392	931	1,318	936	1,285
1972	25,460		14,327	1,530	1,764	1,698	1,941	1,955	2,245
1973	39,017	12,606	9,737	2,113	2,127	2,012	3,694	2,759	3,969
1974	47,451	11,996	11,011	3,096	1,642	7,888	5,303	2,765	3,750
1975	63,368	15,972	13,241	4,965	1,806	11,198	7,770	3,900	4,516
1976	87,319	20,477	15,898	6,853	2,381	16,648	12,040	7,199	5,723
1977	89,516	20,258	16,953	8,783	2,078	16,445	10,124	6,744	8,131
1978	104,566	28,566	20,251	12,852	2,103	14,979	14,051	10,656	6,108
1979	126,726	26,505	22,638	18,140	1,823	20,472	15,517	11,877	9,754

* Other includes Eastern Europe, Japan, Australia, New Zealand, South Africa and unallocated.
Source: Bank of England Quarterly Bulletin, various issues.

Deposits from the United States and Canada remained fairly constant in proportionate terms over the six-year period, amounting to roughly 12% and 10% respectively of total deposits. The Bank of England also noted that United Kingdom residents' deposits of Euro-currencies rose some two and a half times from £200 M. to £500 M. between 1967 and 1969. Half of this increase was believed to represent holdings of the insurance market and a further third the proceeds of borrowing awaiting investment. These operations were only possible where Bank of England permission had been obtained (by residents) to hold foreign currencies.

The most obvious trend during the 1970s, and after 1973 in particular has been the deposits received from oil exporting countries – largely in the Middle East but also including countries such as Algeria, Nigeria, and Venezuela. These deposits represented only 5% of the total in 1971 and 16% in 1979, having reached a peak in 1976 when they amounted to 10% of total Euro-dollar deposits.

Deposits from the United States tended to decline as a proportion of total deposits in the early part of the 1970s, but after 1973 they recovered their share, and by the end of the period had again reached the proportion they had achieved during the 1960s. This was largely a result of the removal of controls on capital outflows from the United States in January 1974 which facilitated the flow of deposits to the Euro-dollar market.

The non-oil developing countries have been heavy borrowers in the Euro-dollar market, but they also use the market to deposit their foreign exchange reserves. It can be seen that since 1976 these countries have been able to build up the amount of reserves they hold in the Euro-dollar market quite considerably. These were years when their balance of payments positions were relatively favourable and they were able to build up reserves.

EMPLOYMENT OF FUNDS

The users of Euro-dollars may be classified in three main groups:

(i) Official institutions
(ii) Commercial banks
(iii) Other non-banking institutions.

(i) Official institutions, although major participants on the supply side, are relatively small users of Euro-dollars. Central banks are theoretically able to borrow directly from the market but have made little attempt to do so probably because of the expansion of credit facilities available through the International Monetary Fund and swap arrangements between major central banks. Government borrowing occurs on a fairly large scale – chiefly by East European countries, Belgium, and United Kingdom local authorities. The latter only borrow on the Euro-dollar market when the covered differential favouring sterling loans through dollar swaps develops. Since they can always obtain finance from one of several sources their objective is to obtain the funds they need at the cheapest rate. In recent years however, West European governments have approached the Euro-dollar market on several occasions. Britain borrowed $2·5 billion in 1974 and other European countries such as Italy have also been substantial borrowers.

Governments in less-developed countries have also increasingly tapped the Euro-dollar market in order to finance development and growing balance of payments deficits. This began about 1970 and grew to very large porportions after 1973. Indeed one of the biggest causes for concern in international banking circles is the exposure of Eurobanks to less-developed countries.

(ii) and (iii) The function of commercial banks on the demand side of the market is mainly to act as an intermediary between the original suppliers and the end-users. Since most of the dollars obtained through the Euro-dollar market are used by the private sector, it is evident that the commercial banks and the non-banks are the dominant institutions on the demand side.

An examination of the evidence provided by Table 27 shows that the pattern of external claims has changed substantially over the years. In 1963 the foreign currency claims on the United States by banks in London represented 23% of total external claims, and had reached 49% or £5,617 M., at the end of 1969. The level of the United Kingdom banks' claims on overseas countries other than the United States grew in absolute terms from £978 M. to £6,389 M.

The U.S. maintained a dominant position until 1969/70 but since then borrowing by American banks and their customers has increasingly been channelled through the offshore banking centres where banking profits are taxed at much lower levels. By 1979 U.S. bank borrowing only accounted for 9% of claims but offshore bank centres had risen to 18% of claims. The table also clearly shows the increasing levels of borrowing by banks in the E.E.C., Eastern Europe, and the developing countries.

Total claims have increased almost one-hundred fold since 1963

Table 27

GEOGRAPHICAL ANALYSIS OF EXTERNAL CLAIMS OF U.K. BANKS IN FOREIGN CURRENCIES

£M. End of Period	Total	Western Europe E.E.C.	Western Europe Other	North America U.S.A.	North America Canada	Oil Exporting	Offshore Banking Centres	Non-oil Developing Countries	Other*
1963	1,268		692	290	37			249	
1966	3,020		1,161	1,244	93			522	
1967	4,376		1,453	1,710	145			1,068	
1968	7,117		2,166	3,061	202			1,688	
1969	12,006		3,570	5,617	267			2,552	
1970	14,691		6,270	4,151	377			3,893	
1971	16,720		8,167	2,007	500	301	1,973	2,339	1,433
1972	24,019		11,165	2,306	900	522	3,383	1,948	3,795
1973	36,274	12,518	3,923	3,011	1,413	825	6,039	2,625	5,920
1974	43,651	12,086	4,987	4,356	710	992	7,662	3,397	9,461
1975	58,440	15,362	6,548	3,385	656	1,677	12,576	4,771	13,465
1976	81,076	21,309	9,016	5,051	971	3,193	17,014	6,904	17,618
1977	82,997	24,431	10,088	5,086	1,863	4,782	15,509	7,283	13,955
1978	99,387	30,943	11,748	5,966	1,348	7,044	18,161	9,993	14,184
1979	121,351	34,263	13,993	11,017	2,016	8,073	22,160	12,938	16,891

* Other includes Eastern Europe, Japan, Australia, New Zealand, South Africa, and unallocated.
Source: Bank of England Quarterly Bulletin, various issues.

demonstrating the huge growth in international financing which has taken place through the Euro-markets.

MATURITY OF ASSETS AND LIABILITIES

The authorities have shown growing concern about the maturity structure of the Euro-currency markets, as evidenced by their now regular requests for analyses of figures. Their anxiety stems from the rapid and continued growth of the market and the tendency for banks to have mismatched maturity positions.

In July 1969 over 25% of the market's assets and liabilities were at sight whilst a further 45% fell due between two days and three months, giving a grand total of 70% of total funds due within three months. As mentioned in the previous section of the chapter, the bulk of borrowing in the market was attributable to the American banks and since the funds were a means of supplementing immediate liquidity needs, it is not surprising that they had net sight assets of over £1,800 M. as compared with £520 M. in April 1968. Significantly, by July 1970 this figure had fallen to some £590 M. thus confirming that as credit restrictions (and Federal Reserve Board reserve requirements) were eased the American banks' needs were substantially reduced. In fact, during the year to end July 1970 their sight assets fell by £850 M. whereas sight liabilities to banks abroad, other than in the United States, rose by £400 M. thus showing that the American banks accounted for the whole of the decline in the net sight position of all London banks at end-July 1970 to £590 M. (as mentioned above).

Taking the cumulative position of all the banks from sight to three months, it can be seen (*see* Table 29) that the change in the sight position of the London banks had substantially affected the total maturities (to three months), giving a net liability of £1,275 M. at end-July 1970 compared with £277 M. in the previous year and £365 M. in April 1968. Similarly, the net liability position up to one year and over had almost doubled from £762 M. in 1969 to £1,429 M. in 1970 as compared with a mere £140 M. increase between April 1968 and July 1969. At the longer end of the spectrum there was an increase of £473 M. in net claims of one year and over on overseas customers other than banks. In addition, and as evidence of the increased use by United Kingdom residents of the Euro-dollar market, the net claims of one year and over of 'other United Kingdom residents' rose by £100 M. to £300 M.

Table 28

MATURITY ANALYSIS OF LIABILITIES AND CLAIMS IN NON-STERLING
CURRENCIES OF BANK IN U.K. JULY 1970

£M. Total Liabilities and Claims	Liabilities July 1970	Liabilities July 1969	Claims July 1970	Claims July 1969	Net Liabilities− Net Claims+ July 1970 Sight	2 Days to Less than Three Months	One Year and Over
British banks	6,891	4,914	6,926	4,963	−154	−360	+784
American banks	9,746	8,891	9,696	8,870	+668	−1,301	+449
Other foreign banks	2,769	2,051	2,754	2,054	+77	−205	−196
	19,406	15,836	19,376	15,887	+591	−1,866	+1,429
				July 1969	+1,823	−2,100	+762
				April 1968	+520	−885	+622

Source: Bank of England Quarterly Bulletin, December 1970.

The trends shown by this analysis indicate that despite the continued growth of the market, the pattern of lending was materially changed. Notwithstanding reduced borrowings by the American banks, the funds released plus new deposits were absorbed by the demands of European and British companies who had experienced liquidity problems and the effects of right monetary policies. There was, therefore, a tendency throughout the market to borrow short and lend longer – to obtain the longest maturities available.

If we examine the position of each group of banks it is noteworthy that the British banks showed the greatest increase in Euro-currency business in the year to July 1970, gross assets rising by 40% to £6,926 M. in contrast to a rise of only 9% to £9,700 M. for the American banks and 35% for other foreign banks in London. Significant also for the British banks was that their net assets at one year and over grew from £320 M. to £870 M. during the year, illustrating once more the trend to longer-term lending to customers other than banks. It would also seem to show the high proportion of Euro-dollar business which the American banks transact with their head offices (some £3,900 M. of gross claims amounting to £5,620 M.) and when this business is not available, that the British banks are more competitive in utilizing the surplus funds.

As would be expected, the America banks' proportionate share of total gross assets declined some 5% during the twelve months to July 1970, but they nevertheless retained 50% of the total market assets. The reduction was largely due to their reduced lending to head offices coupled with an increase in deposits received from banks abroad, which led to a fall of £1,100 M. in net claims on banks abroad; the main decline occurring in the sight category (net sight claims fell from £2,300 M. to £1,040 M.). Their borrowing in the London interbank market also fell £550 M. and a similar drop occurred in their net borrowing from overseas customers other than banks.

The position of the third group of banks – 'other foreign banks in London' – registered a fall in the net sight assets from £150 M. in 1969 to £77 M. in 1970 comprising lending in the inter-bank market and by Japanese banks to their head offices. The majority of the lending in this sector was from sight to three months.

A development, of which quite considerable use is now being made, is the standby credit whereby many London banks make available foreign currency lines of credit. The facility may be used by either private customers of the bank or by other banks abroad. Of total credits granted amounting to £1,475 M. at the end of July 1970, £1,175 M. was to overseas companies but this figure also include the balance of any normal commercial credits sanctioned but not fully utilized. It is estimated that over two-thirds of the total credits were given by branches of American banks in London. Many foreign banks in London had informal arrangements with their head offices for 'last-resort' backing in case of need, and this probably accounts for the low figure of £450 M. reported for standby credits received.

The Bank subsequently published further figures in the *Quarterly Bulletin* (March 1972) (*see* below), which show that the size of the London market (in Euro-currencies), as measured by total assets, rose by an additional £5,000 M. to £24,743 M. during the period from July 1970 to October 1971. Most of this increase was accounted for by borrowings of £2,320 M. by overseas customers other than banks, and some £618 M. more borrowed by United Kingdom residents. This domestic borrowing was, however, restricted in January 1971.

An indication of the extent to which Euro-dollars were borrowed to finance speculative foreign exchange operations can be seen by the fact that despite repayments of over £2,200 M. on loans by

FOREIGN CURRENCY CLAIMS ON BANKS IN THE UNITED KINGDOM

	July 1970	February 1971	Change over Period	October 1971	Net Change Since July 1970
Other banks in U.K.	5,508	5,906	+ 398	6,893	+1,385
Other U.K. residents	811	1,190	+ 379	1,429	+ 618
Banks overseas	9,202	8,801	− 401	10,246	+ 1,044
Other overseas residents	3,855	5,469	+ 1,614	6,175	+ 2,320
	19,376	21,366	+ 1,990	24,743	+ 5,367

Source: Bank of England Quarterly Bulletin, December 1970 and March 1972.

United States banks, the net lending to banks abroad increased by £1,044 M., thus showing that manifestly over £3,000 M. was lent to other banks overseas.

These changes made a substantial impact on the maturity structure of the Euro-currency market at end-February 1971. The market's net sight position had deteriorated by some £750 M. (after due allowance for the fact that the sight figures for February 1971 included holdings of dollar certificates of deposit and foreign currency bills, whereas previously these items had been reported by date of maturity). Nevertheless the banks still had some £300 M. in net assets of up to seven days. The position of the market at less than one year was, however, less satisfactory since net liabilities increased by £440 M. to be matched by a broadly similar increase in net assets of one year and over.

By October 1971, however, there was a significant improvement in the market's short-term position with net sight assets amounting to £1,059 M. and a cumulative net asset position of £69 M. up to one month's maturity. There was also a continuing trend towards longer-term lending as loans with one year or more to run increased by £640 M. and loans of three years or more amounted to £1,900 M.

This relief to the market's short liquidity position was welcomed by the Bank of England and was probably brought about as the result of a number of contributory factors.

Firstly, in January 1971 $1,000 M. of very short-term lending by the London branches of United States banks to their head offices was converted into three-month Eximbank notes and also by the

%	Oct. 1971	Oct. 1972	Sept. 1973	Nov. 19⬛
LIABILITIES				
Less than 8 days	18·0	17·8	19·1	22·2
8 days − < 1 month	18·8	17·5	19·5	20·8
1 month − < 3 months	33·0	31·8	26·1	28·2
3 months − < 6 months	19·4	19·4	20·9	16·9
6 months − < 1 year	6·5	8·1	8·8	5·2
1 year − < 3 years	2·6	2·5	2·5	2·3
3 years +	1·7	2·9	3·1	4·4
Total	100·0	100·0	100·0	100·0
CLAIMS				
< 8 days	19·8	14·8	14·9	17·4
8 days − < 1 month	15·2	15·9	18·8	17·2
1 month − < 3 months	26.2	28·2	24·8	24·1
3 months − < 6 months	18·3	18·9	20·8	15·1
6 months − < 1 year	6·8	8·0	8·2	5·6
1 year − < 3 years	6·1	6·5	4·8	5·7
3 years +	7·6	17·7	7·7	14·9
Total	100·0	100·0	100·0	100·6

Source: Bank of England quarterly Bulletin, various issues.

CLAIMS OF BANKS
RENCIES 1971–9

v. 1975	Nov. 1976	Nov. 1977	Nov. 1978	Nov. 1979
19·0	21·7	21·9	20·1	21·0
18·0	18·5	17·3	17·8	18·7
28·5	28·0	28·4	29·0	28·6
20·8	17·6	18·7	19·0	19·3
6·9	7·5	7·4	8·4	7·4
3·4	5·0	4·5	3·9	3·3
3·4	1·7	1·8	1·8	1·7
100·0	100·0	100·0	100·0	100.0
15·3	16·8	16·0	15·1	16·6
15·2	14·5	14·0	14·2	15·4
23·3	22·6	22·9	23·2	23·7
16·4	14·8	16·3	15·8	17·2
6·2	7·2	7·5	8·2	6·9
7·4	9·7	9·5	8·8	6·7
16·2	14·4	13·8	14·7	13·5
100·0	100·0	100·0	100·0	100·0

issue of U.S. Treasury notes. Later, in August 1971 when the convertibility of the dollar was suspended, the notes were not renewed as they matured thereby assisting the liquidity of the market. Secondly, the borrowing of foreign currency by U.K. residents for domestic use was restricted (in January) to periods of five years or more, and thirdly, the foreign currency operations of U.K. banks were limited by preventing them from converting foreign currency deposits into sterling unless their spot currency assets exceeded their spot currency liabilities. The efficacy of this step can be seen from the fact that claims on other overseas residents increased by £1,614 M. during the period July 1970 to February 1971, but increased by only £700 M. in the following period to October 1971.

Since October 1971 the Bank of England has provided data on the maturity structure of the Euro-dollar market on a far more regular and comprehensive basis. Table 29 gives an indication of how the maturity structure of the market has changed over time. It is clear that until 1974 the market matched its assets and liabilities reasonably closely as regards maturity. In October 1971 69·8% of liabilities were for less than three months while 61·2% of claims were for a similar maturity. Even at this time, however, there was a certain tendency for banks to borrow short and lend long.

By November 1974 this situation had changed considerably. 71·2% of liabilities were for less than three months while only 58·5% of claims were for this maturity. At the other end of the maturities only 6·7% of liabilities were for one year or more, while 20·6% of claims were in excess of one year. The reason for this sudden increase in maturity mismatching can be found in the huge oil price increases of 1973. This resulted in the OPEC countries having oil revenues far in excess of their requirements for investment which they deposited to a large extent at very short maturities in the Euro-dollar market. At the same time the oil price increases resulted in 'non-oil less-developed countries' suffering very substantial balance of payments deficits. To finance these deficits the less-developed countries turned to the Euro-dollar market where they sought the longest possible maturities. In order to satisfy both the OPEC depositors and the borrowing requirements of the developing countries, the Euro-banks were forced to extend the practice of borrowing short and lending long. This clearly involves a liquidity risk. In order to continue funding their long-term loans, banks need to renew deposits as they mature and in the event of fresh deposits being unobtainable the bank concerned will be in serious trouble. This risk is particularly important as there is no formal

Table 30

A COMPARISON OF MATURITY TRANSFORMATION BY BANK IN THE U.K.

% as at 16 May 1979	British Banks	American Banks	Con-sortium Banks	Japanese Banks	Other Overseas Banks	Total
LIABILITIES						
< 8 days	21·0	26·3	14·8	15·1	20·9	21·4
8 days – < 1 month	17·5	18·6	20·7	16·3	18·8	18·2
1 month – < 3 months	28·1	26·4	31·1	27·1	28·7	27·8
3 months – < 6 months	20·2	17·9	24·6	18·2	19·6	19·3
6 months – < 1 year	8.3	7.3	5.4	9.1	7.6	7.7
1 year – < 3 year	2·4	2·2	2·0	11·0	3·0	3·8
3 years +	2·5	1·3	0·6	3·2	1·4	1·8
Total	100·0	100·0	100·0	100·0	100·0	
CLAIMS						
< 8 days	16·5	17·5	11·0	12·4	15·6	15·6
8 days – < 1 month	11·5	14·1	10·5	14·6	16·0	14·0
1 month – < 3 months	17·5	25·8	16·3	24·3	25·9	23·3
3 months – < 6 months	13·3	18·1	12·4	17·8	18·0	16·7
6 months – < 1 year	8·1	7·5	7·9	6·1	8·1	7·6
1 year – < 3 years	10·3	6·0	18·1	7·0	6·3	7·8
3 years +	22·8	11·0	23·8	17·8	10·0	15·0
Total	100·0	100·0	100·0	100·0	100·0	100·0

Source: Bank of England Quarterly Bulletin, December 1979, Table 13.

lender of last resort in the Euro-dollar market. Banks do try to minimize the risk by inserting a 'dollar availability clause' in loan
agreements which gives the bank the right to demand repayment of
the loan if sufficient funds are not available. However, in many
cases the borrower would be unable to repay at short notice. It is
also likely that in the event of a liquidity crisis the Bank of England
and other central banks would provide some form of 'lender of last
resort' support (as indeed was done at the time of the fringe
banking crisis in 1974). However, the Bank of England does keep a

close watch on the maturity position of banks in the United Kingdom to ensure that the liquidity risk does not become too great.

It is in some ways surprising that the degree of maturity transformation has not increased since 1974. Table 30 shows that the proportions of assets and liabilities of various maturities have remained relatively stable. In view of the intense competition and the very low profit margins in the Euro-dollar market one might have expected banks to increase maturity mismatching. One way of increasing profitability is to shorten deposit maturities and lengthen loan maturities. Since the yield curve for deposits and loans is normally upward sloping this has the effect of increasing the spread between deposit and loan rates.

As Table 30 shows there are considerable differences in maturity transformation between banks. Consortium banks tend to spread their deposits the thinnest, taking only 2·6% of deposits for one year or more and lending 41·9% of claims for one year or more. This is presumably because they have strong banks as shareholders on whom they can rely in the event of a liquidity crisis. On the other hand the Japanese banks have a more conservative maturity structure – 14·2% of deposits and 24·8% of claims were for one year or more in May 1979.

9 The Euro-dollar market II

STRUCTURE OF THE MARKET

If one examines figures, and it does not matter whether you choose deposits or advances as the yardstick or whether you look at the figures for numbers of branches or other ventures such as consortium banks, the growth of overseas and foreign banks in London has been staggering. Since 1963 there have also been some fundamental changes in the structure of the market – not only amongst the groups of banks and their relative importance to the whole market, but also within the various groups.

There would seem to be little doubt that the prime reason for this tremendous expansion was the growth in demand for Euro-dollars by the United States dometstic banks, initiated as a direct result of credit stringency in the United States. Subsequently more banks have followed simply because the Euro-dollar market is so large and London is its main centre. There are now probably in excess of 328 foreign banks established in London maintaining either a full branch service, a subsidiary or a representative office. There are also approximately 59 other banks which have minority interests in United Kingdom registered banks. The growth of foreign bank representation in London is shown in Table 31.

An examination of Table 32 indicates the major changes that have taken place in the market's structure.

Given the caveat entered in the note to Table 32 concerning discontinuities in the figures, the outstanding feature of the data is the dominant position of the American banks although this has been steadily eroded every year since 1971. The loss of approximately 18% of total market share by U.S. banks is reflected in the rising proportion of the market taken by Japanese, other overseas and other U.K. banks. The deposit banks share of total liabilities

Table 31

FOREIGN BANK REPRESENTATION IN LONDON

Year	Directly* Represented	Indirectly Represented‡	Total
1967	113	–	113
1968	134	–	134
1969	137	–	137
1970	161	–	161
1971	174	25	199
1972	213	28	241
1973	230	35	265
1974	262	72	334
1975	261	72	333
1976	263	78	341
1977	298	55	353
1978	311	69	380
1979	328	59	387
1980	351	50	401

* Directly represented through a representative office, branch or subsidiary.
‡ Other banks indirectly represented through a stake in a joint venture or consortium bank.
Source: C.Parker, *Banker*, November 1980, p.87.

has increased slowly over the decade but may show greater growth and volatility in the future as the abolition of exchange controls influences banking business. The accepting houses have however lost considerable ground until 1975 but have maintained their position at approximately 3% of the market since. The likely reason for this is that they have suffered from a relative lack of capital as compared with the large banking groups and thus their activities in the project financing field have been somewhat curtailed, even though in total their liabilities have increased four-fold since 1970.

KEY FACTORS IN THE MOVEMENT OF ASSETS AND LIABILITIES OF EURO-BANKS

The precise causes of the highly volatile movements of funds within various centres in the Euro-markets are always difficult to identify and what follows therefore is intended to provide the reader with an outline of the principal factors involved. A detailed analysis of the position can be found in the quarterly analysis of the Bank of

Table 32

TOTAL FOREIGN CURRENCY LIABILITIES OF BANKS IN THE U.K.

(£M.) [%] December make-up date	1970	1971	1972	1973	1974
Deposit banks	–	460 (1.9)	1264 (3.7)	2019 (3.7)	3,351 (5.1)
Accepting Houses	1,620	1,825 (7.4)	2,198 (6.4)	2,985 (5.5)	2,649 (4.1)
British oversea & Commonwealth	3,813	4,516 (18.2)	6,428 (18.6)	9,551 (17.7)	11,081 (17.0)
American banks	10,474	11,908 (48.0)	14,980 (43.4)	21,676 (40.1)	24,671 (37.7)
Foreign banks	1,768	2,382 (9.6)	3,899 (11.3)	7,349 (13.6)	9,379 (14.3)
Other overseas	1,279	1,556 (6.3)	2,879 (8.3)	6,145 (11.4)	9,651 (14.8)
Other U.K. banks	1,633	2,143 (8.6)	2,880 (8.3)	4,380 (8.1)	4,584 (7.0)
TOTAL	20,587	24,790 (100.0)	34,528 (100.0)	54,105 (100.0)	65,366 (100.0)

(£M.) (%) December make-up date	1975	1976	1977	1978	1979
Deposit banks	4,408 (5.2)	5,691 (4.9)	6,267 (5.2)	7,388 (5.2)	9,465 (5.6)
Accepting Houses	2,802 (3.3)	3,680 (3.2)	3,647 (3.0)	4,523 (3.2)	5,258 (3.1)
American banks	32,770 (38.5)	42,514 (36.9)	43,668 (35.9)	46,152 (32.7)	51,321 (30.3)
Japanese banks	11,612 (13.6)	16,027 (13.9)	15,038 (12.4)	19,225 (13.6)	28,452 (16.8)
Other overseas banks	19,495 (22.9)	28,256 (24.5)	32,348 (26.6)	39,939 (28.3)	46,292 (27.3)
Other U.K. banks	9,237 (10.8)	11,597 (10.1)	13,021 (10.7)	15,652 (11.1)	19,649 (11.6)
Consortium banks	4,827 (5.7)	7,068 (6.1)	7,577 (6.2)	8,314 (5.9)	9,060 (5.3)
TOTAL	85,151 (100.0)	115,103 (100.0)	121,566 (100.0)	141,193 (100.0)	169,497 (100.0)

Note:　Between 1974 and 1975 changes were made by the Bank of England in the various groups of banks when Japanese and Consortium banks were separately identified.

Source: Bank of England Quarterly Bulletin, various issues.

International Settlements:

(1) The key stimulus to change in the assets and liabilities of Euro-banks stem from the operation of U.S. monetary policy and controls. Thus a tightening (or easing) of U.S. monetary conditions, especially the imposition (or lifting) of, or changes in the level of reserve requirements for banks, may induce a competitive advantage for the Euro-market. Consequently, $ holders shift their balances from the U.S. to banks in the Euro-market. Similarly, it may also encourage U.S. banks to raise reserve free funds in the Euro-market.
(2) Transactions between parent banks and overseas branches.
(3) The valuation effects of $ depreciation also cause major fluctuations as fear of depreciation of the $ tends to give rise to additional anticipatory borrowing of $.
(4) the widening of OPEC balance of payments surpluses increase Euro-market deposits and encourage fund movements.

INTEREST RATES

(1) Readers should note that this section discussing interest rates offers, because of the complexity and volatility of the Euro-market rate structure, no more than a general analysis of broad trends and development seen over the last 15 years.

THE POSITION TO 1971

It is a difficult problem to resolve whether Euro-dollar interest rates determine national interest rates (outside the United States) or whether the converse is true. The Euro-dollar market is perhaps the economist's dream in so far as it is the only market in the world where price is really governed by supply and demand. Moreover, since there are no controls on arbitrage between Euro-currencies, covered interest rate differentials do not exist between the various Euro-currency interest rates. Indeed foreign exchange dealers set the forward exchange rates by reference to the relative Euro-currency interest rates. Clendenning* gives an exhaustive survey of

---

* W. Clendenning, *The Euro-dollar Market*, pp. 82–91.

the factors affecting Euro-dollar interest rates and their interaction with national interest rates. In the statistical analysis the rates chosen were the three-month Euro-dollar rate, the three-month local authority rate and the United Kingdom Treasury bill rate. These particular rates were chosen because of the 'ready availability of data' and no doubt give a broad indication as to the efficacy of the findings. One point should be emphasized, however, that in charting the development of London's money markets this book has been especially concerned with short-term funds – the general definition of which has been from sight to say one year. Admittedly, Clendenning's researches fall well within this period, but it is important to realize that the majority of the funds lent to the London discount houses, local authorities, and in the inter-bank market are very short-term funds (that is, seven days or less). These very volatile funds flood in (or out) depending on the strength of sterling and level of interest rates usually on an uncovered basis, whereas three-months' money is invariably negotiated on a covered arbitrage basis.

Clendenning observed that there is a high degree of independence enjoyed by Euro-dollar and United Kingdom interest rates *vis-a-vis* each other because the elasticities of supply and demand for arbitrage funds are probably higher in the United Kingdom than in the Euro-dollar market. However, exchange controls* which restrict the transfer of capital from the United Kingdom to the Euro-dollar market partially offset the impact of the relatively high elasticity of supply of arbitrage funds in the United Kingdom on Euro-dollar rates. Furthermore, United Kingdom and Euro-dollar interest rates may gain a considerable degree of independence due to the impact of the forward exchange mechanism chiefly as the result of substantial official intervention in the forward market which was aimed at maintaining the forward rate as close as possible to its interest parity value. This naturally resulted in covered arbitrage flows being cut off before their full impact was felt in interest rate structures.

It becomes apparent from an examination of Graph 4 that a close relationship existed between the three-month Euro-dollar rate and the local authority rate between 1964 and 1970. The two rates rise and fell approximately together albeit not to the same extent. In particular the large change in the local authority rate in 1965 should be noted compared with the modest reaction in the Euro-dollar

---

* Abolished in 1980.

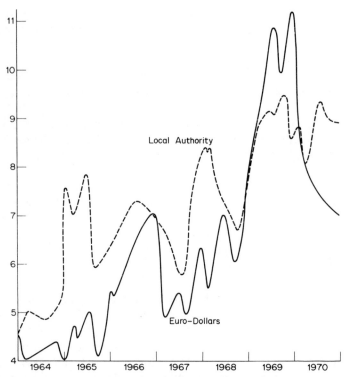

Graph 4. The behaviour of three-month Euro-dollar and three-month UK local authority rates 1964–70.

rate. This indicated that Euro-dollar rates were to a considerable extent independent of United Kingdom rates.* However, although the behaviour of the differential between the two rates showed some degree of interdependence, the fact that United Kingdom rates were able to change to a greater extent than Euro-dollar rates and did on occasion, moved in the opposite direction – particularly in 1965, early 1968, and 1969–70 – seems to indicate that United Kingdom rates were not greatly dependent on Euro-dollar rates. The underlying reasons for these fluctuations are legion – e.g. numerous internal market forces such as the correlation between the gilt-edged market and monthly trade figures, speculation as against a revaluation of the German mark in May 1971 or against

---

* But see also Paul Einzig, op. cit. chapter 11, p. 100. From 1964 to 1969 inflows of Euro-dollars to local authorities and hire purchase finance houses bolstered United Kingdom's reserves and thus avoided an even higher bank rate.

sterling devaluation in 1967, and lastly political factors.

The effect of official support for forward sterling during the 1960s is readily apparent from Graph 5. There is a near identity of

Graph 5. Covered differential between Euro-dollar and UK local authority rates three months' deposits. *Source: Bank of England Quarterly Bulletin*, March 1970, p. 41.

covered yields which is entirely attributable to the fact that between November 1964 and devaluation in 1967 the authorities supported the rate for forward sterling, keeping the discount to a very small figure. After devaluation the forward rate for sterling was allowed to find its own level, so much so that the cost of three months' cover has fluctuated between 8% per annum to as little as ⅛% in early 1970.

A high Bank rate and high interest rates generally do not of themselves necessarily attract overseas funds to London although on many occasions in the past they have done so. This is easily illus- trated by comparing past performance with the situation which pertained early in 1971. Official interest rate policy may be direc- ted at achieving internal or external equilibrium for the economy. The usual instrument for such policy is the central bank discount rate, which generally influences the level of those key arbitrage rates that attract foreign funds. It is not enough, however, to look merely at discount rate action – other aspects of monetary policy must be examined. Where, for example, borrowing from the lender of last resort is not an unlimited right, rationing or the giving of assistance at a higher cost than usual may exert significant upward pressure on market short-term interest rates. Arbitrage rates may be affected in other ways, such as by the extent to which those offering the rates can obtain funds outside the market – this was exemplified by the ability of United Kingdom local authorities to borrow from the Public Works Loan Board. Bill rates are, of course, also influenced by the monetary authorities open market operations, as is also the cash base of the banking system and through this the general level of interest rates. Helping to bring on the general escalation of the international interest rate war is the fact that the theory of achieving international payments balance by equilibrating short-term capital movements broke down in practice. Of fundamental importance is that deficit countries did not always gain an inflow of funds when they raised their interest rates, because the balance of payments deficit was accompanied by weakness of the currency in the foreign exchange markets. Consequently, the forward discount was sufficient, and frequently more than sufficient, to absorb the interest rate differential. This is precisely what happened to the United Kingdom in the past. If we look at the situation in 1971, however (when admittedly we had a balance of payments surplus) we see that the United Kingdom had experienced massive inflows of Euro-dollars. The reason for this was largely because of the then relatively high level of Bank rate (7%) which prevailed throughout most of 1970 and early 1971, whilst other countries such as France, Germany, and Canada had reduced their central bank discount rates to nearer the United States rate of 5% (January 1971), albeit with reluctance, in an endeavour to control 'hot money' flows. Between November 1970 and January 1971 the Federal Reserve discount rates were lowered four times to 5% and American banks replaced their Euro-dollar borrowings with cheap domestic funds causing a drop in gloss liabilities of United States banks to their foreign (mainly London) branches of some $7,000 M. This reflux of funds to the Euro-dollar market had a marked impact on interest rates which fell from 8% in December 1970 to under 5% in March 1971. We now come to two paradoxes as a result of these discount rate falls (American and European); West Germany reduced its rate from $7\frac{1}{2}$% to 6% during the period under review and yet in May 1971 was under enormous pressure following the exchange of some $10,000 M. for Deutsche-marks, notwithstanding a $1\frac{1}{2}$% reduction in central bank discount

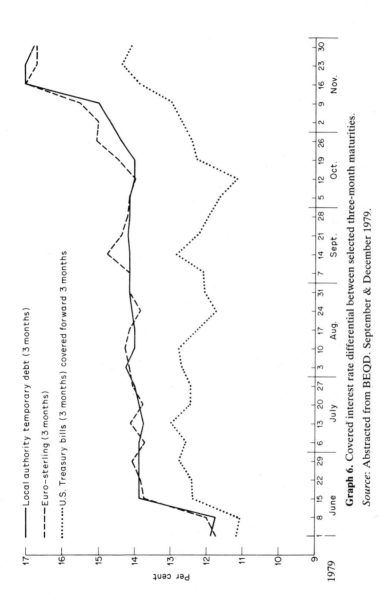

Graph 6. Covered interest rate differential between selected three-month maturities.

Source: Abstracted from BEQD. September & December 1979.

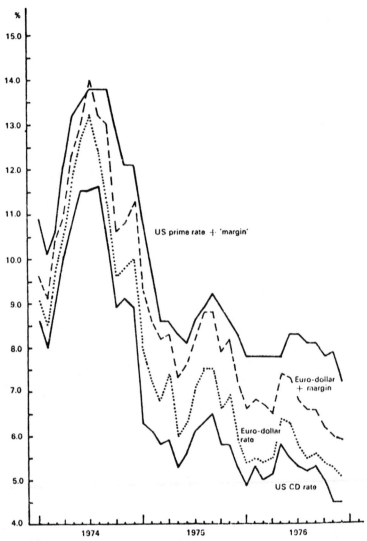

Graph 7. Domestic and Euro-dollar borrowing and lending rates, 1974–6.
Source: S. Frowern, *A framework of International Banking,* 1979.

rate. This situation arose as a direct result of the actions of international speculators who hoped for a revaluation of the mark. The
eventual outcome was that the mark was allowed to float, and
speculation subsequently lessened. The second paradox arising

from this speculation was that the demand for Euro-dollars became so strong that Euro-dollar rates of interest started to rise sharply. These high rates may well have encouraged holders of other currencies, including the Deutschemark, to convert into dollars. In the meantime it is of interest to note what had happened to the local authority three-month rate, covered forward and uncovered. Most of the key market rates in the United Kingdom remained substantially the same at end-January 1971 as they were three months earlier – the local authorities' rate varying between 7% and 7⅞ whilst the Euro-dollar three-month rate fell below 6%. However, the key arbitrage rate – the local authority rate adjusted for the cost of forward cover – had significantly dropped below 5% at end-January 1971. The above explanation serves to give some indication of the complex interactions in the determination of Euro-dollar interest-rates in the real world.

The pattern in short-term interest rates has remained largely the same throughout the 1970s. Graph 6 shows the trends from 1973 to 1977 and this has been maintained into 1980. The graph shows that covered three-months Euro-sterling and covered Euro-dollar rates are very highly correlated indeed. Covered three-month Euro-sterling and local authority rates are also highly correlated, especially after the abolition of exchange control.

In this review of the Euro-dollar market we have seen its tremendous expansion since the early sixties and seventies. It was at first thought that the market would bring about a reduction in world interest rates by making capital readily available and evenly spread throughout the world. Instead, interest rates have shown a continuing upward trend despite occasional set-backs. The market has, in fact, provided a large and highly mobile body of international short-term capital, facilitating the use of the interest rate weapon for external purposes, as well as more quickly communicating interest rate policies between countries. Since the market is denominated in one currency and with a single supply price (the Euro-dollar rate of interest), Euro-dollars have made the task of achieving the level of short-term rates necessary to attract foreign funds much easier for national monetary authorities. It has brought closer links between domestic money markets and as a result interest rate movements in the Euro-dollar market are increasingly being reflected in, and have greater significance for, domestic money markets. That United States monetary policy seems to be the linchpin there appears little doubt: many commentators consider the market to be no more than an appendage of the United

States money supply, and whilst this is perhaps an over-simplistic view, American influence on Euro-dollar interest rates is over-whelming.

Graph 7 shows that United States interest rates set the upper and lower limits for Euro-dollar lending and deposit rates respectively. Moreover it is evident since 1974 that the direction of causality is from the United States domestic interest rates to Euro-dollar interest rate, since movements between the Euro-dollar market and the domestic dollar market leave the latter market unaffected.* Prior to 1974 U.S. capital controls prevented rates from equalizing. See also the comment at the end of section I of the Euro-market.

CONTROLLING THE MARKET

The Euro-dollar market, because of its international nature and the freedom with which it operates, facilitates the mobilization of vast quantities of short-term funds which are dispersed throughout the world in accordance with supply and demand considerations. There is, and has been since the inception of the market, much debate and controversy as to whether or not it has generally been a beneficial development. It is undoubtedly a major factor in promoting and financing world trade, although this has brought in its wake difficulties in international monetary management, the ramifications of which are not yet fully understood.

The market has posed problems in three general areas: (1) for individual branch banks; (2) for countries individually, and (3) for the international monetary system. The risks faced by each sector of the market are essentially similar, stemming from well-known characteristics of the Euro-dollar market. Moreover, the impact and consequences of the risks as they affect the market at each level are by no means the same, nor are the methods employed to deal with them uniform in each sector.

As any banker knows, his chief risk when lending funds un-

---

* For further detailed discussion of euro-currency interest-rates, see 'Some aspects of the determination of euro-currency interest rates', *Bank of England Quarterly Bulletin,* March 1979 and 'Conditions in the Syndicated medium term Euro-credit market,' *Bank of England Quarterly Bulletin,* September 1980.

secured, is that the borrower will renege on his debt. The Euro-dollar system adds a new dimension to this risk resulting from and compounded by its international character, and the long chain of transactions involved in the majority of Euro-market operations. Although it is possible for each bank to establish how much it has lent to another bank, the course of funds moving through the market cannot be established with any precision. Consequently, one bank can never know how much the borrower is indebted to other banks in the system. The generally long chain of transactions which exists between the original lender and the end-user further complicates matters since the lending banker cannot determine either the destination or use to which funds are put. Ultimately, each bank must rely on the integrity of the original borrower for repayment in the event of someone defaulting along the line.

Critics of the market frequently raise the spectre of borrowers and bankers becoming over-committed where Euro-dollars have been converted into domestic currency for internal use, or if borrowers of Euro-dollars defaulted on a large scale. In such circumstances the banks would have to obtain United States dollars through the foreign exchange market to meet their obligations, but there is always a danger that the foreign currency reserves of the country would be insufficient to meet the demand. Alternatively exchange controls could be imposed preventing the reflux of Euro-dollars and effectively precluding banks in other countries from repatriating their Euro-dollar deposits. Taking such a situation to its ultimate position, the probable outcome would be a severe shortage of Euro-dollars throughout the international monetary system culminating in an acute lack of liquidity and failure at some point or points in the chain.

Other areas of concern at the individual bank level include maturity mismatching; country risk; and the question of the 'lender of last resort' in the Euro-dollar market.

Maturity mismatching of assets and liabilities could be a cause for concern for two reasons. First, the weighted average maturity of deposits in London is between three and four months, while most Euro-dollar loans have interest rates adjusted at six monthly intervals in relation to six month LIBOR. Thus sudden increases in short-term Euro-dollar rates could result in serious losses for banks. Secondly, maturity mismatching may cause problems in the event of a crisis of confidence in the Euro-dollar market which results in a withdrawal of deposits. If these short-term deposits are tied up in longer-term assets banks may be unable to find the liquidity to meet deposit maturites. This leads on to the question of the lender of last resort in the Euro-dollar market. In the traditional money market the Bank of England via the discount market acts as a lender of last resort to the banking system, providing it with liquidity in times of need. There is no such formal arrangement in the Euro-dollar market. However, the Bank of England has obtained 'comfort letters' from foreign banks with branches in London, agreeing to stand behind them in the event of crisis as well as agreement from major central banks to assist in the provision of liquidity to these branches.

A further area for concern is the exposure of Euro-banks to country risk on both sides of their balance sheets. This is the result of the recycling of OPEC deposits to less-developed countries. The country risk relating to LDC lending is widely recognized but concern is also expressed in some quarters over the risks resulting from the heavy concentration of deposits by official institutions in OPEC countries.

The idea of regulating Euro-banks at an international level has been rejected by the Committee on Banking Regulation and Supervisory Practices (Cooke Committee), but the Bank of England does supervise individual bank activities, in particular by calling for regular returns on such things as concentration of lending and deposits; maturities; and foreign exchange positions; as well as by laying down regulations on liquidity, capital adequacy and foreign exchange positions.

At the national level two major risks manifest themselves: first, the Euro-dollar market provides an additional channel facilitating the movement and volume of international short-term funds. Secondly, and a corollary of the first point, is the danger that domestic banks will over-reach themselves through imprudent or excessive lendings, thereby placing a strain on official foreign exchange reserves. Corrective measures which need to be taken undoubtedly exert a downward movement on the exchange rate leading to further depletion of the foreign currency reserves. These two factors obviously influenced the Bank of England when in August 1971 they required that banks must maintain net spot asset positions in their foreign currency dealings.

Clendenning* concluded that the problems stemming from substantial and highly volatile capital movements were of greater significance at a national level than considerations concerning

* W. Clendenning, *The Euro-dollar Market*, chapter 10.

individual bank liquidity. The Bank of England has, of course, intimated on various occasions that it would, in a crisis situation, bale out an individual bank in difficulties rather than expose the standing and integrity of the City as a whole to doubt. The possibility of increased capital movements arises from the covered interest rate differential between Euro-dollars and domestic interest rates since these are crucial in determining the direction and extent of covered arbitrage and whether speculation and hedging will occur in the spot and forward market. Consequently, there is now an additional interest parity to which the forward rate can adjust, which complicates the problem of achieving equilibrium in the forward exchange market. The assumption however, is that, if the Euro-dollar market ceased to exist, exchange rate instability would diminish. On the other hand, of course, capital flows are only responses to disequilibrium situations which already existed, rather than the cause of such disequilibrium. Moreover, now that many of the barriers to international capital movements (e.g. exchange controls) have been released, many other channels for capital flows are available.

In addition, with increasing experience of these volatile monetary flows, central bank authorities have become much more sophisticated in dealing with the problems which arise. There is no doubt that although the autonomy of national credit policy is being reduced, national authorities are developing techniques which can be utilized to exploit the Euro-dollar market to further their own policy aims. For example, the Bank of England has made increasing use of the Euro-dollar market as an instrument of liquidity policy, especially during 1970 and 1971. In times of tight domestic credit the Bank has allowed the Euro-dollar market to act as a channel for funds to boost United Kingdom currency reserves. This has been achieved, in general, by maintaining a higher discount rate than other competing countries. It should be emphasized, however, that this would not be a practice to be recommended since it could ultimately create fundamental adjustment problems if balance of payments deficits are persistently financed in this way.

The position could also be eased by the authorities improving the interest rate differentials through the forward market, thereby creating an inflow of funds. (Such a policy was followed by the Bank of England from 1964 to 1967 although at that time it was to prevent the outflow of funds and encourage capital inflows so as to support the sterling spot rate.) Fortunately for the United Kingdom speculation against other currencies, principally Deutschemarks, United

States dollars and the Japanese yen, have to some extent alleviated similar pressures on sterling. The Germans have used the Euro-dollar market, albeit not always successfully, to support their endeavours to siphon-off excess domestic liquidity and reduce immense increases in currency reserves when a revaluation of the Deutschemark was anticipated in 1969 and 1971. More recently, wide use has been made by many European countries of swap operations carried out between the central bank and the commercial banks, or dollar operations effected in the forward market at preferential rates. Intervention of this nature has the effect either of raising the premium on dollars or reducing the cost of forward cover, which results in the interest rate differential moving against the domestic currency and in favour of the Euro-dollar market. As mentioned above, the Bank did pursue such a policy of regular intervention from 1964 to 1967. There is, however, one inherent difficulty in swap operations which appears in times of crisis or speculation. A boomerang effect is often created stemming from the increased quantity of funds in the Euro-dollar market thus heightening the effects of speculative pressures. (*See* comment earlier in the chapter covering the German currency crisis.)

It is the impact of these facets of the Euro-currency markets which have caused much official concern the world over, and which have led to an increasing interdependence between the short-term money markets and monetary policies of the participating countries.

It is clear that despite the market's obvious advantages in mobilizing substantial quantities of funds and thereby easing international liquidity problems, it has nevertheless made it increasingly difficult for a country to implement national monetary control and isolate itself from other countries within the system. Indeed, it is probably true to say that the monetary policies of countries in Western Europe are conditioned to a considerable extent by United States monetary conditions. That this is so is evidenced by the various periods in 1967, 1968, and 1970–1 when tight money conditions prevailed in the United States and funds were attracted from other centres, thus spreading the tight monetary conditions. Repayment of the borrowing when the monetary situation ceased in the United States brought an equally rapid fall in European rates of interest.

At the international level the most frequent criticism of the Euro-markets is that they have contributed to worldwide inflation by adding to the supply of world money or credit. This argument rests on the view that the Euro-dollar market can create money over and above that created by domestic banking systems. Certainly it is true that a shift of deposits from a bank in the United States to a Euro-bank will increase the amount of dollar deposits as the size of deposits in the United States is not reduced while new Euro-dollar deposits have been created. However, most opinions now seem to agree that the Euro-dollar market does not possess an 'autonomous' credit creation potential and that its function is to transmit rather than create credit.

A second criticism, recently voiced by the German Bundesbank is that the Euro-dollar market has resulted in 'over-recycling'. While it is accepted that the Euro-dollar market initially played a useful role in re-cycling OPEC funds, thus preventing a deep recession, the market has enabled countries to finance bigger balance of payments deficits and for longer periods than was justified by the increase in oil prices. More-over since Euro-dollars are lent without conditions (unlike say, I.M.F. loans) countries do not have to take deflationary action to reduce their deficits. This is perhaps the only way in which the Euro-dollar market could be said to add to world inflation.

Even if we accept that there might be some need to control the Euro-dollar market it is still difficult to conceive an affective way of doing so. It is accepted that it is not feasible for controls to be imposed at an international level, which means it is up to individual countries to impose restrictions. One frequently proposed solution is to introduce reserve requirements. This would certainly reduce the competitive advantage that Euro-banks enjoy, but the chances are that this would simply cause a shift to unregulated offshore centres with a resultant loss of invisible earnings for London. Certainly when Germany imposed a 100% reserve requirement on external liabilities in excess of the level at November 1968 the only result was to remove Frankfurt as a major centre and to cause German banks to operate from Luxembourg.

At present it would seem that the best that can be hoped for is closer co-ordination of existing exchange controls to achieve better multilateral harmonization of exchange positions. The predominant influence in this respect must be the United States which holds the key to the problem, although at times the influence of other countries such as Germany can also be significant. The capricious behaviour of the Euro-dollar market between 1969 and 1971 stemmed principally from the ever-changing 'stop-go' tactics of the United States monetary authorities thereby fuelling the crises

which followed. What is required for the future is that all governments will endeavour to pursue economic and monetary policies
which will take more account of the international implications of
the Euro-dollar market, thus curtailing the incidence of extreme
monetary fluctuations of the recent past.

10 The finance house market

The instalment credit industry had, by 1979 set a new record by extending credit amounting to £4,841 M. with outstandings to Finance House Association members totalling £5,989 M.

The growth of the market since 1967 is shown in Graph 8 with outstanding instalment credit* growing from approximately £1,200 M. to £2,000 M. by 1972 and over £2,700 M. by 1977.

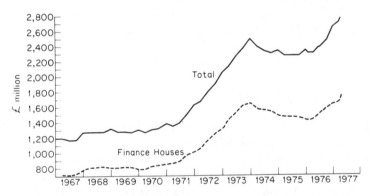

Graph 8. Outstanding Instalment Credit. *Source:* Finance Houses Association.

Finance houses accept deposits from the public and industrial and commercial concerns, and from banks and financial institutions. Other funds are also obtained through bank borrowing, and the money markets. The funds are then chanelled into the industrial, commercial and consumer sectors by means of loans, hire purchase, conditional sales, credit sales, and leasing.

---

* This excludes leasing, stocking finance and other non-instalment credit extended by finance houses, which accounts for the apparent differences between total credit and instalment credit of finance houses.

The finance houses have always been adversely affected by various credit controls imposed by successive governments since the 1950s. The restrictions have been effected through Control Orders laid down by the Department of Trade specifying the minimum amount of initial deposits and maxium repayment periods. One of the chief difficulties for the finance houses has been the frequency with which changes have been made. For example between 1961 and 1969 term controls were changed eight times and in mid-1971 they were lifted completely. The finance companies have also been subject to ceiling controls on their lending and the Bank of England has from time to time requested the banks to curb their lending to finance companies.

THE RANGE AND DIVERSIFICATION OF BUSINESS LENDING

In the 1950s most finance houses were concerned with providing consumer finance for the purchase of motor cars and credit sales for domestic goods. Provision of finance for working capital was rare apart from stock financing for motor dealers but many companies had begun to develop industrial financing techniques primarily for industrial and commercial vehicles.

LEASING

The early 1960s were a time of considerable innovation when finance houses were the first institutions to offer leasing. This development opened up a whole new market for finance houses, so much so that by 1980, leasing had become a mainstream business for many companies. By 1976 the amount of leasing business written by members of the Equipment Leasing Association* was £421 M. (approximately 30% of total finance leasing) rising to over £1,800 M. by 1979 illustrating the size and growth of the market.

BLOCK DISCOUNTING

Finance houses also provide block discounting facilities to retailers who undertake their own instalment credit business. The retailer sells 'blocks' of existing instalment credit agreements to the finance

---

* The majority of Finance Houses Association members are members of both associations.

houses who provide immediate cash sums to the retailer, improving his cash flow. The retailer usually continues to collect the instalments on the finance companies' behalf and it is this feature which generally distinguishes block discounting from factoring.

FACTORING

This financial technique, along with leasing, was the second major innovation pioneered by the finance houses. Both techniques have provided a major long-term stimulus to industry and commerce through access to a broader range of services and sources of funds.

Factoring involves the purchase of a company's book debts against immediate cash payment less an agreed commission charge. Debt collection and bad debt recovery is undertaken by the finance house.

CONSUMER FINANCE

Finance companies provde instalment credit at the point of sale as well as direct to the consumer for the purchase of a wide range of consumer durables. The houses have however extended their services to include personal loans, revolving credit schemes, term loans and current account services for personal customers. By 1980 consumer credit business constituted approximately 40% of total lending, the remaining 60% being with industrial and commercial companies.

SOURCES OF FUNDS

It was not until December 1961 that detailed statistics of the assets and liabilities of finance houses were published. This was brought about as the result of recommendations made by the Radcliffe Committee. Previously the only composite statistics published were for the years 1954 to 1958 and were given to the Committee in evidence. The current statistical series is produced by the Department of Trade (formerly the Board of Trade) and published quarterly in *Business Monitor*.

Finance houses rely for the greater part of their funds on borrowed money. The predominance of deposits was a significant feature of the houses' financing in 1958. Indeed, at that time they accounted for two-fifths of total funds. This proportion increased

Table 33

SELECTED LIABILITIES OF FINANCE HOUSES 1962–79

(£M.) End of	1962	1964	1966	1968	1970	1971	1972	1973	1974	1975	1976	1977	1978	1979
Deposits by:														
(a) U.K. Banks	49	84	94	118	97	212	116	114	260	167	317	398	381	419
(b) Other U.K. Finan-cial Institutions	40	55	55	79	115	139	129	134	32	28	42	82	91	85
(c) U.K. Industrial and Commercial Companies	128	203	255	269	316	294	136	169	93	133	210	215	239	279
(d) Other U.K. Residents	34	66	114	103	110	115	50	52	54	54	93	64	84	157
(e) Overseas Residents	86	86	130	43	50	63	6	8	20	33	41	50	60	65
Total Deposits	337	494	648	612	688	823	437	477	459	415	703	809	855	1,005

– Bills Discounted with U.K. Banks	65	111	106	109	97	103	58	150	151	142	149	216	424	716
– Other Borrowing	98	132	55	87	30	73	95	140	175	196	540	649	929	1,205
– Unearned Finance Charges	64	88	86	102	110	144	113	122	97	105	169	209	283	434
– Issued Capital and Reserves	142	172	189	198	230	257	172	173	195	215	N/A	N/A	N/A	N/A
Total Selected Liabilities	706	997	1,075	1,108	1,155	1,400	875	1,062	1,077	1,073	1,561	83	2,491	3,360

Note: From January 1972 figures exclude finance houses recognized banks.
From March 1976 a number of other companies whose main business is consumer credit were included therefore the series is not strictly comparable.

Source: Business Monitor: SD 7 Assets and Liabilities of Finance Houses.

to about one-half by June 1962, and at 31 March 1972 deposits amounted to over 60% of the total liabilities of the houses. By 1979 however deposits had fallen to approximately less than a third of total liabilities. Table 33 shows the changes in the position from 1962 to 1979 but these figures must be regarded with utmost care as a major discontinuity arose in 1972 when four major finance companies were recognized as banks causing a significant fall in the aggregate totals. Moreover, in 1976 a number of other companies whose main business is consumer credit were included.

Further complications have arisen since the implementation of the Banking Act which has re-classified* most Finance Houses Association members as licensed deposit takers, notwithstanding the fact that the four major finance houses – Forward Trust, Lombard North Central, Mercantile Credit and United Dominions Trust still remain for statistical purposes as banks. A number of finance companies have however, decided not to apply for licensed deposit status and consequently have had to re-finance much of their deposit base from new sources, to avoid being in breach of the Banking Act. Clearly it is impossible to take any one official statistical series which gives a true reflection of the size of the finance house market.

Table 34

DEPOSITS OF SELECTED LARGE FINANCE HOUSES (£M.)

	1976	1977	1978	1979	1980
Mercantile Credit Co. Ltd.	48	54	150	388	N/A
Lombard North Central	443	415	391	424	474
Lloyds Scottish Ltd.	226	314	437	531	N/A
United Dominions Trust	557	480	510	557	570
Forward Trust	191	262	333	545	N/A

Sources: Annual Accounts of the Companies

A more accurate picture of the size and importance of the finance house market can be obtained by reference to Table 34 which shows the deposits of five selected large finance companies. The figures are for the parent company in each group and not for

---

* Companies must apply for licensed deposit taker status.

the group itself as the intention is to exclude other group activities. The figures also include a considerable element of bank borrowing and this would seem to be reflected in the 'other borrowing' figure in Table 33 which has almost doubled since 1977 from £649 M. to £1,205 M. in 1979. Table 35 shows the approximate proportion of various liabilities as a percentage of total liabilities for Finance Houses Association members as a group in 1980.

Table 35

PERCENTAGE OF TOTAL LIABILITIES

	1980 (%)
Retail deposits	3
Wholesale deposits	35
Overseas deposits	8
Shareholders funds	15
Unearned finance charges	10
Discounted Bills	9
Acceptances	20
	100

Source: Finance Houses Association

In the official statistics deposits are divided into five main divisions: United kingdom banks, other United Kingdom financial institutions, United Kingdom industrial and commercial companies, other United Kingdom residents, and overseas residents. Basically in this market there are two types of deposit: those, which are obtained in the money market, and those, which are obtained through advertising in the press. The bulk of a finance company's deposits are usually in the money market since this is now a natural outlet for the institutional treasurer with surplus funds. Quite obviously the money market has the attraction that very large sums can be obtained in single amounts whereas advertising will generally only attract the relatively small saver. Some companies endeavour to obtain the best of both worlds by obtaining their deposits exclusively from the small investor in the manner of a deposit bank, whilst others will only accept minimum deposits of £25,000 and consequently operate almost exclusively through the money market.

During the 1950s many finance houses attracted deposits

through advertising, offering rates of interest which were several points higher than the prevailing rates on bank deposits. Regrettably, many houses had insufficient capital resources and a small number became insolvent resulting in the loss of depositors' money. Subsequently in 1963 legislation was passed to safeguard future investors. Under the Protection of Depositis Act it became compulsory for finance houses which advertise for deposits to publish fuller details of their liabilities and also on the nature of their lending. Following the implementation of the Banking Act finance houses will be required to meet new regulations. The devaluation of sterling in 1967 was the factor which engendered the renewal of interest in the small investors' deposits. One large company was caused acute embarrassment by the withdrawal of many large deposits particularly by overseas residents. This trend in the market as a whole can be seen by examing Table 33. Deposits of overseas residents fell from £130 M. in 1966 to £43 M. in 1968. Subsequently, many companies commenced a concerted campaign to attract the smaller deposit to obviate such a sudden loss of funds arising again. The wisdom of this practice was demonstrated in December 1972 when deposits of overseas residents fell to £6 M. as pressure built up on sterling in the foreign exchange markets. It is now a matter of policy of many houses to spread their risks by taking a larger proportion of small deposits.

We must not, however, overstate the problem: it is estimated that there are approximately 1,600 finance houses engaged in the business of providing credit on an instalment basis. The major proportion of deposits is handled by eight leading companies, whose deposits range for £90 M. to £700 M. In 1967 the members of the Finance Houses Association (with a membership of some forty-one companies) held 75% of the market. By 1980 the proportion was 85% of total deposits. It follows then that the giants of the industry must depend to a high degree on large deposits borrowed in the market. If Table 33 is examined it can be seen that the figures appear to bear this out: of total deposits amounting to £823 M. at end 1971, some £645 M. was obtained from United Kingdom industrial and commercial companies. Presumably even some of the deposits of other United kingdom residents must also have been obtained through the market. The same would undoubtedly be true of a proportion of the £6 M. recorded for overseas residents. Over the period total deposits have risen from £33 M. to £1,005 M. and apart from the setback occasioned by devaluation in 1967, they grew steadily throughout. From December 1962 to December 1965 hire purchase debt increased from £622 M. to £894 M. and this increase of £272 M. was almost entirely financed from increased deposits during the years 1963–4 (£104 M.) and 1964–5 (£160 M.). Following the lifting of hire purchase restrictions in 1971, there was a 20% increase in hire purchase debt to £1,051 M., most of which was financed by a rise of some £135 M. in deposits and £27 M. in issued capital. Between end-December 1970 and end-December 1971 there was a significant fall in deposits of United Kingdom industrial and commercial companies from 46% of total deposits to 35·7%, whilst the United Kingdom's banks' sector increased by over 100% to 25·7%. The withdrawal of funds by the company sector no doubt stemmed from the very competitive rates offered by the banks on Certificates of Deposit as they endeavoured to attract funds. The increasing participation of the banking sector in the finance house market was a direct result of the revised banking and monetary policies in 1971. This trend in the pattern of depositors was repeated during 1972 with the banking sector increasing its deposits to £307 M. and the company sector falling a further £28 M. by 31 March 1972. The figures after March are not comparable with earlier statistics because of the decision of a number of finance houses to be designated as banks with the resultant loss of some £700 M. of assets. As a proportion of total liabilities, deposits increased from 47·7% in 1962 to 60·2% in 1966. In 1967, the year of devaluation, the percentage dropped to some 55% which was no doubt attributable to the withdrawal of overseas funds.

An examination of the individual sections of deposits ((a) to (e) in Table 33) indicates where the major growth took place prior to 1971. By far the biggest expansion occurred in funds deposits by United Kingdom industrial and commercial companies which increased from 38% of total deposits in 1962 to 46% in 1970 and illustrates the realization by company treasurers that high interest rates were obtainable in this market. The other sectors showing most growth have been other United Kingdom residents (d) with 6% and other United Kingdom financial institutions (b) 4%. Deposits by United Kingdom banks remained substantially the same at 15% of total deposits. As already mentioned those of overseas residents declined both in total from £136 M. in 1965 to £50 M. in 1970 and also as a proportion of total deposits from 25% to 7%. The dramatic reduction which occurred in 1967 of £42 M. was followed by an even bigger fall in 1968 of £45 M. as foreign investors showed their continuing doubts about the strength of sterling. The year 1969–70 subsequently showed an increase of some £24 M.

which no doubt reflected the improved position of sterling and the strong balance of payments position.

The credit restrictions imposed on the banks during the 1960s severely curtailed the extent to which they could lend to finance houses. The peak year for bank borrowing was 1964 when the amount outstanding was £116 M., but this ultimately declined to a mere £23 M. in 1970. The position of bills discounted or acceptance credits is essentially similar to that of overdrafts because they were also the subject of severe restraint.

Both overdrafts and acceptances serve a dual purpose for a finance house: first, as a source of funds, and secondly, as a reserve to be used in case of need. The five quarters ending December 1972 demonstrate the volatility of this particular liability which, commencing in December 1971 at £56 M., were £17 M., £54 M., £92 M., £74 M., and £97 M., respectively. Quite obviously from the finance house standpoint the bank advance is the easiest element to adjust to meet seasonal and unforeseen requirements. It is quite usual for a company to finance its increased debt initially during the main car buying season by drawing on its bank account pending the receipt of other funds. Table 33 shows that of total liabilities 'other borrowing' from United Kingdom banks of £30 M. in December 1970 amounted to a mere 2%. By end-1979 the proportion was 35%. Bank borrowing for a small company may, however, account for as much as 50% of its total liabilities.

Acceptances averaged about 7–9% from 1962 to 1971, but thereafter steadily grew to 14% by 1973 and 21% by 1979 notwithstanding constant surveillance by the Bank of England. The acceptance market has strong links with the finance houses, heavy involvement in leasing and group banking connections. The bills are, of course, 'accommodation bills' and therefore have no underlying trading transaction. They are drawn by the finance houses on merchant banks who then accept the bills by adding their name to them, thus adding to their security and marketability. The banks charge an acceptance commission which varies with the standing of the finance house and it is quite usual for one company to maintain several lines of credit. These will, in all probability, not be utilized to the full since, to the extent that they remain unused, they constitute a form of reserve for the finance house.

The only figures in Table 33 which have not been commented on are the issued capital and reserves. In assessing the scale of shareholders' participation, it is evident that the proportion of issued capital to total liabilities is approximately 5:1, and has been consistently at the level since 1962. No figures are available after 1975.

THE IMPACT OF THE INVOLVEMENT OF THE BANKS

The clearing banks have a major interest in all the larger finance houses, indeed some like Forward Trust are wholly-owned subsidiaries. Many non-clearing banks and insurance companies also have minority interests in finance houses. It became obvious in the early and mid-1950s that instalment credit was a fast growing field and the banks decided that they must endeavour to develop this line of business. Despite this fairly early move it was not until 1958 and after, when the government removed restrictions on instalment credit, that the real impetus for bank involvement occurred. The growth of hire purchase debt from £480 M. in September 1958 to £961 M. in July 1960 was a period of unfettered competition for the finance houses. Many houses were unprepared with staffs that were too small and inexperienced to cope with the plethora of business that had been unleashed. The interest of the banks and of their incursion into the field of instalment finance then became manifest, either by offering personal loans or through their participation in hire purchase companies. There is no doubt that the banks engendered tremendous prestige and enhanced financial resources by lending their names to the houses they acquired. This was demonstrated in two ways: firstly, finance company bills were more readily accepted by the merchant banks, and in their turn, by the discount houses. It also meant that finance house paper generally commanded finer rates of discount than hitherto, although actual rates naturally depend on the standing of individual companies or their parent insitutions. Secondly, this ability to borrow at more advantageous rates was coupled with the ability to attract a greatly increased volume of deposits from all sources. There is, of course, no cartel agreement between finance houses in respect of interest paid on deposits. Generally speaking rates varied from house to house and remained static regardless of changes that occurred in Bank rate. The average cost of borrowing is a matter of crucial importance to a finance company since it is in the very nature of their business to lend from one to three, or even five years. For this reason then they endeavour to obtain funds on the longest periods of notice of withdrawal. For example, many houses do not accept deposits at less than seven days' notice and deposits for one month, three months and six months or more constitute the majority of their funds. It is clear then that the dangers for finance houses manifest themselves particularly during periods of rising interest rates when the regular renewal of short-term deposits at increased interest rates may well result in losses for the company. This pattern of borrowing may well change in times of falling interest rates, when the maturity pattern will tend towards much shorter periods of say from overnight to seven days.

INTEREST RATES, MATURITIES AND PROFITABILITY

The nature of the business carried out by a finance house makes it particularly sensitive to changing levels of interest rates and demand on the market. In general they are providing credit facilities of up to three years' duration, whilst the average life of outstanding credits is approximately eighteen months. Consequently, during periods of rising rates such as was experienced in the late 1960s and during 1972–3 when rates virtually doubled, they are forced into the unenviable predicament of renewing maturing deposits at the higher prevailing rates. Similarly, between 1978 and 1979 rates rose over $4\frac{1}{2}$ percentage points, drastically reducing profitability. As mentioned earlier, the majority of finance house deposits are held for 1–6 month periods.

The demand for funds in the finance house market is unusually responsive to changes in government economic policy which are intended to stimulate or dampen industrial activity and consumer spending. The twin expedients of increasing purchase tax (now VAT) and tightening hire purchase regulations were found to be a highly effective method of controlling the demand for consumer durables during the 1960s. Relaxation of these measures naturally has the reverse effect.

Seasonal considerations, especially the cyclical nature of the motor trade and pre-Christmas trade, also can have a marked influence on the rates paid for funds by the smaller finance houses. A further consideration, which also applies to the local authorities' market, is the fact that there is no secondary market available to the investor. The problem manifests itself for the houses when money is tight in the market with rates rising; the determining factor governing the rate of interest will be the willingness of the investor to renew his contract for a further period. It is then that the question of liquidity will be important to the depositor and the knowledge that once the deposit is lent it cannot be recovered

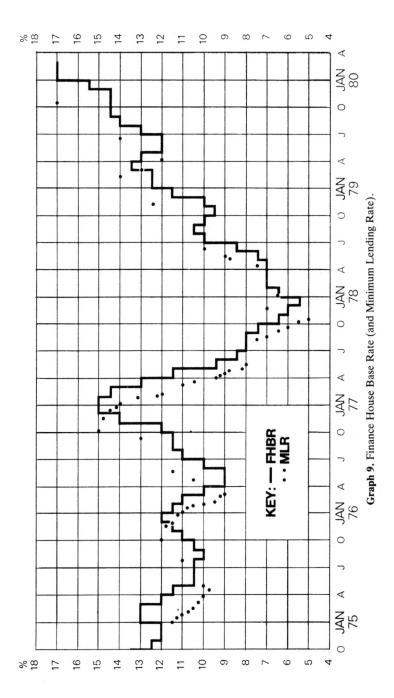

Graph 9. Finance House Base Rate (and Minimum Lending Rate).

before maturity, may inhibit a renewal unless the interest rate offered is above average. In periods when funds are plentiful finance houses never directly refuse to accept deposits but overcome the difficulty by quoting unattractive rates.

It is apparent that because of the magnitude of the funds they require, and the often violent fluctuations, which can occur in the demand for them, the finance houses are forced into a high degree of dependence on large deposits bought in the money market. Clearly, however, the larger companies and especially those linked to major banks, can obtain funds at the finest rates. This reliance on bought money and bank borrowing is confirmed by an examination of the position at end of 1976, 1978 and 1979 where 85%, 71% and 65% of total funds were in deposits and other borrowing. It is also probable in 1979 that a high proportion of the £65 M. obtained from overseas depositors and the £157 M. from other United Kingdom residents represented money-market money.

The principal factor determining the rate of interest in the finance house market on a day-to-day basis is the current interbank sterling rate. In turn, this rate is determined by many factors, apart from technical ones, depending on the day of the month, such as the rates obtainable day-by-day on other investments – call money, Certificates of Deposit, local authority bonds, Euro-commercial paper, etc., the yields on which are determined by market circumstances.

Graph 9 compares the Finance House Base Rate with Minimum Lending Rate from 1975 to April 1980. The difficulties that occur for the finance houses which follow sudden increases in Minimum Lending Rate and the market volatility of rates over the period are very evident. In an effort to counteract this problem many companies have moved towards fluctuating rate business for large industrial business but this has not been possible with small and medium balances.

11 Certificates of Deposit

DEVELOPMENT OF A NEW CREDIT INSTRUMENT IN THE U.S.A.

The significance of the emergence in New York in 1961 of the Certificate of Deposit market and of its subsequent importance in bringing about a fundamental change in the thinking and methods of the British banker, were not fully recognized until some ten years later when the Bank of England introduced competition and credit control (*see* Appendix II). Since then it is probably fair to say that there has been an intellectual revolution in the thinking concerning how a U.K. bank should manage its assets and liabilities.

The development of the New York market was important to London on two counts: first, it brought home the advantages to be gained from the issue of Certificates of Deposit, and secondly, it enabled the London banker to acquire and ultimately develop the necessary specialized techniques which were later to prove invaluable to the successful creation of the market in sterling Certificates of Deposit in 1968. The British banker's attitude on investment and loans is now much more aggressive than could possibly have been conceived 15 years ago. At the hub of that fundamental reappraisal of banking operations has been the Certificate of Deposit.

It is of interest, therefore, to examine the reasons why the American banker launched the negotiable Certificate of Deposit in 1961. When the Second World War ended in 1945, total deposits of the commercial banks in the U.S.A. were $150 billions, of which some $30 billions, or 20% was held in New York. By 1960, however, total deposits were $230 billions and New York's proportion had fallen to 14% or $33·7 billions.

This loss of deposits by the New York banks to the country banks was to some extent predictable following the substantial industrial

expansion which took place after the war in the west, south-west
and north-western areas of America. That New York remained the
financial centre of the country, and that much of the investment
supporting the industrial growth was provided by the New York
banks, is evidenced by the fact that their loans to deposit ratio
increased from 24% to 55% between 1945 and 1960. The massive
industrial complexes brought in their train a new breed of corporate treasurer who was trained in highly sophisticated investment techniques and was constantly seeking higher yields on liquid
reserves. Because of the operation of Regulation Q, which limited
the rate of interest to be paid on time deposits, the treasurers channelled their funds into the more profitable areas of the money
market. It became imperative that measures be taken by the banks
to stem this loss of interest-sensitive funds and a number of
schemes were devised before the Certificate of Deposit was eventually introduced. The adoption of the new instrument proved out-
standingly successful in reversing the trend away from the New
York banks, and indeed by 1972 approximately 40% of the U.S.
bank deposits were held in the form of Certificates of Deposit.

LONDON DOLLAR CERTIFICATES OF DEPOSIT

The London dollar Certificates of Deposit market was created primarily to attract fresh funds into the Euro-dollar market. They
were introduced, with the Bank of England's permission, in May
1966 by First National City Bank, which was the first American
bank to launch the new instrument in New York in 1961. One of the
salient features of the dollar Certificate of Deposit is that it is
issued in amounts from $25,000 whereas the more usual figure for
deposits in the Euro-dollar market is $1 M.; thus the Certificate of
Deposit was meant to appeal to the smaller non-bank lender. Most
of the advantages and disadvantages of Certificates of Deposit will
be enumerated in the later section of this chapter covering sterling
Certificates of Deposit: only those that have especial relevance to
the dollar Certificate of Deposit will therefore be discussed in this
section.

GROWTH OF THE MARKET

The market in London for dollar Certificates of Deposit has shown sustained growth throughout its life, as shown in Table 36. This shows the size of the market when measured both in sterling (which follows the Bank of England presentation) and in dollars (which is the more appropriate measure). Dollar Certificates of Deposit now represent approximately 10% of total currency deposits of banks in the U.K.

While the figures indicate a considerable increase in resources, they are not perhaps as rapid as originally envisaged bearing in mind the advantages offered by the Certificates. One explanation of this caution by investors is that since the inception of the market Euro-dollar rates have tended to rise.Therefore, when investors anticipate further rises in interest rates the Certificate of Deposit loses its attraction, since if they wish to redeem their funds before maturity they can only do so at a loss. It would seem then that investment in Certificates of Deposit will only expand during a period of declining interest rates; at other times investors will tend to invest their funds in Euro-dollars overnight or at call.

If we test this thesis empirically, however, by examining the pre-1970 periods of greatest growth in the Certificates of Deposit market, we find that the argument is only partially correct. Between December 1967 and September 1968 Certificates of Deposit outstanding rose by some £319 M. and the hypothesis seems to hold good because between December 1967 and March 1968 Euro-dollar rates fell by approximately 1% from 6½% to 5½%, only to rise again to over 7% by June and tail off quickly again to just over 6% by September 1968. Looking at the period from March 1969 to December 1969 the total of Certificates of Deposit outstanding almost doubled (to £1,541 M.) and yet during this period Euro-dollar rates went from 8½% in early March to over 11% in mid March, remained there or thereabouts until June, and then fell rapidly to 10% by September only to rise sharply again from October to December 1970. This apparent anomaly was probably due to the enormous demand for Euro-dollars generally over the period, but particularly by the American banks in London.

An appraisal of the position during 1970 again presents us with another paradox – Certificates of Deposit outstanding actually fell from £1,684 M. to £1,649 M. at end-December, whilst Euro-dollar rates, apart from a brief upward surge in the early part of the year, fell steadily from 9½% to just over 5% by March 1971. If our hypothesis is correct then we should have witnessed a substantial increase in Certificates of Deposit holdings instead of a fall. The

Table 36

SIZE OF LONDON DOLLAR CERTIFICATE OF DEPOSIT MARKET

DECEMBER	1966	1967	1968	1969	1970	1961	1972	1973	1974	1975	1976	1977	1978	1979
MEASURED IN £M.	80	249	597	1,541	1,653	1,924	3,072	4,429	5,088	6,419	9,860	12,455	14,132	19,775
MEASURED IN $M.(1)	225	599	2,020	3,699	3,957	4,910	7,213	10,291	11,954	12,966	16,782	23,895	28,843	43,459

Note (1): Converted from £'s at ruling spot rate on last working day of the year.
Source: Bank of England Statistical Abstract Nos. 1 and 2 and update.

	Turnover $M.	Turnover as a % of outstandings
December 1973	646	6·2
December 1974	759	6·8
December 1975	991	7·6
December 1976	1,798	10·9
December 1977	2,921	12·7
December 1978	4,883	17·1
December 1979	6,363	14·7

most likely explanation would seem to lie in the greatly reduced Euro-dollar borrowing by the United States banks which continued throughout 1970, coupled with reductions in United States discount rate and other world rates when borrowings were reduced by $1,500 M. during the three months ended January 1971. Thus Euro-dollar rates fell significantly below comparable United Kingdom rates before allowing for the cost of forward cover, rendering an investment, say in local authorities, more profitable than Euro-dollars. Since the early 1970s the growth in issues has increased approximately tenfold to over $47,000 M. which is entirely in concert with the huge growth in the Euro-dollar market over the same period. It is almost impossible to attribute specific causes for the expansion of the $ CD market except to say that it undoubtedly offers the issuing banks with new sources of deposits, and investors achieve competitive rates for any maturity they wish to purchase or sell. An important factor in this respect has been the proven stability of the market which has continued to quote prices even at times of extreme pressure and difficulty in the foreign exchange markets.

The turnover, as a percentage of total issues, increased from 6.2% in 1973 reaching 17·1% in 1978 but fell to 14·7% in 1979. The sales figures reflect purchases in both the primary and secondary markets and show the increasing activity in the market as investors adjust their portfolios to the volatile interest rate structure.

The growth in the number of issuing banks has risen gradually in concert with the increasing size of the market. In 1967 there were approximately fifteen issuers amongst the American, foreign and British overseas banks in London; by 1968 the Bank reported that the number had risen to twenty-six, by 1970 it was said to be over thirty and by August 1980 the total was 147. The American banks introduced this new monetary instrument in an effort to increase their share of the Euro-dollar market in London by enticing deposits away from their competitors. To what extent this gambit has succeeded it is hard to estimate, but what does seem certain is that it precipitated the entry of other banks (particularly British) into the market on the grounds that those who do not enter the market will lose deposits to those who do.

One important feature of this financial instrument which is of particular importance to overseas investors is that maturity monies are paid without deduction of tax (as are many equivalent sterling short-term investments); thus the attraction of the short-term Certificate of Deposit would be reduced considerably if non-residents were forced to follow complicated procedures to reclaim tax deducted at source.

Certificates are issued in multiples of $1,000, with a minimum of $25,000 for short-term Certificates of Deposits, and a minimum of $10,000 for medium-term Certificates of Deposit. They are available at varying maturity dates in addition to the more usual fixed calendar months. The minimum initial maturity period is three months and the maximum five years. Most issuing banks will create Certificates for specific periods or maturity dates up to one year, these being described as short-term Certificates of Deposit. Medium-term Certificates of Deposit are issued from one- to five-year periods. These are issued in three ways:

(a) By 'tranche' in denominations of U.S. $10,000, commonly with investors who do not normally enter the money market direct. There is an active secondary market in the form of $ Certificates of Deposit with daily quotations widely published.

(b) 'Tap' Certificates of Deposit are issued on demand for differing settlement and maturity dates and yields through International Certificates of Deposit Market Association members. Issues are in multiples of U.S. $1,000 (sometimes $5,000) with a minimum of $25,000. Very fine rates are quoted for amounts of $1,000,000 or more.

(c) Floating Rate Certificates of Deposit (which are similar to floating rate notes) where the interest rate is fixed every six months at a pre-determined spread over LIBOR for six month deposits.

MATURITY STRUCTURE

Table 37 analyses the maturity structure of $ Certificates of Deposit from mid-November 1975 to mid-February 1980. It should be borne in mind however, that the figures relate to remaining and not original maturity. Thus the shorter categories are swollen by the inclusion of longer dated Certificates of Deposits approaching maturity. An examination of figures reveals that the market is fundamentally a short-term one with approximately 75% or more of maturities lying in the period up to one year and of those 40–50% in the up-to-three months band.

Taking the mid-November figures for 1975, 1977, 1978 and 1979 the 8-days to one month band has moved between 10% and 14%.

Table 37

MATURITY STRUCTURE OF LONDON $ CERTIFICATES OF DEPOSIT
OUTSTANDING
$ M.

Maturity band	Mid-Nov.75	Mid-Feb.76	Mid-Nov.76	Mid-Feb.77
Sight	69	128	60	133
0 – 8 days	402	391	442	274
8 days – 1 month	1,364	1,476	1,599	1,536
1 – 3 months	3,541	3,650	4,326	4,056
3 – 6 months	3,317	3,435	3,512	3,466
6 months – 1 year	1,564	1,777	2,293	2,989
1 – 3 years	1,811	2,055	2,970	3,193
3 – 5 years	684	609	757	742
5 years +	2	2	18	53
Total	12,754	13,523	15,977	16,442

Maturity band	Mid-Nov.77	Mid-Feb.78	Mid-Nov.78	Mid-Feb.79
Sight	67	177	114	321
0 – 8 days	746	593	665	1,068
8 days – 1 month	3,084	2,055	3,328	4,375
1 – 3 months	6,748	6,648	8,090	8,018
3 – 6 months	5,051	5,528	6,127	6,939
6 months – 1 year	2,505	2,875	2,330	2,777
1 – 3 years	3,055	3,055	3,547	3,964
3 – 5 years	992	935	981	1,305
5 years +	38	21	17	36
Total	22,286	21,837	25,199	28,803

Maturity band	Mid-Nov.79	Mid-Feb.80
Sight	111	424
0 – 8 days	1,661	1,542
8 days – 1 month	6,920	8,178
1 – 3 months	13,574	14,363
3 – 6 months	9,742	9,249
6 months – 1 year	4,209	5,212
1 – 3 years	5,481	5,217
3 – 5 years	1,820	1,768
5 years +	65	84
Total	43,583	46,037

Source: Bank of England 1980, Financial Statistics
Division.

The 1–3 month band has fluctuated between 27% and 32%, while the 3–6 month maturities have remained around 23% of the total. The analysis confirms the need to keep investment portfolios 'short' at times of high and volatile interest rates.

The rates at which issuing banks will issue Certificates vary considerably from day to day but generally will yield $\frac{1}{8}$% less than the comparable Euro-dollar maturity with a swing from $\frac{1}{16}$% to $\frac{3}{16}$%. The fluctuations in rates as between issuing banks arise from the differing views on future tendencies in the course of interest rates, coupled with the particular bank's commitments in Euro-dollars for various maturities and the demand for Certificates of various maturities. The banks are also much keener to attract deposits on Thursdays and Fridays or at year-end window-dressing dates, by reducing the differentials to capture the necessary funds.

THE SECONDARY MARKET

A strong secondary market for Certificates of Deposit is of course vital to their success since without it they will not be easily realizable and will therefore lose their main advantage over fixed time deposits. The question of the viability of the secondary market in dollar Certificates of Deposit was never in any doubt. In the later section of this chapter the difficulties and fears encountered by those participating in the market for sterling Certificates of Deposit are highlighted in some detail. In contrast, in 1966 when the dollar Certificate of Deposit was introduced, the London branch of White Weld & Co. announced that it would provide the nucleus of a secondary market by discounting outstanding certificates. They did this with the knowledge that the London branches of the American banks, who were instrumental in launching the market, would provide substantial last-resort facilities through the media of the head offices in the United States. The major issuing banks in the United States do have access to ultimate funds from the Federal Reserve, not necessarily against Certificates of Deposit, but against their liquid assets: government bonds, Treasury bills, etc. The significant difference in the United Kingdom is, of course, that the non-clearing bank issuers do not have such facilities at the Bank of England, but it is generally accepted that the banks would provide limited last-resort facilities in case of need. The discount houses have also played an important part in providing the necessary liquidity in the market. Initially houses which acted as brokers in Euro-dollar deposits were not permitted to act as dealers in dollar Certificates of Deposit, but after 1971 licences to deal in dollar Certificates of Deposit were available to all houses. The discount houses act primarily as jobbers in this market and as is clear from Table 5 (p. 36) their holdings of Dollar Certificates of Deposit are relatively small.

STERLING CERTIFICATES OF DEPOSIT

The market in London for sterling Certificates of Deposit came into being on 28 October 1968; again on the initiative of First National City Bank.

The first difficulty to be overcome in dealing with the new instrument concerned exchange control regulations. The Certificates of Deposit were to be bearer securities which created problems of physical control as all such documents had to be held by authorized depositories (for example, banks, solicitors, and stockbrokers) to prevent unauthorized switching out of sterling by residents. Eventually, after much discussion the Bank concluded that appropriate changes in the law would have to be made and the necessary provisions were made in the Finance Bill of 1968.

It would be useful at this stage to define briefly a Certificate of Deposit and outline the conditions of issue. A sterling Certificate of Deposit is a document certifying a deposit made with the United Kingdom office of a British or foreign bank. It states the rate of interest, the date of repayment, is fully negotiable and in bearer form. It may be issued in multiples of £10,000, with a minimum of £50,000 and a maximum of £500,000 for any one certificate. Issuers will split certificates into multiples of £10,000 if required, as this enables depositors to reduce or use as security only part of a certificate. Certificates may be issued for periods of from three months up to five years and, a very important point, tax is not withheld on transfer or maturity. Certificates are issued at par. The number of banks issuing certificates increased from 79 in December 1968 to 144 in September 1972, and include the accepting houses, British overseas banks and the foreign banks, whilst the clearing banks initially became involved through the medium of their subsidiaries. After the introduction of the changed arrangements for credit control in September 1971, however, the clearers commenced issuing in their own right and have subsequently made considerable use of the new instrument as a means of attracting additional resources at times of high demand for credit. By 1980 some 200 banks had a history of issuing Certificates of Deposit.

ADVANTAGES OF THE CERTIFICATE OF DEPOSIT

When sterling Certificates of Deposit were introduced as a medium for the investment of short- or medium-term resources in 1968, there were already in existence many other outlets for such funds within the parallel money markets. It is therefore of some interest to examine the reasons underlying the emergence of this new credit instrument, to define some of the benefits to issuer and investor, and to consider some of the technical problems involved. There is little doubt that the acceptance houses in particular welcomed the opportunity to issue Certificates of Deposit because of fundamental differences* in their secondary banking *modus operandi* from clearing or 'deposit' banking. The chief distinguishing feature is that banks in the secondary system match their advances on the asset side of their balance sheet with their 'term' deposits on the liabilities side: thus the new vehicle enabled them to match medium-term credits in which they are increasingly involved, to liabilities of a corresponding tenor.. This advantage acquires special dimensions if, through the issue of Certificates, the banks concerned were able to secure a substantial volume of three to five years' money. This does not yet seem to have happened as interest rates have generally fluctuated too much for investors to wish to commit themselves for long periods, although the demand for medium-term finance is growing rapidly. In August 1979 only 17% of issues were due to mature in more than one year. The advantage of term loans is that the bank has an exact figure for the total requirement of the borrower, for the length of maturities, and for the rate of return; in each case, therefore, he can match off his outgoing loans by issuing Certificates of Deposit of appropriate amounts and maturity, and be certain in advance of the sort of return he can look for. Other advantages to the issuer are:

(1) Initially it was hoped to attract more funds from the clearing banks to the inter-bank market by virtue of the higher interest rates offered. This was, of course, prior to clearing bank participation in the Certificate of Deposit market which commenced late in

---

* J. R. S. Revell, 'Changes in British Banking. The Growth of the Secondary Banking System'. Hill Samuel Occasional Paper No. 3, March 1968, pp. 15–27.

September 1971.

(2) Because on occasion funds in the Euro-dollar market had dried up when the market was under intense pressure, and it was feared that a similar situation might arise in the inter-bank market (which has no lender of the last resort). For this reason the secondary banker liked the security of firm deposits for a fixed length of time extending into the future.

(3) It was hoped they would obtain their funds more cheaply because the holder of Certificates of Deposit would accept a lower rate of interest in exchange for the benefit of immediate liquidity.

(4) It enables banks to obtain funds from a wider range of sources. It is noteworthy, and doubtless reflected the more traditional attitude of the clearing banks, that the Midland Bank* observed in 1969 that (Certificates of Deposit) 'have no special advantages for the isssuing banks'. During 1971–2 the Midland Bank became one of the largest issuers of sterling Certificates of Deposit indicating their recognition that the Certificate of Deposit market now provides attractive employment for their second line of resources.

In the early days of the market two possible criticisms were levelled against it. Firstly, it was thought, especially by the clearing banks, that the Certificate of Deposit would merely erode existing deposits and certainly, under the traditional deposit bankers' restrictive cartel on interest rates, the clearers would probably have lost funds to the secondary markets. The likelihood of similar losses occurring to the non-clearing banker were, of course, minimal since they were already paying market rates for their funds in the inter-bank market and relatively few would have captive deposits held at bankers' deposit rate.

Secondly, it was feared that the Certificate of Deposit might cause a deterioration in the personal relationships between the merchant banker and his customer, created by the inter-position of the secondary Certificate of Deposit market between borrowers and lenders. The position of the secondary market in Certificates of Deposit is, however, precisely the same as that for inter-bank deposits where the market is broker-based and lenders and borrowers are therefore seldom in direct contact with each other. Such anonymity moreover might well be seen to be advantageous in some cases.

Turning to the investor, there are special advantages of invest-

---

* *Midland Bank Review*, November 1969, p. 5.

ment in Certificates of Deposit as opposed to the other existing diversified array of investments available for short- to medium-term deposits. Obviously, the main advantage lies in the negotiability of the instrument, the crux of which depends on the flexibility of the secondary market. The attraction of a Certificate of Deposit may not, of course, be in any straight interest advantage, but lies in the fact that at any given interest rate, the Certificate of Deposit could be more attractive to the active investor than the straight deposit. This is because of the existence of the secondary market which is the equivalent of a call-option, enabling the holder to sell at any point and, by 'riding the yield curve', avoid ever-running his investment into the lower-yielding short maturity zone thus raising the investor's average yield. This is a practice carried out by many corporate treasurers both in this market and the gilt-edged market.

The Certificate of Deposit market enables sophisticated bankers and company treasurers to manipulate and shape their portfolios without increasing their actual size. This practice is not viable when running a book on inter-bank term deposits only. For example, if recently it had been sensible to borrow for one year and to lend for one week and it then became necessary to reverse the situation, the only method of achieving this was inter-bank deposits would be by doubling the size of one's book; that is, by doubling the book you would return to a neutral position and still further funds would be required to reverse the position to take up a stance as a net lender for one year and a borrower for one week. However, with a book of Certificates of Deposit the position is easily controlled by buying and selling Certificates of Deposit of different maturities without increasing the total size of holdings. The final advantage of Certificates of Deposit to investors is that interest is paid without deduction of tax and the secondary dealers now have substantial quantities of Certificates of Deposit for broken periods to meet the needs of particular investors.

STRENGTH OF THE SECONDARY MARKET

Prior to the inception of the Certificate of Deposit market there was a good deal of concern about the organization and control of the secondary market, particularly from the members of the London Discount Market who are the primary operators in this field. Their concern was described in detail by Mr I. W. K. Smith of Alexanders Discount Co. Ltd.* Briefly, his argument was that because secondary banking had developed into 'matched deposit banking' the acceptance houses and other issuers had a vested interest in promoting the new market. They could, however, hardly claim that their new instrument was truly negotiable unless a strong and viable secondary market existed, and this was not possible unless some form of 'last-resort' facility was made available to ensure liquidity in times of stress. Whilst not strictly comparable, the American Certificate of Deposit market in New York was cited and more particularly the London market for dollar Certificates of Deposit. Issuers in the latter market have provided substantial last-resort facilities (estimated at 10% or more of the market) which have been instrumental in enabling the market to overcome crises which have occurred from time to time. Mr. Smith also emphasized the importance of each issuer supporting the market as a whole – supporting the paper of all other first-class issuers. It is the practice in the dollar Certificate of Deposit market that the majority of issuers specify that they will not take in their own paper except, of course, in the ultimate situation where finance has run out.

These points then were considered of fundamental importance by the discount houses, prompting the comment 'it looks . . . as if the issuing banker is trying to get the best of both worlds. He is attracting a volatile short-term deposit and yet is absolving himself from the responsibility of providing the liquidity to cover it. . . .' It is doubtless possible to argue that the Bank of England is the chief cause of discontent because they refuse to accept Certificates of Deposit as eligible paper from the discount market. This was no doubt a ploy by the authorities to limit the amount of Certificates of Deposit held by the discount houses and their ability to create liquidity through the new medium. Understandably, the issuing houses were not enamoured by the views of the discount houses despite the fact that they fully appreciated the secondary market's difficulties.

Mr J. R. H. Cooper,† in defence of the issuers, pointed out that the primary object of issuing Certificates of Deposit for, say, three years, was that 'by doing so one obtains one's money for three years and there is no question of early repayment. . . .'. He also

* I. W. K. Smith, 'The Sterling Certificate of Deposit Secondary Market in London', p. 23–34. Report of a one-day conference.

† J. R. H. Cooper, 'The Sterling Certificate of Deposit Secondary Market in London', op. cit. p. 43. Report of a one-day conference.

rejected the idea of a liquidity requirement of 10%* as this would 'destroy a large part of the attraction of the Certificate of Deposit idea'. Neither did he consider the analogy of the Euro-dollar market (in London) a relevant comparison because the American banks in London (the principal issuers of dollar Certificates of Deposit) were safe in the knowledge that their head offices in the United States would always stand behind them as lenders of the last resort for dollar funds. In contrast, the London issuers of sterling Certificates of Deposit had very limited last-resort facilities and it would therefore be quite wrong for them to offer such facilities to the secondary market. This particular fear for the solvency of the market was subsequently overcome in 1972 by the full participation in market of the clearing banks. At one stage the future growth of the market was questioned on the grounds that certain issuers dominated it so that there was an insufficient diversity of names amongst the primary issuers.

INTEREST RATES AND MATURITIES

THE CHOICE OF THE ISSUER

As one might expect, the level of rates in the Certificate of Deposit market is governed, like any other price, by demand and supply considerations. The difficulty for the issuer lies in arriving at a rate which will attract the investor but, at the same time, will be advantageous to the bank. In the present climate of volatile, if increasing, rates, such decisions are not made any easier. The bank must take into consideration its need for funds at the time since it might be faced with the need to replace a large deposit which has been withdrawn, especially where loans have already been sanctioned and a deposit is required of the appropriate amount and maturity to cover the position. If funds are not forthcoming the bank has the choice of either increasing the rate offered or waiting until the rates on other alternative outlets change.

In the main, Certificate of Deposit rates are determined by the level of rates in the money market generally but have a special iden-

---

* In practice a 10% requirement for last-resort facilities would amount to only, say, one-tenth of ½% on profitability; e.g. if the issuer was working on a margin, or a differential between day-to-day funds, as against long-term funds of 4–6 months at ½%, the secondary market is asking the issuers to invest 10% of their long-term funds in the day-to-day market. A 3% requirement would mean therefore one-thirtieth commitment.

tity with the movements in the inter-bank and local authority sectors. When the Certificate of Deposit market was in its embryo state, it was thought that Certificate of Deposit rates would tend to follow those in the inter-bank and local authority sectors rather than have a decisive influence on them, since both of these sectors have a much higher turnover than the Certificate of Deposit market. The range of Certificate of Deposit rates, therefore, tended to fall between the inter-bank rate and the local authority rate.

However, in establishing the level of a rate structure in which Certificates of Deposit must find their place, two conflicting factors must be borne in mind. Inevitably, as we have seen, Certificates of Deposit are issued on fine margins stemming firstly from the fact that they are fully negotiable, thus the issuing bank would hope to pay a slightly lower rate than it would pay on comparable inter-bank money. Conversely, as Certificates of Deposit are not eligible for rediscount at the Bank, or as security for loans from the Bank, this is reflected in generally higher rates than those quoted for comparable eligible securities.

During the period September 1971 to mid-1973 there was a very close identity of rates between the Certificate of Deposit market and the inter-bank market with a differential of rarely more than $\frac{1}{8}\%$ between the two rates with neither being consistently higher than the other. Quite obviously the banks have found the Certificate of Deposit to be a close substitute for inter-bank deposits. It is significant also that the Certificate of Deposit rate has generally tended to be higher than the local authority rate, sometimes the differential exceeding $\frac{1}{8}\%$, indicating that, although retaining a close relationship, the Certificate of Deposit rate has led the local authority rate as the result of competition between the banks for funds. The Certificate of Deposit has usually maintained a differential of $\frac{3}{8}\%$ over the prime bank bill rate, although the margin was considerably wider between end-June and the beginning of September following the large outflows of sterling. The banks' demand for funds at one time pushed the differential as high as $1\frac{3}{4}\%$. As can be seen from Graph 10 CD's held a yield advantage over prime bank bills and Treasury bills from 1971 to 1976.

THE MATURITY PATTERN

The pattern of maturities in the Certificate of Deposit market depends ultimately on the resolution of the conflicts between the

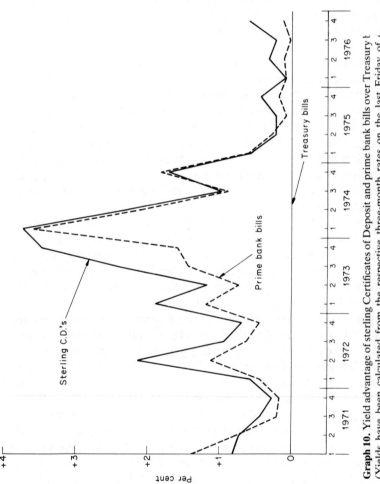

Graph 10. Yield advantage of sterling Certificates of Deposit and prime bank bills over Treasury t (Yields have been calculated from the respective three-month rates on the last Friday of c quarter.) *Source:* Abstracted from various issues of *Bank of England Quarterly Bulletins.*

needs and expectations of the banker and the expectations of the investor. During a period of rising interest rates the banker will endeavour to issue longer maturities at the prevailing rates, safe in the knowledge that even if they have no matching loan commitment, they can always re-lend the funds in one of the alternative short-term money markets at a profitable margin. If the expectation is for the interest rates to fall, then the issuer will offer short maturities until such time as the expected reduction materializes, when longer maturities would again be offered. The choice of the depositor, however, will be quite different; when interest rates are rising he will prefer to invest in the short maturities at existing rates and defer longer-term placements until rates rise. On the other hand, long-term maturities would be preferred if rates were expected to fall, thereby obtaining the benefits of prevailing rates.

Between October 1970 and September 1971 Bank rate fell from 7% to 5% during which time there was a noticeable shift of emphasis in the maturity pattern in the Certificate of Deposit market. By November 1971 there was a clear movement to the longer maturities with an increase of over £400 M. in the six months to one year range, giving this sector over 28% of total issues. The less than three months range increased in total by some £212 M. but their percentage share of total issues fell from 43% to 31%. The one-year to two-year range increased from £37 M. in November 1970 to £122 M. by November 1971, representing over 4% of total issues. Certificates with a maturity of over two years increased by over £73 M. and had increased their share of the market to nearly 1% of total issues. The position had not changed substantially by end-September 1972 with little more than 10% of certificates due to mature in more than one year, over 60% maturing within six months, and approximately one-third within three months.

Table 38 shows the maturity structure of the sterling Certificates of Deposits market from 1975 to July 1980. Certain general trends can be discerned; the 1–3 month band is consistently the largest individual sector and has never fallen below 31% of total issues. This is only to be expected as the Certificates of Deposit market is closely linked with the 3 month sterling inter-bank market and Euro-markets. Total issues up to 3 months have fluctuated between 45% and 63% while maturities up to 6 months have never fallen below 71%, moving as high as 82% and 84% in 1976 and 1978 respectively. Thus the market is predominantly short-term, indeed maturities up to 1 year have never accounted for less than 91% of total issues (in 1975) reflecting the maturity preferences of

Table 38

STERLING CERTIFICATES OF DEPOSIT
MATURITY STRUCTURE AND TOTALS OUTSTANDING
(£M. END DECEMBER)

MATURITY BAND	1975	%	1976	%	1977	%	1978	%	1979	%	1980 (July)	%
Less than one month	568	19	644	20	584	13	751	20	701	18	675	14
1 – 3 months	927	32	1,205	36	1,491	32	1,619	43	1,426	38	1,445	31
3 – 6 months	740	25	886	26	1,171	26	784	21	855	23	1,233	26
6 – 12 months	486	15	437	13	1,010	22	389	10	636	16	1,064	23
1 – 2 years	193	7	133	4	231	5	124	3	105	3	184	4
2 – 3 years	54	2	27	1	32	1	50	1	91	2	75	2
3 years and over	15	–	9	–	121	1	91	2	20	–	14	–
Total	2,983	100	3,340	100	4,641	100	3,808	100	3,833	100	4,689	100

Source: Abstracted from data provided by Bank of England Statistical Division.

	1975	1976	1977	1978	1979	1980
Minimum Lending Rate	11¼	14½	7	12½	17	16
% of total issues						
up to 3 months	51	56	45	63	56	45
up to 6 months	76	82	71	84	79	71
from 1 year to over 5 years	2	1	2	3	2	2

both bankers (issuers) and investors to maintain short books.

A development which emerged during the early 1970s in the secondary market in Certificates of Deposit and worthy of note is the use of forward dealing which has gained favour amongst the more astute dealers. The need had arisen for bankers to attract longer-term deposits without imposing upon the purchaser the disadvantages of holding longer-dated Certificates*. The difficulty has been overcome by the issuing bank offering, say, a one-year Certificate embodying an agreement that at the end of the year it will be 'rolled-over' for a further period of a year or a number of years. Generally, the rate of interest is fixed at the outset and remains unchanged throughout each roll-over period notwithstanding changes that may occur in prevailing interest rates. A second and alternative form of forward contract was also noted by the Bank, which bears a closer identity to the more usual forward deals carried out in the foreign exchange markets. This device enables the banks, discount houses, and other participants to enter into contracts to buy or sell Certificates at some future date when they foresee a surplus or scarcity of funds. These contracts are often linked with rollover transactions as described above. Contracts are arranged for the sale of one-year Certificates for delivery in two years' time, or the operation might be fixed to cover, say, three or five years, with equal amounts of one-year Certificates delivered at the end of each year. The contracts have two chief advantages in that they provide an opportunity to obtain a higher yield, and since the interest rate is fixed at the inception of the contract, they may also provide a hedge against adverse movements in interest rates. The risks involved for the operators in the market are appreciable as the criteria outlined in the previous section demonstrate.

GROWTH OF THE MARKET

The growth of the Certificate of Deposit market can be seen in Table 39. It is clear that until Competition and Credit Control growth was relatively slow, particularly since the clearing banks were precluded from participating by reason of the deposit rate cartel. Although the clearing banks themselves did not issue Certificates of Deposit their affiliates were among the principal issuers and this may have given some indirect relief to the parent institu-

* *Bank of England Quarterly Bulletin,* December 1972, p. 494.

tion when it was close to its lending ceilings. This arose by the clearing bank passing on a particular demand for facilities to its affiliate which issued Certificates of Deposit to cover the position. To that extent then the clearer's position was relieved. There is ample proof in the Bank's published figures that clearing bank subsidiaries did compete more effectively for deposits by offering higher rates of interest than the parent institution. In view of the extent of the growth of the subsidiaries' deposits they may well have attracted funds which would otherwise have gone to finance houses and local authorities. The growth of the market was undoubtedly inhibited, prior to the participation of the clearing banks, by the tendency of certain issuers to dominate the market. The concern of discount houses on this restriction was noted by the chairman of Gilletts in 1971.* The value of sterling Certificates of Deposit outstanding expanded rapidly after September 1971. However, with the entry of the clearing banks into the market and the general increase in bank lending at that time, the sterling market quickly outpaced the size of the dollar market. The discount houses made significant losses on Certificates of Deposit when interest rates rose in the second half of 1972. These losses may even have been as large as those incurred on their gilt portfolio, but this experience did not bring any serious reduction in turnover; the tendency was simply to keep portfolios shorter, and the forward market dwindled in size. The market peaked in November 1973 with total issues outstanding of £6,111 M. and then contracted. The principal reason for this is that the clearing banks use the market as a residual source of funds when loan demand is particularly strong. Thus when the demand for bank credit fell the clearing banks no longer needed to rely as heavily on Certificates of Deposit and inter-bank funds.

HOLDINGS

(1) *Bank sector*

Certificates of Deposit were originally conceived as a way of attracting funds from outside the banking system, but, from the start, as is clear from Table 39, banks have held a significant proportion of the total, and the market has really developed as an extension of the sterling inter-bank market.

The introduction of Competition and Credit Control in Septem-

---

* Annual Accounts, 31 January 1971.

Table 39

THE STERLING CERTIFICATE OF DEPOSIT MARKET
(£M: (%) TOTAL)

December Make-up date	Total in Issue	Holders Banking System		Discount Houses	
		(£)	(%)	(£)	(%)
1968	83	N/A		56	(67)
1969	176	N/A		97	(55)
1970	1,062	568	(54)	246	(23)
1971	2,242	1,160	(52)	418	(19)
1972	4,926	2,945	(60)	420	(9)
1973	5,983	3,296	(55)	923	(15)
1974	4,318	2,658	(62)	401	(9)

End December	Total	Banking System (£)	(%)	Overseas	Private	Discount Houses (£)	(%)
1975	3,117	2,235	(72)	76	806	303	9
1976	3,420	2,299	(67)	40	1,081	404	12
1977	4,706	3,499	74)	65	1,142	509	11
1978	3,892	2,828	(73)	82	982	333	9
1979	3,922	3,221	(82)	38	463	84	2
1980	5,405	3,905	(72) (Sept.)	96	1,404	N/A	–

Source: Bank of England Financial Statistics Division 1980.

ber 1971 not only brought the clearing banks into the market but also increased the attractiveness of investing in Certificates of Deposit for banks. Certificates of Deposit generally yield more than reserve assets while having the advantage over other non-reserve assets that holdings may be deducted from eligible liabilities when computing reserve asset requirements. Thus the banks have an obvious incentive to maintain their liquidity needs in the form of Certificates of Deposit and inter-bank deposits rather than in reserve assets. By September 1980 banks in the U.K. held 20% of their sterling assets in this form although only 3% or £3,905 M. was held in sterling Certificates of Deposit. Thus it is clear that the Certificate of Deposit market is now dwarfed by the sterling inter-bank market.

In 1978 the Bank of England authorized the issue of variable rate sterling Certificates of Deposit and also fixed or variable rate Certificates with a term to maturity not exceeding five years. For the purpose of establishing eligible liabilities, Certificates of Deposits both issued and held are taken into the calculation of individual bank's liabilities on a net basis, irrespective of term.

(1) *Private sector*

Sterling Certificates of Deposit have undoubtedly broadened and increased the flexibility for the investment of funds by the private sector – the definition of private sector covering all holdings other than banks, discount houses, and overseas residents. The growth in this sector has been very substantial indeed from just under £200 M. in 1970 to £560 M. in March 1972, and then more than doubling to over £1,200 M. by September 1972. The Bank* reported that much of the increase was due to the activity of the building societies, Crown Agents, and investment unit trusts, which had doubled their holdings to over £280 M. by September 1972. Accurate identification of other private sector holders is extremely difficult, but it is known that approximately 200 of the largest industrial and commercial companies held some £250 M. of certificates at the end of June 1972, compared with £100 M. in the previous March. The banks were very successful in attracting these additional funds by following a much more aggressive policy engendered by the highly competitive atmosphere of the changed monetary regulations.

The Bank* also indicated that the sterling crisis in June 1972 contributed indirectly to the already rapid growth in private sector holdings of Certificates of Deposit. This stemmed from the very substantial movements of funds abroad which created acute shortages of sterling in the money markets causing steep rises in short-term money market rates. This made it profitable for bank customers to engage in 'hard arbitrage' or 'round-tripping' – drawing on their bank overdrafts to invest in Certificates of Deposit and earning a higher return than they had to pay on their overdrafts. This causes serious distortions in the £M3 money supply figures and was a major factor leading to the imposition of the corset in 1973.

---

* *Bank of England Quarterly Bulletin*, December 1972, p. 492.

(2) *Discount market*

As with the dollar Certificate of Deposit market, the discount houses play an important role in making the sterling secondary market and their holdings represent about 15–25% of the total. This of course means that the Bank of England is able to exert considerable indirect influence on this market by making money tight in Lombard Street and so discouraging the houses from investing. From 1968 until the end of 1973 the Discount Houses built up their holdings of sterling Certificates of Deposits, such that by 1973 they represented 35·2% of total assets. Since that time, however, holdings of sterling Certificates of Deposit have fallen both in percentage and absolute terms. The main reason for this is the relationship between relative rates of return on short-term assets. The discount houses respond very rapidly to small changes in the differential between yields on various short-term assets as a slightly higher rate of return on one asset can significantly affect running profits. Graph 10 shows the yield differential between Treasury bills and both Certificates of Deposit and bank bills. It can be seen that during 1973 especially (which was the time when discount houses were investing particularly heavily in Certificates of Deposit), the yield on Certificates of Deposit was considerably above that on bank bills, which in turn was well above that on Treasury bills. Following the introduction of the 'corset' at the end of 1973, however, issues of Certificates of Deposit declined and rates fell. At the same time this measure also increased the use of bills of exchange and caused the discount houses to switch from Certificates of Deposit to bank bills and Treasury bills, both of which also have the advantage of being 'eligible' at the Bank of England.

Since 1975 the market's holdings have fluctuated between £300 M. and £500 M. but usually nearer to the lower figure. By end December 1979 they had fallen to only £84 M.

12 Euro-commercial paper

DIFFICULTIES OF ESTABLISHING THE MARKET

The latest of London's parallel markets came into existence in June 1970 with the introduction by J. Henry Schroder Wagg, in collaboration with White Weld, an American investment bank, of short-term company promissory notes issued by major industrial companies. Before embarking on a description of the market a brief résumé will be given of the factors leading to the establishment of this credit instrument as a viable proposition within the Euro-currency field. Some of the difficulties which Schroder's had to overcome will also be mentioned.

Parallel to the widely publicized growth of the Eurobond market in the latter half of the sixties, another market was staging equally fast but quite unheralded growth, namely the market for unquoted short- to medium-term credit instruments. These instruments in themselves had nothing new conceptually as they were already being used widely in Canada and the United States, but what was new was the development of the concept and its mechanics to the special characteristics of the international Euro-dollar market. Notwithstanding numerous difficulties put in their way, the new securities found a ready market for themselves. It is difficult to determine precisely which factors created the initial pressure for development of the market, but it does seem clear that the increasing rate of inflation made investors opt for shorter maturities than Eurobonds. Another factor was the higher yield that such paper offered when compared with Certificates of Deposit. In fact the market can be viewed as an extension of the Certificate of Deposit market.

In general, higher yields involve the investor in higher risks, but such risks were minimized by the marketing of short-term debt by industrial companies of prime credit rating. Thus, with judicious distribution of risks, investors were able to maximize their earnings. Finally, additional impetus was given to the market in the late sixties, when short-term rates were from time to time long-term rates, a marked preference by investors for short-term investment becoming evident. From the borrowers' point of view, it meant that they were able to tap a source of international finance to meet short- to medium-term requirements that not only complemented traditional bank borrowings but also proved to be competitive with bank finance. It also provided companies with greater flexibility in their portfolio management and some publicity which was useful when embarking on a Eurobond issue at a later date.

The establishment of this market by Schroder's was only achieved after almost a year of sustained effort by a team of technical staff who travelled widely in North America and Europe. The chief problems encountered were legal ones and those associated with the exchange control regulations of the various countries involved. Before issues could be contemplated it had to be established, for example, which borrowers could issue commercial paper, where it could be marketed, and whether or not the ramifications of American and English law could be reconciled. Amongst the legal problems to be overcome, for example, was the precise form the paper should take. It is well known that the wording of certain promissory notes might well be construed as debentures, and as such would require registration on the Companies Register. It could also give rise to difficulties under the Companies Act in respect of the company's balance sheet and the regulations governing the issue of a prospectus.

Of all the difficulties to be overcome, however, probably the most significant were those concerning United States exchange control regulations. In particular, the approval of the Office of Foreign Direct Investments of the United States Department of Commerce, that borrowings by United States companies would qualify as long-term borrowings, was especially important. It should be emphasized that 'long-term' in this context is for balance of payments purposes and has nothing to do with 'long-term' in the investment sense. It therefore meant that such borrowings would be treated as an inflow in United States balance of payments accounting. The distinction drawn between long-term and short-term foreign borrowings is extremely important to American companies as it affects the level of investment they can make abroad and the amount of retained earnings that they can keep abroad. Thus, since long-term foreign borrowing can be set-off against foreign investment (whereas short-term borrowing cannot), it means that the proceeds of long-term borrowings can be invested outside the United States free of regulations limiting such investment.

To ensure that the issue of Euro-commercial paper qualified as long-term foreign borrowing, when the tenor of individual notes issued were of three or six months' duration, Schroder's obtained special dispensation for their paper and subsequently (in June 1970), the Office of Foreign Direct Investments' definition of long-term borrowing was duly amended. The present ruling is that any foreign borrowing that is not in fact repaid within twelve months of the original borrowing, as in the case of four three-monthly renewable promissory notes, would qualify as long-term borrowing.

RISKS ASSOCIATED WITH THE MARKET

Since the inception of the market much criticism has been voiced against it. This stems from the concern which already existed in many banking and financial parlours over the risks which exist in the Euro-dollar market. It seemed to many observers that Euro-commercial paper was adding to, or even compounding, these hazards. The critics of the market expressed their fears on several counts: first, there were doubts about the marketability of the paper and whether or not the interest rates would render it attractive to banks (who already deal in Euro-dollars) as well as to companies and the private sector. Some sections of the banking community were also concerned that the market might, to some degree, poach on their preserves since this type of borrowing can effectively bypass the banking system. The lie must surely be put to that particular argument by the fact that Schroder's are first and foremost merchant bankers and pioneers of the market. Questions were also raised about the wisdom of bringing to an already uncontrolled Euro-market industrial risks which holders of Euro-dollar funds may not be able to assess. In this context the case most frequently cited is that of the bankruptcy of Penn Central, and certainly Schroder's feel that to raise the spectre of this particular failure as an argument against the viability of Euro-commercial paper is quite unjustified. That is as it may be, but the critics were right to draw attention to what they felt was a growing tendency towards risk taking which would not be countenanced in more prudent banking circles. Whichever view one takes, the Penn Central affair merely served to underline to all practitioners in Euro-currency markets the need for serious and professional assessment of credit risks accepted by them. Schroder's take the practical step of insisting on back-up lines of credit being available to support the issue of Euro-commercial paper if they are not completely satisfied with the borrower's ability to meet his obligations on maturity. Under the old monetary and credit control arrangements, the Bank were known to look upon one-named paper with disfavour since it represented an extension of financial facilities over which they would have little control. They were known to have similar inhibitions with regard to the closely linked inter-company market. Under the present framework of controls, however, it seems that the Bank have imposed adequate safeguards. Commercial paper held by the discount market would fall into the category of private sector assets whilst Euro-commercial paper held by the banking system would be equivalent to normal commercial lending.

Those in favour of the market point to the success of company promissory notes in the United States where outstanding paper now amounts to well over $100 billion. They say that the advantages to supra-national corporations are numerous, providing companies of high repute with an alternative source of funds outside the banking system. It is hoped that eventually, when the market has expanded, it will also enable companies to borrow more cheaply. It also allows the sophisticated company treasurer much greater flexibility in timing his borrowings to meet fluctuations in cash flows.

THE MARKET, ITS METHODS, AND SCOPE OF OPERATIONS

Commercial paper is merely another term for a promissory note issued by a commercial or industrial company in order to raise short-term funds. There has been an active market for such paper in London for many years. The issuers were Canadian finance and industrial companies, and a secondary market was maintained by Canadian brokers in London. However, as non-governmental Canadian paper is subject to a withholding tax, brokers usually buy the paper back from the investor one day prior to maturity. The paper is generally on offer but the present rate structure renders it somewhat unattractive to investors operating in the Euro-dollar markets.

In the context of commercial paper one must also mention development in a closely related field which is the Euro-dollar acceptance or foreign currency Bill of Exchange. This is a bill drawn on a merchant bank or accepting house and sold through bill brokers such as Allen Harvey & Ross, who have buyers for such bills. The advantage of this paper for an investor over an ordinary bank Certificate of Deposit is a slight premium in the rate of interest which varies from about $\frac{1}{16}$% to 1% per annum. This is an approximation since rates vary with market conditions. The paper appears principally in two forms depending on whether the money being raised is purely a general purpose finance raising operation, or is linked to an underlying trading transaction involving the movement of goods. In the former case the paper takes the form of a promissory note made to bearer or to the sponsor of the note (e.g. Schroder's) who would then endorse it with or without recourse (usually without recourse), when placing it with other lenders of funds. The paper is usually issued on a discount basis, although sometimes a rate of interest is quoted. When an underlying trading transaction is involved the note takes the form of a Bill of Exchange with two signatures on it. This last point may well be the decisive factor in deciding which of the two types of paper becomes the more popular. The London money market has a well-known preference for 'two-named' paper and a marked dislike of the 'one-name' variety. Sometimes a bank accepts the note, thus adding the prestige attached to its name and, of course, its commitment to meet the liability. All major Euro-currencies have been used (for bills of exchange but not company paper) to meet the requirements and choice of the borrowers with maturities varying from one month to five years. Medium-term notes are usually sold at floating rates of interest adjustable every six months.

Many types of paper are marketed: the earliest type to appear was South American paper. Mexico was the largest borrower followed by Brazil and Argentina. The majority of this paper is issued purely as fund raising operations, although some from Central American countries originates from export orders. Far Eastern paper is issued by the Philippines, South Korea, Formosa, and Indonesia but has limited negotiability. It is difficult to generalize about rates which vary widely depending on the political and economic stability of the country as well as the commercial viability of the borrower. The same problem arises with East European paper because many of the names are little known to investors. The main borrowers are exporters in Rumania, Yugoslavia, and Hungary. More recently, however, the trend has been towards simple fund raising operations evidenced by promissory notes. The paper, which is usually guaranteed by one of the main state banks in the respective countries, was becoming increasingly popular by mid-1971 and margins on better-known risks were diminishing. Very little West European paper has emerged, no doubt inhibited by the fact that a number of countries have a withholding tax that renders short-term international investment unattractive to lenders. Furthermore, full negotiability of paper has been hampered by difficulties encountered where certain double-tax treaties exist. Broadly speaking, countries of Western Europe are not short of foreign exchange, and they have managed to encourage their borrowers, possibly by inducement or perhaps by strict exchange control regulations, to borrow long-term rather than short-term. Consequently the paper that does emerge tends to be from borrowers with little-known names, thus restricting its negotiability. There is a flourishing market in paper issued by South African Government agencies, usually by means of promissory notes under the government's guarantee. In addition, there are roll-over credits which the agencies have arranged with banks. There is little activity in the secondary market even though the paper is highly negotiable, chiefly because demand for South African notes far exceeds the supply.

The procedure adopted in the placing of promissory notes in the London market is quite simple. The minimum denomination for Euro-commercial paper is $50,000 and it can be issued in multiples of $10,000 above that minimum. When a primary issue is arranged, an agreement is reached with the issuer regarding the amount, the maturity, and the rate. The bank introducing the paper then places the notes at a rate that would take into account its placement commission. In the secondary market dealings are transacted in the usual money market fashion on the telephone or telex and are generally done two working days prior to the settlement date. This is standard procedure in the Euro-currency markets. It is customary for the sponsoring bank to offer to hold any notes sold in its custody free of charge. This practice has lessened the administrative problems involved in the delivery of notes and reduced insurance costs.

The early issues of Euro-commercial paper were modelled closely on the U.S. commercial paper market, being issued in small denominations and on a discount basis. In June 1980 however, Merrill Lynch arranged a $100 M. Euro-commercial paper facility for IC Industries of Chicago. Denominations are from $250,000 upwards and the investor has the choice between an interest-bearing or a discount note. On the interest-bearing note interest is payable at maturity in the same way as on a Certificate of Deposit. Interest is based on LIBOR plus a small margin. For discount notes interest is deducted in advance from the principal paid and the note is repaid at par on maturity, as with a Treasury bill.

Secondary market transactions and settlement procedures are similar to those in the Certificate of Deposit market and as with the Certificate of Deposit market, the main investors in Euro-commercial paper will be banks and other financial institutions.

13 Inter-company loans

One of the characteristics of the London money market is its ability
to adapt itself to new situations and develop new techniques to deal
with them. A fitting example of this ingenuity is the way in which
inter-company loan business grew in the latter half of 1969. The
two prime factors in the expansion of this market were the credit
squeeze and amalgamations of the money brokers who are the
dealers in this market. Undoubtedly, the initial momentum came
from industrial companies themselves as they found it increasingly
difficult to obtain funds from their bankers who were subjected to
strict ceilings on their lendings. It seems unlikely, however, that
inter-company loan business would have flourished without the
many amalgamations which took place between the brokers, bringing together groups which cover a broad spectrum of interests.
From the brokers' standpoint this step was necessary to enable
them to offer prospective clients a comprehensive assessment of
the whole range of short-term investments available.

The importance of such a service in a complex money market
cannot be over-emphasized. In the inter-company loan market it
was essential if the difficulties of matching a willing lender with a
willing borrower were to be overcome. To achieve this, three vital
factors had to be reconciled: the sum involved, the rate of interest
and the maturity. In addition there were other somewhat fundamental drawbacks which created problems for the pioneers of this
market. Not the least of these was the lack of marketability or
negotiability of such loans. Companies lending or borrowing in this
sector must assume that their money is locked in for the term fixed
by the loan. The only method therefore of circumventing this
problem would have been by setting up a secondary market, but it
is well known in the City that the Bank would never countenance
such a move. The authorities were also known to have serious mis-

givings about inter-company loan business on two other counts. First, they were concerned that no record existed, official or other-wise* of the total business done, and secondly, they were unhappy about the integrity of some 'fringe' operators in the market – firms of indeterminate lineage and perhaps, by City standards, doubtful business practices, who might persuade companies to over-stretch themselves and borrow too much. These objections were largely overcome, however, by the mergers and amalgamations under-taken by the major operators in the market whose business methods and integrity are beyond reproach, in the best traditions of the City.

Understandably, stemming from the foregoing, the reputable dealers in the market agreed that business must be limited to the top 200 or so companies; deposits were for a minimum of £50,000 but preferably of £100,000 or more. Mostly, sums of £250,000 or larger were dealt in, the larger sums being preferred since they pro-vided a substantial profit to the broker whereas small sums would not justify the work involved. Commission was generally charged at the rate of $\frac{1}{8}$% to $\frac{1}{4}$% per annum.

Substantial use was made of bank guarantees in an effort to over-come the difficulties encountered with regard to the status and cre-ditworthiness of borrowers. In the early 1970s the larger brokers estimated that as much as 20% of total business was backed by bank guarantee and several United States banks were known to ad-vertise the service openly to would-be borrowers. This develop-ment proved to be doubly useful to the market: in the first place it involved the banking sector in transactions which by their very nature, had formerly bypassed the banking system, and in fact had given rise to certain misgivings on the part of the clearing banks and merchant banks alike. Not unnaturally, they felt that their function was being usurped by the brokers who were not subject to official restrictions as they were. Furthermore, there were instances of companies borrowing from clearing banks at 1% over Bank rate and on-lending the funds to other companies at a higher rate thus making a profitable turn for themselves. This practice subsequent-ly ceased with falling interest rates. Secondly, the use of the guarantee resulted in banks providing a link between the broker

---

* It is interesting to note that in Australia the official bill market was set up, partly to offset a similar problem in their own inter-company market, by drawing funds from it, and placing them where a company's liabilities are known. Other parallels with the Australian market could be drawn as interested dealers in London studied the working of the market in Australia at some length.

and their customers, especially when the bank's lending had reached its ceiling. For a nominal commission (the charge for the guarantee) the bank hoped to gain much goodwill, an attitude no doubt engendered in the knowledge that large and complex industrial groups utilize two or three banks and therefore owe no loyalty to one particular bank.

Loans were made for any period from three months to five years and are frequently 'tailor-made' to suit the parties concerned. The reduction of Bank rate in March 1970 from 8% to 7½%, and subsequently to 7% in April, had, however, caused companies to be less willing to take a long view on interest rates. Consequently, long-term money became more difficult to obtain and rates hardened as companies became increasingly concerned at the effects of inflation on fixed-interest loans. The following figures give an indication of the changes in the spread of rates during the twelve months to January 1971. Early in 1970 the difference on the spread between seven-day and one-year money was ½% to ⅜%, but in January 1971 it was 1⅜% or more. The differential between one-year and three-year money in mid-1971 was ⅜% or more whereas in 1970 it was ¼%. Actual rates of interest vary with market conditions but in general tended to be 2% or 3% higher than on the local authorities' market. Estimates as to size of the market during 1971 varied considerably with observers quoting figures of from £100 M. to £300 M. Similar guesses made in 1970 bordered around £50 M. to £100 M. The figures, however, only represented estimates of the volume of funds going through brokers and do not take into account the proportion of loans fixed direct.

When the Banks' revised arrangements for competition and credit control came into operation in 1971 the ceiling on bank advances was lifted, thus removing one of the prime reasons for the initial development of the market.

The market continued to flourish in the mid and later 1970s with estimates of its size varying between £50 M. and £100 M. By 1979/80 only occasional deals were being transacted so that it would strictly be untrue to say that a market now exists. Furthermore, the introduction of the Banking Act 1979 calls into question the legality of inter-company trading since it may constitute a deposit-taking barrier in contravention of the Act. At present the position is unclear and the Bank of England will monitor prospective deals with care.

Part IV

The Economic Environment

The final part of the book provides a critical analysis of the present role of the discount houses and the complementary markets within our financial and monetary structure. The special function of the discount market within the Bank of England's monetary regime and changes in the anatomy of the money market as a whole are examined. Far-reaching changes in both monetary and credit control are likely to be made in the near future and the possible effects of these changes are discussed in the light of past and present difficulties which have arisen in the money markets. The structural changes which have occurred and possible future developments, such as a market in financial futures are also assesssd. Appendix III sets out the board rationale underlying the Bank of England Monetary Base Control Paper.

14 The economic function of the discount houses

It has been suggested from time to time that as a result of the development of the complementary markets, the City would subsequently witness the demise of the traditional discount market. Ignoring the present wide diversification of business undertaken by the discount houses, they have a vital function to perform in the operation of the Bank's monetary policy. Indeed, it is probably no exaggeration to say that the discount market's function is indispensable – not in the sense that it is beyond the wit of men to devise an alternative mode of control, or another institution to fulfil its function, but in the sense that the function *per se* is of fundamental importance and must be undertaken.

Much criticism of the market has been voiced over the years (in evidence given to the Radcliffe Committee in 1959 and to the Select Committee on Nationalized Industries in 1969), but nevertheless it is now the widely accepted view that the market performs its function with great efficiency and at minimum cost to the community. This opinion was expressed by the Radcliffe Committee as long ago as 1959 and was confirmed in the recent report by the Wilson Committee. The principal functions of the discount houses may be summarized as follows:

(1) They make the call money market in London.
(2) They cover the Treasury bill market in London.
(3) They assist the merchant banks by providing an independent market for the discounting of bills accepted by these banks. They also discount non-government paper.
(4) They indirectly assist the Bank in re-financing the public debt by dealing in short-bonds and other gilts nearing maturity.

(5) They provide an alternative source of short-term funds for trade and industry.
(6) They make the secondary market in sterling and dollar Certificates of Deposit.
(7) They provide a source of reserve assets for banks.

From the standpoint of the Bank of England the points of particular significance are numbers (1), (2), and (4) stemming from the fact that the Treasury is far and away the largest borrower of money in the country. The Bank's chief interest in the market is that it provides a sophisticated instrument for operating credit control policy. Some idea of the magnitude of the Treasury's task can be gained from the totals of Treasury bills offered in recent years. The figures for the years ended 28 February 1975 and 1974 were £6,820 M. and £4,990 M. respectively. Thus it becomes readily apparent that the Bank must have a stable and assured market for its bills. The discount houses provide part of such a market by applying each week for an amount of bills roughly equal to the total on offer. The market's ability to absorb large quantities of bills in a short space of time was amply demonstrated in 1970 when their Treasury bill holdings rose from £158 M. in March to the record total of £813 M. in December.

At the same time it must be pointed out that when money is in short supply, the Bank of England must first provide the market with the funds to take up the Treasury bills. As a corollary to this Treasury bill mechanism the houses also provide a highly efficient short-loan market which enables the clearing banks and secondary banks to work to minimum cash ratios. The discount market is always prepared to exchange Treasury bills for cash, or cash for Treasury bills and in turn the banking sector lends a proportion of its surplus cash to the market on call. If one bank is short of money it calls its funds from the market knowing that the market can probably recoup this loss from another bank which is in surplus. If there is no surplus cash to be found then the houses can always go to the Bank as lender of the last resort. This intermediary role is advantageous to the authorities in two ways: first, the Bank knows that there is one centralized point to which surplus cash will flow, which obviates the difficulty of dealing with each individual bank. Furthermore, it facilitates the use of open-market operations to inject central-bank cash into the banking system. It also enables them to initiate cash shortages in the system. However, it has special significance in giving the authorities close control over short-term money rates. If, for example, the Bank wishes to force short money rates up it can create a shortage of cash in the market which ultimately will cause the discount houses to go to the Bank as a last resort. The Bank can then impose whatever penal rate it chooses to alleviate the shortage. The authorities have now achieved great finesse in this mechanism both in the variable rates that may be charged and the number of days that the market may be forced to borrow. The system also has merit for the clearing banks, who do not, of course, tender for bills on their own behalf, in that they know they can always find bills of a particular maturity when required to assist their future liquidity pattern. For example, they may not wish to hold three-month bills but prefer, say, six-week maturities.

The discount market plays a significant role in Treasury financing also by providing an active market, along with the Stock Exchange, in short-bonds. The market will buy (in particular) long-bonds which are approaching maturity, which renders the redemption and re-financing of public debt much easier. The source of these securities is industrial and commercial investors who wish to replace their maturing bond with another more appropriate long-term investment. These investors know that as professional bond dealers the discount market can afford to pay slightly higher prices than the ordinary investor, thus a substantial proportion of these 'short' maturities is channelled through the market. Again, this pool of near-mature bonds enables the Bank to take up when required large amounts of stock of precise maturities.

It is evident then that the Bank would be most unlikely to sacrifice these advantages which it derives from the operations of the discount market. Indeed, probably the most important conclusion to be drawn from the Bank's regulations on competition and credit control and the 1980 proposals to introduce new liquidity requirements, is that they have seen fit to draw up arrangements that go out of their way to favour the continued existence of the discount market largely in its present form. Thus, in outline at least, the official attitude to the market appears similar to what it was when the Bank of England gave evidence to the Radcliffe Committee more than twenty years ago.

In providing a pool of liquidity for the banking system it is obvious that the discount market, together with the Bank and Treasury, plays a central role. In the early 1950s the market was the only source of inter-bank liquidity, but with the emergence of the parallel markets the increasing importance and effects of the sterling inter-bank market cannot be ignored. This market, in fact, provided a pool of liquidity between the non-clearing banks (or secondary banks); thus there were two distinct groups of banks in the City operating by and large independently. This did not mean, however, that the 'old' and the 'new' markets operated in isolation from each other, but there is no question that since the inception of the newer markets the discount market's participation in secondary banking operations had diminished substantially. At the same time the houses' reliance on the clearing banks was also increased to a material extent. The deterioration of the discount market's position with regard to the liquid assets of the non-clearing banks can be clearly seen by comparing the figures for 1958, when roughly 40%–45% of the secondary banks' total deposits were placed with the discount houses, with those for 1970 when they had fallen alarmingly to, at best 7% and at worst 0·6%. The houses were therefore forced into an ever-increasing reliance on the clearing banks, a trend which was apparent in the statistics; in 1959 total borrowing by the market amounted to £789 M., of which £433 M. was borrowed from the clearing banks and £184 M. from the non-clearers. At end-March 1971 the relative figures were £1,190 M. and £294 M. (of some £1,713 M. total borrowed funds). As a proportion of borrowed funds then the clearing banks' share had risen from 55% in 1959 to 70% in 1971, whilst the secondary banks' percentage fell from 23% to 17% over the same period. It must be emphasized, however, that statistics can be notoriously ambiguous and there are admittedly discontinuities in the Bank's presentation of the figures. In this instance, however, it takes nothing from the efficacy of the conclusions drawn since one of the principal differences in the figures is that the later ones include more banks in the non-clearers' group (following the enormous growth of foreign banks in London).

Nevertheless, this line of argument must not be overstated, because although the general trend in the 1960s was towards a preponderance of clearing bank money since 1971, the non-clearing banks have maintained approximately 30% of their borrowed funds in the traditional market. Stimulus in this direction was boosted in 1972 after the Bank had specified call money with the discount market as a reserve asset. The reason for the substantial sums retained by the secondary banks in discount market assets stems from the fact that the traditional market is, of course, underpinned by the Bank.

The situation is very different in the inter-bank sterling market where there is no lender of the last resort, and the dangers of over-borrowing in this and the Euro-dollar market have already been examined in some detail in earlier chapters. It must be borne in mind that the dangers of a collapse in these secondary markets, however minimal, are very real as the fringe banking crisis showed and could be transformed into fact in the event of some major international financial crisis.

The ties between the two markets then do exist and both are subject to the same basic influences (e.g. minimum lending rate of the Bank of England), but to a different degree in the same circumstances. The secondary market in sterling Certificates of Deposit is possibly the discount houses' most direct link with the newer markets. The discount market's holdings of sterling Certificates of Deposit has grown rapidly from £56 M. in 1968 reaching a peak of £923 M. in December 1973. Since then holdings have declined and fluctuate between £300 M. and £500 M. Whilst most of this 'book' is held for tradng purposes, a certain proportion is retained for investment and speculative purposes to assist the market in times of stress. For example, sterling Certificates of Deposit are becoming used to an increasing extent as collateral for borrowing by the houses, from the clearing banks (but not, of course, from the Bank). Thus is the event of official intervention in the market (to create a shortage) the houses can obtain loans from the clearing banks against the security of sterling Certificates of Deposit, thereby alleviating the shortage. From September 1971 to July 1973 the discount houses were unable to hold more than 50%* of their assets in the new markets due to the requirement to hold at least this proportion of their assets in public sector debt. Furthermore, one of their prime functions is to provide a pool of liquidity for the clearing banks when required. Therefore, if the clearing banks made sudden substantial calls on the market, the houses would probably be driven into the Bank and at rates determined by the authorities.

As mentioned earlier the secondary banks keep considerable funds in the traditional market and a substantial amount of this is in bills as well as call money. Whether or not they retain these bills is usually a question of interest rate differentials between the markets. If rates are higher in the inter-bank market then they may well sell their bills to the discount houses thereby forcing them to borrow from the clearing banks or, if the latter cannot provide

---

* See Appendix II.

funds, from the Bank. To some extent then the traditional market is in an impasse in that either the clearing banks or the secondary banks (and parallel markets) may cause considerable embarrassment and loss of profitability.

The differentials which can occur between, say, overnight loans in the discount market and the rates for short-term money in the sterling inter-bank market, can fluctuate to an almost incredible degree. For example, in 1967 when the money market reopened after the devaluation of sterling, such was the acute shortage of sterling in the inter-bank market (caused by dealers previously selling sterling and purchasing foreign currencies) that rates quoted for overnight money reached 125% per annum. At the peak of the sterling crisis of mid-1972, inter-bank money reached 200%. At worst, money rates in the traditional market would not have exceeded Bank rate under the old monetary regime.

Despite the foregoing it can be seen that although the discount houses are subject to many pressures, the dominant factor is still the fluctuating needs of the clearing banks. As we saw in Chapter 7 the liquidity requirements of the secondary banks were provided in the main by the inter-bank market and that such demands are generally much more volatile. The requirements of the clearing banks, however, tend to follow a predetermined pattern controlled by such factors as fiscal policy, tax demands, public debt redemptions, and so on. Consequently, their deposits tend to be highest at the close of the year, and lowest in February and August when tax payments are being met.

There was an obvious temptation for the clearing banks to invest some funds in the more lucrative new markets, but their strict liquidity base generally prevented this. By and large the problem was solved for them by operating in the new markets through the medium of their subsidiaries and affiliates, which were not subject to the same constraints. With Competition and Credit Control and in particular the change in the liquid assets ratio and the abandonment of the interest rate cartel, the clearing banks have become directly involved in the parallel money markets, and Table 5 shows that there has been a substantial shift in liquid assets towards the parallel markets.

It is apparent that although there are quite clear associations between the 'old' and the parallel markets, the link between the discount market and the clearing banks is still the significant factor. That the Bank intends this strong relationship to continue is undoubtedly confirmed by the tenor of its recent liquidity paper.

There has been criticism voiced in many quarters concerning the Bank's policy towards the inter-bank market and also the market in sterling Certificates of Deposit on the grounds that it had lost its control over the volume of 'credit'. Certainly it is clear that the authorities had not anticipated the dramatic increase in the size of the inter-bank and Certificate of Deposit market or the trend towards the use of liability management. The result was a change in the way banks responded to a traditional liquidity squeeze, as outlined in Chapter 7, which brought serious distortions to the structure of interest rates and money supply.

It should not be forgotten that the Bank and the Treasury are perpetually on the horns of a dilemma; on the one hand they must try to fund the National Debt in the most economical way, and on the other they are burdened with the task of controlling credit, tasks that do not always run in harmony. Seen in the light of such problems and in addition the need to keep sterling strong, it is not surprising that the Bank takes a fairly liberal attitude to the complementary markets. The principal operators in the inter-bank and Euro-dollar markets are the foreign banks in London. The Bank is therefore most anxious to encourage any and all spheres of operation of such banks in order that London can maintain its position as the world's leading financial centre. This aspect of London's international dealings has achieved an even greater significance since the U.K. joined the E.E.C. and the subsequent abolition of exchange controls in 1979.

15 The structure of interest rates

STRUCTURE OF INTEREST RATES PRIOR TO 1971

A. *The traditional market*

Prior to 1971 the keystone of the rate structure which existed between the discount houses and the clearing banks was Bank rate. It was on the basis of Bank rate that all other rates in the traditional market were built. Consequently, when Bank rate was changed, adjustments were made in the overall pattern of rates. Briefly, the arrangements* between the discount houses and the clearing banks were as follows:

(1) The minimum rate for call money to the discount market was $\frac{3}{8}\%$ over the rate the banks paid on deposits (i.e. $1\frac{5}{8}\%$ below Bank rate). Not all call money was lent at this rate, only that proportion known as 'basic' money – the remainder being lent at a higher rate. Money lent at the 'basic' rate accounted for approximately 40% of the total and was generally left with the houses semi-permanently and was only called in an emergency. Other funds known as 'night' money were lent late in the day, if a house was short of cash for its nightly balance, at rates which fluctuated widely depending on market conditions. Additionally, there was privilege money which in total did not exceed £5 M. for the whole market. This was money which houses could claim as a small additional loan, if at the close of business the market was still short of money to balance its book. The rate for privilege money was $\frac{1}{2}\%$ over the clearing banks' rate for basic money and had to be repaid automatically the next day. Since Bank rate determined the clearing banks' deposit

---

* See Chapter 3 for details of changes in the Bank's techniques with regard to borrowing by the market and rates charged during the mid-1960s and 1970s.

rate it also governed the cost of money to the discount market. It follows then that this was the base of the pyramid on which all other rates in the traditional market were set.

(2) The clearing banks did not compete with the discount houses by tendering for Treasury bills at the weekly tender, but bought them from the houses after they had held them for seven days or more.*

(3) The houses bid collectively at a single price for the bills at the tender and allocated the bills to each individual house on a quota basis; the quota being related to its capital resources.

(4) The discount houses agreed to cover the total tender at their bid price.

In the same way the discount rate for commercial bills was also related to the Bank rate, with differing rates quoted for fine bank bills and trade bills. The differential which arose between the Treasury bill rate and commercial bill rates fluctuated from time to time and the rate for fine bank bills was generally about $\frac{3}{16}\%$ above Treasury bills during the latter part of the 1960s, but had widened more recently to as much as $1\frac{3}{16}\%$. The cause of this change in the differential was no doubt attributable to the ceilings placed on the banking sector's holding of commercial bills and the shortage of Treasury bills. The discount houses also adopted the same deposit rate as the clearing banks and this restrictive practice prevented the market from competing effectively for non-bank funds. In point of fact, this arrangement lost some of its sting following the emergence of the sterling Certificate of Deposit market, which enabled the houses to finance rate-free funds from non-bank sources to the extent that they operated in this field.

B. *The complementary markets*

An important respect in which the complementary markets and the discount market differed was the way in which interest rates were determined. As has been shown, in the traditional market they were closely related to Bank rate, but the operations of the Bank only had a limited effect on the newer markets where the links with the Bank rate were becoming increasingly tenuous. The rates of interest ruling in the complementary markets varied in response to changes in supply and demand, fluctuated more widely, were more

---

* Under existing monetary measures (*see* Appendix II) the clearing banks continue to refrain from competition for tender of Treasury bills.

volatile, and consequently were readily adapted to specific needs. Other points of difference between the traditional market and the new markets are seen in some of the (later) established practices, such as the quoting and fixing of a rate of interest for the period of deposit regardless of any change which might have occurred in Bank rate. In this context it is interesting to note that in 1966 the *Midland Bank Review** reported that it was then possible to 'indicate a typical – though by no means invariable – structure of rates in the complementary markets which was generally based on Bank rate'. In 1969, however, it reported that it was no longer possible to discern such a pattern. Nevertheless, it would be quite wrong to suppose that Bank rate did not affect transactions in the new markets, for although its influence had lessened considerably, some account had to be taken of the influence of movements in Bank rate, stemming from competition with the discount market. This inevitably arose, say after a 1% increase (or decrease) in the central banks' rate and operators in the complementary markets had to 'take a view' as to the next change in Bank rate. Thus it, becomes evident that they must shorten or lengthen their book, which in turn affected the differential between long- and short-term rates. To that extent then Bank rate affected the rates quoted in the complementary markets.

Other major influences that also had an important effect† on the structure of rates in both the traditional market and the complementary markets were changes in international rates which were reflected in Euro-dollar rates in particular, currency crises such as the Deutschemark and dollar/yen confrontations, and United States monetary policy. Apart from these international influences other factors which affected the relationships between the parallel markets are technical ones such as the day of the week/month and year-end balance sheet 'window dressings'. Other influences which have grown in importance are the rates obtainable on other short-dated fixed interest investments, such as sterling and dollar Certificates of Deposit, commercial paper, government securities and so on, the yields on which are determined by market forces. It will be appreciated, therefore, that the rates in the individual markets did not necessarily respond to these numerous influences to precisely the same degree; in fact, there were frequently wide divergences in

---

* *Midland Bank Review*, 'London's "New" Markets for Money', August 1966, p. 10, and November 1969, p. 10

† These influences are, of course, still important in determining the interest rate structure.

the pattern. Such fluctuations were particularly evident in currency crises. (*See* Chapter 6 where it was shown that although there is frequently a close relationship between three-month Euro-dollar rates and three-month local authority rates, they have at times moved in opposite directions – especially in 1965, 1968, and 1969–70.) Again, such factors as swap rates, forward exchange, and arbitrage also have a substantial influence on the Euro-dollar market which may eventually be reflected in the other complementary markets.

Consideration must also be given to the degree to which rate differentials varied within a particular market resulting from the changing responses of the varying maturities: thus call money may have been affected to a greater extent than three-month money, or vice versa. It is also possible for arbitrage to occur between the various parallel markets as brokers attempted to benefit by switching funds from one sector to another in response to interest rate differentials moving outside their normal levels. This factor should not be overstated, however, because an equilibrium situation should soon be achieved if any really large-scale switching were to occur.

As mentioned earlier, it was observed that it was possible, certainly until 1966, to discern a fairly regular pattern to the interest rate structure, based on Bank rate. Typically, rates for periods up to one week were usually related to rates for lending in the traditional market, and varied from $\frac{1}{4}$% to $\frac{3}{8}$% above them in the inter-bank market. Rates in the local authority sector were generally $\frac{1}{8}$% to $\frac{1}{4}$% higher. Maturities for one month or more were usually related to Bank rate, although running at a margin above it that increased slightly with the duration of the period. The following figures give some idea of the magnitude and variability of the movement which occurred following changes in Bank rate.

	Bank Rate	Clearing Bank Call Money	Local Authority 3 Months	Finance Houses 3 Months
26 March 1965	7	$5\frac{3}{4}$	$7\frac{3}{4}$	$7\frac{1}{2}$–$7\frac{7}{8}$
25 June 1965	6	$4\frac{3}{4}$	$6\frac{3}{4}$–$6\frac{1}{2}$	$6\frac{1}{4}$
24 June 1966	6	$4\frac{5}{8}$	$6\frac{5}{8}$	$6\frac{1}{2}$–$6\frac{7}{8}$
29 July 166	7	$5\frac{3}{8}$	$7\frac{3}{8}$–$7\frac{1}{2}$	$7\frac{5}{8}$–$8\frac{1}{4}$

Source: Bank of England Quarterly Bulletin, Table 24, March 1967, p.97.

As can be seen when Bank rate fell (in 1965) by 1% the call money rate fell in unison whereas the local authority rate fell by $1\frac{3}{8}$% to $1\frac{1}{4}$% and the finance house rate showed (at most) only $1\frac{1}{8}$% change. In 1966 when Bank rate was increased by 1%, again the call money rate moved to the same extent but the local authority rate 'spread' on this occasion was only 1% to $1\frac{1}{8}$%. The finance rate moved up by $1\frac{1}{8}$% to $1\frac{5}{8}$%.

By 1969 the links with Bank rate were becoming increasingly tenuous, so much so that it was given practical recognition by the finance houses in September 1970 who introduced a new 'base rate' which reflected the trend of the costs of three-months' interbank deposits. (The 'base rate' was devised as an alternative to Bank rate for the determination of rates charged by Finance Houses Association members on industrial and commercial lending.)

	Bank Rate	Clearing Bank Call Money	Inter-Bank Overnight	Local Authority 3 Months	Finance Houses 3 Months
27 February 1970	8	$6\frac{3}{8}$–$7\frac{7}{8}$	$8\frac{1}{2}$–20	$9\frac{1}{2}$	$9\frac{3}{4}$–$9\frac{7}{8}$
26 March 1970	$7\frac{1}{2}$	$5\frac{7}{8}$–$7\frac{1}{4}$	$7\frac{1}{4}$–8	$8\frac{7}{8}$	9–$9\frac{1}{4}$

Source: Bank of England Quarterly Bulletin, Table 29, March 1971, p. 134.

This general trend away from the influence of Bank rate is further demonstrated by the above random selection of rates subsequent to a reduction in Bank rate. Clearly the inter-bank rates were extremely volatile, and surprisingly indicate that the minimum rate actually fell below Bank rate on March 26. On October 16 it dropped even further to 1% indicating just how much this rate is governed by supply and demand influences in the market. The local authority and finance house rates, however, show less relative change than in the previous comparison for 1965–6, but they nevertheless indicate that the differential over Bank rate has increased substantially. Thus in 1965 the differential was $+\frac{3}{4}$ for the local authority rate and $+\frac{1}{2}$ to $+\frac{7}{8}$ for the finance house rate. The comparative figures in 1970, however, are $+1\frac{1}{2}$ and $+1\frac{3}{4}$ to $+1\frac{7}{8}$ Table 40 shows the changes in interest rates in the traditional markets and selected complementary markets between 1964 and 1970.

C. *The inter-bank market and Certificate of Deposit market*

The complexity of transactions which take place between the complementary markets were discussed in Chapter 7, but an attempt

Table 40

SHORT-TERM INTEREST RATES 1964–9

Per cent per annum—end of period	1964	1965	1966	1967	1968				1969				1970
					Marc.	June	Sep.	Dec.	Mar.	June	Sep.	Dec.	Spread of Rates
Bank rate	7·00	6·00	7·00	8·00	7·50	7·50	7·00	7·00	8·00	8·00	8·00	8·00	8–7
Clearing banks:													
Deposit rate	5·00	4·00	5·00	6·00	5·50	5·50	5·00	5·00	6·00	6·00	6·00	6·00	5
Call money rate*	5·375	4·375	5·375	6·25	5·875	5·375	5·375	5·375	6·25	6·375	6·375	6·375	$5\frac{3}{8}$–$6\frac{5}{8}$
Treasury bills (yield)	6·74	5·60	6·64	7·62	7·24	7·37	6·69	6·90	7·93	8·04	7·97	7·80	6·93
Bank bills (three months)	6·84	5·91	6·91	7·78	7·41	7·66	6·97	7·28	8·41	8·88	8·88	8·88	8–$8\frac{1}{8}$
Deposits with local authorities:													
(seven days)	8·00	6·25	7·38	8·44	9·00	8·13	7·44	7·25	8·69	8·69	9·63	8·88	$6\frac{1}{4}$–$6\frac{7}{8}$
(three months)	7·69	6·38	7·28	7·63	8·06	8·13	7·40	7·75	8·88	9·38	9·88	9·03	$7\frac{1}{4}$
Deposits with finance houses:													
(three months)	7·69	6·56	7·38	8·19	8·75	8·50	7·56	8·00	9·13	9·81	10·38	10·38	$7\frac{3}{4}$–$7\frac{7}{8}$
(six months)	7·63	6·75	7·44	8·25	8·00	8·50	7·56	8·13	9·19	9·94	9·56	9·63	$8\frac{1}{4}$–$8\frac{3}{8}$
Euro-dollar deposits (three months)	4·50	5·25	7·75	6·31	6·38	6·38	6·25	7·13	8·53	10·56	11·25	10·06	

* Minimum

Source: Monthly statistics, published with the permission of the Controller of Her Majesty's Stationery Office

must now be made to establish the influence of each market on the other sectors. The inter-bank market was the key link in the chain of new markets; it was the entrepôt through which funds were fed into the other markets. The deposits borrowed in this market were used to finance investment in the alternative markets and the rate quoted in the inter-bank market tended to be regarded as the 'base rate' for the market as a whole. As the clearing banks' call money rate was the dominant one in the traditional market, so the inter-bank rate set the level in the other complementary sterling markets. It follows then that all the operators in this market, the local authorities, the money brokers, finance houses, etc., set their rates at the beginning of each business day when the rates in the inter-bank market were known. The market for sterling Certificates of Deposit is also closely associated with the inter-bank market. This stems from the fact that the non-clearing banks were the chief source of funds in the latter market until 1971, and also substantial issuers of Certificates of Deposit. Whenever there was a choice for the secondary banker between issuing Certificates of Deposit or borrowing in the market, not unnaturally they preferred to issue Certificates of Deposit because, by and large, the rate paid* was lower than the inter-bank rate and the period of deposit fixed. The lender accepted the lower rate of interest because of the liquidity afforded by the secondary market. Some of the basic influences which we noted affected the traditional market also affected the newer markets. Cash shortages occurred particularly on the third Wednesday of every month when the banking system was obliged to render an analysis of its cash position to the Bank of England, or at the end of the year when 'window-dressing' activities were engaged in. The operations in the gilt-edged market by the authorities (or through speculation on the Stock Exchange) may create shortages (or surpluses) which generally affect the whole range of maturities in the inter-bank market, and as there are no last-resort facilities the full impact of circumstances are reflected in rates quoted.

D. *Local authority and finance house markets*

It is of course the case that the local authority temporary money market has tended to become increasingly dependent on banking

---

* In fact, during 1972 this was not always true as there was a close identity between Certificate of Deposit rates and the inter-bank rate. Nevertheless it remains a possible advantage of the Certificate of Deposit.

money as a residual or marginal source of supply of funds and it is, therefore, closely geared to activity in the inter-bank market. There have been many instances where this close relationship was very apparent, particularly at times when the banks were short of funds at the height of the tax payment season, Moreover. they may well have been speculating (say) against an early reduction in Bank rate by lending long and borrowing short. The Bank of England, in endeavouring to combat the situation, often decided on a penal corrective policy and withdrew support from the (traditional) market which effectively drew funds from the banks, causing keen competition for money, which in turn carried inter-bank rates up steeply.

There is no doubt that over the years the markets for money in London have become highly sophisticated. It would seem, however, that at times of crisis (say devaluation) speculative elements aggravate already difficult situations. For example, although a high proportion of loans are called in for genuine reasons, either window-dressing or other end-of-year reasons, there would seem to be little doubt that not only do interest rates get 'talked up' in anticipation of scarcity value, but that a difficult situation is frequently accentuated by lenders creating an element of artificial shortage by calling in funds merely to put them out again at a higher level.

This has been very evident in the local authority sector because lenders know that municipal treasurers must have funds to cover their needs. They are also handicapped (as the finance houses) by the fact that there is no secondary market since this at times may inhibit investors who demand liquidity. This difficulty may be overcome by investors lending overnight, or at call, but it still may have an adverse effect on longer maturities, particularly when funds are tight or there is excessive speculation in the market; at such time investors will tend to opt for the short maturity in the hope of renewing at a better rate. It is apparent then that any increase in interest differentials, in favour of local authorities or finance houses, attracts funds from the inter-bank market, but any increase in differentials in favour of the inter-bank market does not precipitate such a large reflux of funds because investors must wait for their deposits to mature.

In considering the ramifications of the many factors which influence the movement of funds from one sector of the market to another and the relative cost of such funds, it is interesting to note some observations made in the periodical, *Local Government*

Finance.* Before municipal treasurers were permitted to pay
'short' interest without deduction of tax, it was argued that the
local authorities were not fully competitive with other outlets for
investment since the ruling involved the depositor in a loss of interest. When the innovation was introduced (in 1969) it was subject
to the discretion of individual treasurers and, as such, was intended
to enable them to secure a fractional reduction in the rate of interest offered to the investor. Thus the advocates of the interest
paid gross arrangement expected a large influx of new money into
the local authority market, with a compensating fall in interest
rates. It was suspected, however, that especially in the case of the
non-banking lenders, that the authorities were merely borrowing
the same money they would have done without any change in the
tax position, but on rather more expensive terms. This arose from
the fact that, broadly speaking, for non-bank lenders wishing to
receive interest gross, the only alternative would be to place funds
on deposit with a bank. If, in turn, a bank placed the funds in the
local authority market on its own account, it is unlikely that it
would pass on to its depositor the full local authority rate received.
To the extent that the bank would expect a 'turn' on the transaction, many municipal treasurers felt that it could well have the
effect of increasing the cost of their money and not of reducing it, as
had been hoped.

E. *The Euro-dollar market*

In attempting to assess the influence of the Euro-dollar sector on
the other parallel markets, we saw in Chapters 8 and 9 that international influences can be overwhelming. That does not mean that
London rates are governed solely or even primarily by the vagaries
of the Euro-dollar market – in fact, London rates have frequently
moved in the opposite direction to Euro-dollar rates. There would
seem to be no question, however, that the interest rate structure in
London is affected to a considerable degree by Euro-dollar rates.
The total funds swapped into sterling for loans to local authorities
and finance houses from 1964 to 1969 mitigated the drain on our reserves. Similarly, in 1970 and 1971 we had tremendous speculative
inflows of funds, so much so that they had become an embarrassment by September 1971, and the Bank imposed embargoes on the
flow of overseas funds into the United Kingdom and also reduced

* May 1969, p. 193.

Bank rate. The United Kingdom was in the unenviable situation of having controls on the flow of overseas funds coming into the country and controls on resident funds moving out of the country. The position was a somewhat anomalous one for Great Britain because in the past we had always been attempting to prevent out-flows of overseas funds. Admittedly, the dollar crisis was a unique one, but the speculation was channelled mainly through the Euro-dollar market which caused changes in the London rate structure. It is also arguable that but for the inflows (mentioned above) in the period 1964–9, interest rates would have had to be kept even higher than they were.

As a large proportion of Euro-dollar funds is invested in London at call, changes in day-to-day Euro-dollar rates are likely to influence from time to time other rates in the London market. A further large proportion of Euro-dollars swapped into sterling was lent to local authorities and finance houses. Consequently, rates on these funds must be influenced by Euro-dollar rates although, theoretically, changes in Euro-dollar rates should be offset by corresponding adjustments of forward rates to their in-terest parities in relation to Euro-sterling. In practice, however, forward rates are often subject to other influences and are not adjusted altogether to changes in their Euro-dollar parities. As a result, Euro-sterling rates, and through them London rates, tend to change. As we have seen then, speculation and arbitrage brought about by the use of Euro-dollar facilities gave rise to situations in which official action became necessary, and moreover, such facili-ties gave rise to a variety of triangular arbitrage and speculative operations liable to affect sterling in such a way as to call for inter-vention which in turn affected London interest rates.

INTEREST RATE STRUCTURE POST–1971

The discount market's sources of funds were examined previously in the inter-bank section, when the former dominance of the clear-ing banks was noted. As the sources of funds have changed, so have the yields obtained on the various securities. The old interest rate structure has therefore been replaced by a highly flexible system which is influenced in the main by supply and demand, within the various elements of the money market.

The hard core of basic money at a fixed rate has been replaced by money at call from both clearing and non-clearing banks. Most banks have, in fact, elected to keep the bulk of their reserve asset ratio in this form as it facilitates the maintenance of the reserve ratio with maximum liquidity and convenience.The significant point about regular money under the old rules was that it was only called in emergencies so the houses could rely on it as semi-permanent money. This had led, under the new regulations, to a new and, from the point of view of the discount houses, unwelcome innovation known as the 'callable fixture'. The nomenclature is a contradiction in terms which has followed from the fact that the Bank will not permit fixed money to count as a reserve asset, hence the bulk of the 'fixed' money is now callable. In practice, the system does not seem to have been disadvantageous to the market although, initially, the banks were borrowing two- or three-month fixtures at the market rate with the option to call if required. During 1972, however, after the market had fully appreciated the strategic significance of call money to the banks, the callable fixture rate was established at a considerable discount below the inter-bank rate. There is, of course, no absolute permanence about this and the day-to-day rate will be determined by supply and demand in the market.

The important factor which characterized the operations of the money market since the adoption of the minimum lending rate was that money rates tended to follow yields on investments, but generally have not exceeded them. By judicious management of portfolios the houses can engineer good profits even during periods of rising interest rates. The previous formalized system often inflicted grievous losses on the market, usually at the most inopportune times.

Although C.C.C. created problems for the discount houses and the banks, especially at times of financial pressure (for example in June/July 1972 when sterling was floated) the then new monetary arrangements provided opportunities both for manufacturing reserve assets and for shifting them between those who required them for ratio purposes and those who did not.

Until July 1973 when the 50% public sector assets rule was abandoned the discount houses were severely constrained in their choice of asset portfolio. Consequently, the houses were unable to reduce their Treasury bill holdings and short-bond portfolio and increase their private sector holdings of more profitable C.D.s and short-term local authority debt. Since July 1973 the only restrictions on the size of the markets portfolio have been through the medium of the 'unidentified assets multiple' which specifies that total assets other than those identified as public sector, shall not exceed 20 times capital and reserves. There is also a general but unquantified supervision exercised by the Bank of England over the relationship between the discount houses' capital and reserves and their total portfolio.

The highly volatile nature of the interest rate structure throughout the 1970s is clearly seen in Graph 11 and Table 41. The importance of this trend for the discount houses is closely linked to the nature of official intervention in the market by the Bank of England and the introduction of M.L.R. and the previously noted changes in asset portfolio control.

The diminution in the importance of Bank Rate throughout the late 1960s continued in 1971. Bank rate did however retain an important psychological influence, especially internationally, on the level of short-term interest rates. In order to lessen this impact the Bank replaced Bank rate with Minimum Lending rate which was market determined, based on the average allotment rate at the Treasury bill tender. The change to M.L.R. appeared to give the discount houses an element of freedom in so far as Bank rate had subsequently been reduced to the single role of the minimum rate at which the Bank of England would lend to the discount house as 'lender of the last resort', whereas the new controlling mechanism was market orientated. The Bank could however make its wishes known to the market and penalize them by use of open-market operations, when its wishes were not complied with.

Despite the change of name the Bank continued to exert pressure on the level of M.L.R. through its influence on the houses. These pressures arose from the conflicting needs of the houses on the one hand and the Bank of England on the other. From the standpoint of the Bank the key importance of the discount market lies in its closeness to the financial community, both domestic and international, and hence its 'market intelligence' as to the general expectations and pressures in London. The houses also uniquely know the wishes of the authorities regarding the current level of interest rates (M.L.R.) but unfortunately, operating as a (relatively) free market and at the same time subjected to Bank of England pressures, to increase or reduce interest rates, were aims which were frequently incompatible. The houses almost invariably acted in accord with the Bank's wishes to the detriment of their own short-term profitability.

During 1976 and 1977 the pressure on the houses was considerable for two conflicting reasons; first there was persistent market

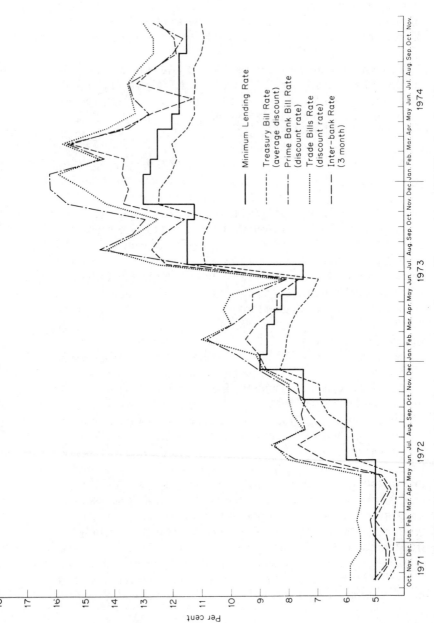

Graph 11. Movements in short-term interest rates   *Source:* Abstracted from BEQB various issues.

pressure for higher interest rates combined with a marked reluctance by the Bank to sanction such a move although it was often forced to reconsider its stance. Secondly, by late October there was a general optimism in the City of a move to lower interest rates which resulted in a sudden rush by the financial institutions to acquire longer dated assets in place of C.D.s or bills close to maturity. Despite continued pressure by the authorities to keep rates up the Treasury bill tender was heavily oversubscribed notwithstanding the efforts of the discount houses to moderate their tender prices, the weight of 'outside' bidding was sufficient to cause interest rates to fall. Ultimately, the Bank reacted by suspending the market determined formula, thereby preventing M.L.R. from following market rates down. Eventually these conflicting needs forced the Bank to abolish the formula completely on 25 May, 1978 when the authorities reverted to its former practice of making discretionary changes in the rate on Thursdays at 12.30 p.m. (instead of 3 p.m. on Fridays).

These changes in the official attitude to the operation of M.L.R. reflect a more fundamental change in economic thinking which has become increasingly evident since the late 1960s. During the 1950s and 1960s the chief aim of monetary policy was to control the interest rate level and lesser importance was given to the actual quantity of money (however defined!). Currently the emphasis is towards controlling the total quantity of money and it would be wrong to conclude that we have returned to exactly the same situation as that which existed prior to he introduction of M.L.R.

Clearly, the Bank can influence market rate movements and decide whether or not to follow them or even anticipate them, whereas in the fifties and sixties Bank rate provided leadership and direction of offical policy.

TWO IMPORTANT RESTRICTIONS ON THE BANKING SECTOR

1. THE CORSET

The authorities introduced a supplementary special deposits scheme in 1973 which ultimately became known as the 'corset' because of its restraining influence on the expansionary aims of the clearing banks. The move represented a significant departure from the one of the avowed aims of Competition and Credit Control, which was to induce greater competition into the financial sector generally. The 'corset' was designed to moderate the increases in interest rates levels which otherwise would have been required to curtail a slowdown in the growth of the money supply.

The scheme operated by the Bank imposed a prescribed ceiling on the bank's interest-bearing eligible liabilities. When the ceiling was exceeded then each bank had to lodge with the Bank of England, non-interest-bearing special deposits. Thus it was highly unprofitable for a bank to expand its lending because the penalties for exceeding the prescribed limits were very stringent indeed.

The supplementary special deposits scheme generally had a greater impact on the clearing banks than on the non-clearing banks. This stemmed from the fact that the clearers lending portfolio is more orientated towards the overdraft system and the structure of its book is therefore more volatile. The 'corset' system thus frequently forced the clearing banks to aim well below their ceiling to be sure that they did not exceed it.

The scheme proved to be an ineffectual control measure and had a somewhat chequered history. It was discontinued in 1975, re-introduced in November 1976, abandoned in August 1977, re-imposed in June 1978 and ultimately abolished in June 1980.

2. INTEREST RATE LIMITATION

In September 1973 a second breach of the spirit of the 'competition' element of C.C.C. occurred when the authorities requested the Banks to restrict the interest paid on deposits of less than £10,000 to 9½%. The restriction was imposed to protect the building societies from the effects of high interest rates and prevent an increase in the interest paid by borrowers on mortgage. In practice the limitation inhibited the banks' ability to be competitive and at the same time discriminated against the bank's smaller depositors.

The chief criticism of the interest rate limitation and the IBEL's scheme was that they both interferred with the free competitive market in the financial sector. More significantly however, they distorted the interest rate structure whenever they were in operation. This manifested itself in two clearly identifiable ways: (1) in 'round tripping' which occurred when bank corporate customers found it profitable to borrow on overdraft and then 're-lend' the funds back to the banks in the form of certificates of deposit; and (2) 'soft arbitraging' which was the exchanging of public sector Treasury bills and local authority deposits for private sector certificates of deposit.

Table 41

STRUCTURE OF INTEREST RATES 1973–80

		Bank of England's Treasury bills			*Commercial bills: discount market buying rates (discount rates)*		London clearing banks		Inter bank				*Sterling certificates of deposit*	Deposits with finance houses
		M.L.R.	*Average discount rate*	Yield	*Prime* bank bills: 3 months	Trade bills: 3 months	*Deposit* account: 7 days notice	Call money	*Over-* night lending	1 month	2 months	3 months	3 months	3 months
1973		13	12·42	12·82	$13\frac{3}{4}$–$14\frac{1}{4}$	15	$9\frac{1}{2}$	2–13	$12\frac{3}{4}$–35	$15\frac{3}{4}$–$16\frac{1}{4}$	16–$16\frac{1}{4}$	$16\frac{1}{16}$–$16\frac{5}{16}$	$15\frac{3}{4}$–16	$16\frac{3}{8}$–$16\frac{5}{8}$
1974		$11\frac{1}{2}$	10·99	11·30	$12\frac{11}{16}$–$12\frac{7}{8}$	$13\frac{1}{4}$	$9\frac{1}{2}$	2–$9\frac{1}{2}$	2–$9\frac{1}{2}$	$10\frac{1}{2}$–$10\frac{7}{8}$	$11\frac{3}{4}$–$12\frac{1}{8}$	$12\frac{1}{16}$–$12\frac{13}{16}$	$12\frac{5}{8}$–$12\frac{3}{4}$	$13\frac{1}{8}$–$13\frac{3}{8}$
1975		$11\frac{1}{4}$	10·64	10·93	$10\frac{53}{64}$	$11\frac{1}{2}$	7	$9\frac{7}{8}$–$11\frac{1}{4}$	9–$11\frac{3}{4}$	$11\frac{1}{16}$–$11\frac{3}{16}$	$11\frac{1}{16}$–$11\frac{3}{16}$	$11\frac{1}{16}$–$11\frac{3}{16}$	11–$11\frac{1}{8}$	$11\frac{1}{4}$–12
1976		$14\frac{1}{4}$	13·51	13·98	$13\frac{5}{8}$	14	11	8–13	6–15	$14\frac{3}{4}$–$15\frac{1}{8}$	$14\frac{3}{4}$–$14\frac{7}{8}$	$14\frac{1}{8}$–$14\frac{5}{8}$	$14\frac{1}{16}$–$14\frac{1}{8}$	$14\frac{5}{8}$–$15\frac{1}{8}$
1977		7	6·29	6·39	$6\frac{3}{8}$	$7\frac{1}{4}$	$3\frac{1}{2}$–$4\frac{1}{2}$	5–7	6–$7\frac{3}{4}$	$6\frac{3}{4}$–$6\frac{15}{16}$	$6\frac{5}{8}$–$6\frac{13}{16}$	$6\frac{9}{16}$–$6\frac{3}{4}$	$6\frac{3}{8}$–$6\frac{7}{16}$	$6\frac{3}{4}$–$7\frac{1}{8}$
1978		$12\frac{1}{2}$	11·56	11·91	$12\frac{7}{32}$	$12\frac{5}{8}$	10	$10\frac{1}{2}$–$11\frac{1}{2}$	$10\frac{5}{8}$–$11\frac{1}{4}$	$11\frac{3}{4}$–$12\frac{1}{8}$	$12\frac{3}{16}$–$12\frac{3}{8}$	$12\frac{7}{16}$–$12\frac{5}{8}$	$12\frac{3}{8}$–$12\frac{1}{2}$	
1979		17	15·84	16·49	$16\frac{3}{4}$	17	15	$14\frac{3}{4}$–17	15–18	$16\frac{11}{16}$–$17\frac{1}{16}$	$16\frac{3}{4}$–$17\frac{1}{16}$	$16\frac{13}{16}$–$17\frac{1}{16}$	$16\frac{11}{16}$–$16\frac{7}{8}$	$16\frac{15}{16}$–$17\frac{1}{8}$
1980	Jan 25	17	15·74	16·38	$16\frac{11}{16}$	$17\frac{1}{8}$	15	$16\frac{1}{2}$–17	16–$18\frac{1}{4}$	$15\frac{3}{8}$–$17\frac{7}{8}$	$17\frac{1}{2}$–$17\frac{11}{16}$	$17\frac{1}{4}$–$17\frac{1}{2}$	$17\frac{1}{8}$–$17\frac{13}{16}$	$17\frac{1}{2}$
	Feb 29	17	16·12	16·74	$17\frac{19}{32}$	$17\frac{13}{16}$	15	16–$16\frac{3}{4}$	12–$18\frac{1}{4}$	18–$18\frac{1}{4}$	18–$18\frac{1}{4}$	$18\frac{1}{16}$–$18\frac{1}{4}$	18–$18\frac{1}{8}$	$18\frac{1}{4}$
	Mar 28	17	16·28	16·89	$17\frac{13}{32}$	$17\frac{5}{8}$	15	14–17	$17\frac{1}{4}$–18	$18\frac{1}{8}$–$18\frac{1}{4}$	$18\frac{1}{8}$–$18\frac{5}{16}$	$18\frac{1}{8}$–$18\frac{3}{8}$	$17\frac{15}{16}$–$18\frac{1}{16}$	$18\frac{1}{4}$–$18\frac{3}{8}$
	Apr 25	17	16·06	16·79	$16\frac{13}{16}$	$17\frac{1}{8}$	15	16–17	17–18	$17\frac{3}{8}$–$17\frac{1}{2}$	$17\frac{5}{16}$–$17\frac{7}{16}$	$17\frac{1}{4}$–$17\frac{7}{16}$	$17\frac{1}{16}$–$17\frac{5}{16}$	$17\frac{1}{2}$–$17\frac{5}{8}$
	May 30	17	16·06	16·77	$16\frac{29}{64}$	$16\frac{7}{8}$	15	12–17	$16\frac{1}{8}$–17	$16\frac{1}{16}$–$16\frac{3}{16}$	$16\frac{1}{16}$–$16\frac{3}{16}$	17–$17\frac{1}{8}$	$16\frac{7}{8}$–$17\frac{1}{16}$	$17\frac{3}{8}$
	June 27	17	15·68	16·37	$16\frac{3}{16}$	$16\frac{3}{4}$	15	14–17	$17\frac{3}{8}$–18	$17\frac{3}{8}$–$17\frac{5}{8}$	$17\frac{1}{8}$–$17\frac{3}{8}$	$16\frac{3}{4}$–17	$16\frac{11}{16}$–$16\frac{7}{8}$	17–$17\frac{1}{4}$
	July 25	16	14·44	15·06	$14\frac{27}{32}$	$15\frac{5}{8}$	14	15–16	$16\frac{7}{8}$–40	$16\frac{3}{8}$–$16\frac{9}{16}$	$15\frac{15}{16}$–$16\frac{1}{8}$	$15\frac{5}{16}$–$15\frac{9}{16}$	$15\frac{1}{4}$–$15\frac{3}{8}$	$15\frac{5}{8}$–$15\frac{3}{4}$
	Aug 29	16	14·95	15·37	$15\frac{7}{8}$	$16\frac{3}{8}$	14	10–16	14–$16\frac{1}{2}$	$16\frac{3}{4}$–$16\frac{15}{16}$	$16\frac{11}{16}$–$16\frac{15}{16}$	$16\frac{5}{8}$–$16\frac{15}{16}$	$16\frac{7}{16}$–$16\frac{11}{16}$	

Source: *Financial Statistics*, August 1980

Table 41 illustrates the high general level of rates throughout the 1970s and also the volatility of the structure especially in 1977 and 1978 and 1979 when rates reached historically high levels. The dominant influence of M.L.R. and the Treasury bill rate on the other rates is also evident as is the wide fluctuations in the call money rate when compared to the period prior to 1971. The extreme volatility of the overnight inter-bank rate is clearly shown through the period and particularly in 1973 and 25 July 1980 and 29 August, 1980, indicating periods of extreme pressure in the money market.

POLITICAL AND INTERNATIONAL INFLUENCES

Quite apart from the factors, which we have analysed above, and the issues discussed in the first part of the chapter, the last decade witnessed a number of critically important political and economic events, the impact of which often totally overrode other considerations. Probably the single most important change in the world economic balance occurred in 1974 when the OPEC countries introduced a four-fold increase in the price of oil. The action caused panic in the financial markets and disrupted economies of both industrialized and developing countries alike.

During 1976 M.L.R. was forced from $8\frac{1}{4}\%$ to 15% by the sheer size of the central government borrowing requirement. The period became known as the 'year of crowding out' because the private sector had tremendous problems in funding its needs. Throughout 1977, when M.L.R. fell to 5% the U.K. economy moved from deficit into surplus as a result of the influx of North Sea Oil revenues. The major influences on the international money market in 1979 were the U.S. Government decision to freeze Iranian government assets and the U.K. authorities abolition of exchange control.

16 Structural changes in the money market

In the previous chapters we have traced the development of each segment of London's money markets, both traditional and complementary. An examination must now be made of the structural changes, which have taken place as a result of the development of the new markets, the extent to which the discount market is involved, and the effect on the markets as a whole.

As can be seen the broad picture is one of an adaptable discount market which, as the 1960s unfolded, was beset with continuing problems created in the main by official monetary and fiscal policies. First of all, the market was faced with a chronic shortage of Treasury bills, then by a ceiling placed on its commercial bills, and then it learned some particularly salutary lessons in the art of bond dealing in 1955, 1957, and 1964, which led to a general reassessment of bond-dealing policy. At the same time the City's new markets were growing rapidly – the local authority market, the Euro-dollar market, and the sterling inter-bank market, all of which were outside the range of the traditional market's activities. It became obvious that if the discount houses were to continue to prosper as in the past they would have to broaden the base of their operations. Many commentators have censured the market for taking so long to appreciate this fact – it was not until the mid-1960s that the houses turned to new outlets in which to fulfil the market intermediary function by creating a secondary market for dollar Certificates of Deposit. Two years later, in 1968, a similar market in sterling Certificates was launched. Today, almost all the houses are involved, directly or indirectly, in all the complementary markets.

The principal arguments between the two factions, the dealers and brokers, were fairly clearly defined. It is probably fair comment to say that the dealers are the more traditionally minded houses. They see a fundamental difference of principle between the house which buys and sells securities on its own account, thereby undertaking a direct liability, and a company which merely acts as the middleman, bringing together buyers and sellers. Furthermore, it is maintained that a discount house's strength is its credit-worthiness and access to relatively cheap money, partly through their (former) special service to the clearing banks, partly because they normally borrow against security (in contrast to the generally unsecured borrowing in the complementary markets). The dealers are, in fact, inferring that they should 'take a view' and buy and sell securities in their own names. Inevitably, the brokers tended to be the younger elements within the discount market and they consider this viewpoint to be somewhat old-fashioned and quite indefensible in times of rapid change and new technologies. They argue that there is no logical reason why broking and dealing activities should not be carried on by the same companies. If they are to provide a truly sophisticated investment service which offers complete information that can quickly identify the deficits and surpluses, then a central marketing organization, which only a broker can provide, must be set up. They claimed that anyone who has used their services would not revert to relying on their own judgement. Certainly no industrial company or local authority could afford the numbers of specialist staff employed by brokers. Therefore, on balance, it would seem that the reasoning of the brokers is more compelling, bearing in mind the increasing complexity of the markets and the influence of the Americans in introducing financial innovations.

During the 1970s as the complementary markets grew in importance the integration between the traditional market and all the other short-term money markets was complete. The discount houses have been extremely successful in marketing their full range of services to industrial and commercial companies through the medium of attractive books and pamphlets and attendance at conferences. Companies with strong export business have always been important customers of the discount houses as commercial bills provide an ideal means of finance for importation of heavy and bulky raw materials or products requiring an extended period to manufacture. Many houses have an acknowledged expertise in the provision of finance to certain industries. In addition, however, the discount market has extended its experience to an increasingly wide range of industrial and commerical companies. This was poss-

ible for two important reasons: (i) the generally high and very volatile short-term interest rate structure; and (ii) the general increased
importance of C.D.s and the frequency with which restrictions
were placed on bank overdrafts. This latter point was frequently
linked with the corset constraints placed on the banks and the now
well-known 'acceptance gap'. These factors created a financial
climate whereby companies of all kinds needed a remunerative
home for temporarily idle funds as well as for normal trade
finance.The banks were able to circumvent the special deposits
scheme by the simple expedient of discounting bills for the customers which were then off-loaded to the discount market. The
discount houses then had to find buyers outside the banking sector
and they have been very successful in developing links with corporate treasurers and overseas buyers. Clearly then there is a two-
way movement in commercial bills, some coming into the discount
market and some moving out of the market. Recent estimates of
the size of the bill market give some indication of the importance of
the instrument to the houses. Total estimated commercial bills in
issue £6,600 M. of which £250 M. are trade bills. £2,500 M. are
bank bills held by the houses, £1,200 M. held by U.K. banks, about
£300 M. held by the Bank of England and £2,300 M. held outside
the banking system. Overseas holdings of bills are thought to be approximately £600/700 M. of non-banking sector holdings.

THE REMOVAL OF THE CORSET AND
THE POSSIBLE INTRODUCTION OF NEW TECHNIQUES
TO CONTROL THE BANKING SECTOR

The authorities published a paper early in 1980 which had a major
impact on the discount market: this was the Bank of England's
Green Paper's on monetary base control. The first major change
announced in the monetary control paper was the abolition of the
'corset' control on the banks. The ultimate long-term effect of this
move is difficult to evaluate but clearly its immediate impact (late
1980) will be for a contraction in the amount of bills drawn as banks
raise funds through certificates of deposit to support their lending
activities – this was formerly done via acceptances. Whether or not
there is a major contraction in the commercial bill market may well
rest on the ability of the discount-market to persuade corporate
treasurers to retain the advantages of bill finance. Moreover it may
prove more difficult for banks to persuade companies to invest in

C.D.s (which is 'one name paper') as opposed to bills which have two names plus the endorsement of the discount house.

It has been suggested that the abolition of reserve asset ratio would adversely affect the discount houses. This seems highly unlikely and indeed the special position of the discount market at the centre of the banking system has been reaffirmed in the Bank of England's liquidity paper. Under the proposed new system, call money with the discount market would qualify as primary liquidity while all the other primary assets are nearly all instruments in which the discount houses are the major market makers (i.e. gilts with less than one year to maturity, Treasury bills, eligible bank bills and local authority bills). In any case the reserve asset ratio when imposed in 1971 merely followed an asset structure which had evolved over many years in the normal course of banking prudence. The presumption must be therefore that even if a 'cash ratio' is imposed on the banking system, that the level chosen would be closely related to current banking practice. Bankers would still wish to minimize such holdings (non-earning asset) to meet either official or their own current needs whichever was the higher. This would be done through call money with the discount market and transactions in short-term paper.

It is not possible, nor indeed is it the purpose of this book to discuss the wide-ranging implications and problems of the Bank of England's two previously mentioned papers. It is however pertinent to point out a major concern which exists at present under the reserve asset ratio control and which would undoubtedly still bedevil the authorities under a cash base regime.

The problem arises from the technical difficulties that manifest themselves when the bank relieves shortages in the market (or absorbs surpluses). Clearly, in an ideal situation the Bank should attempt to act to neutralize shortages and surpluses without causing wide fluctuations in short-term interest rates, that is, causing them to depart from some perceived level for monetary control purposes, nor should they require banks to hold excessive holdings of liquid assets.

The inability of the present intervention techniques to cope with abnormal situations in the money market are evidenced by the periodic need for sale and repurchase agreements and erratic movements in market rates. A problem which emerges from the banks' need to observe a fixed reserve asset ratio is that they are frequently faced with a shortage of reserve assets and sharp divergences then arise between reserve asset rates and other short-term rates. A similar difficulty would exist under a cash base system if specific liquidity norms were imposed and the supply of primary assets was too limited. The resolution of this problem is not an easy one for the Bank of England because they are placed in a 'catch 22' situation since the forms of intervention are a major determinant of a bank's requirement to hold liquidity. On the other hand, the nature of the liquidity requirement influences the effectiveness of different forms of intervention. Thus, there is a strong two-way link between liquidity and intervention and there is therefore an obvious need for flexibility on the part of the authorities if any new system is to operate satisfactorily.

POSSIBLE FUTURE DEVELOPMENTS IN THE DISCOUNT MARKET

Trying to envisage or pinpoint major new business developments in the market has never been easy but the houses are inevitably subject to powerful outside and official influences. There does however, seem considerable scope for the market to extend their services to the commercial and industrial sectors. If as is hoped there is a major resurgence of small and medium-sized companies over the next decade then the financial expertise in the market could be a significant factor in the successful management and growth of these companies.

A number of houses have developed their international activities stemming from the growth of the dollar C.D. market and as the key element in the secondary market, Smith St Aubyn have opened an office in New York and Allen Harvey & Ross, Gerrard and National, Jessel Toynbee and Gilletts have close relationships with U.S. broking houses. The recent removal of exchange controls provides new opportunities for the houses to revive the 'bill on London' by using sterling to finance third country trade. The houses already have close contacts with many overseas companies and banks arising from their traditional bill business. These links are now strengthened by new investors such as Japan and others purchasing Treasury bills and other short-term paper, following a combination of high U.K. interest rates and a strong pound.

An interesting recent development which emphasizes the strength of the discount houses incursion into the complementary markets is the sale of money broking subsidiaries by all but one of the houses which had formerly diversified into this field. The houses have formed an increasing overlap between their now extensive business connections and their broking subsidiaries. Now only Gilletts retains it broking subsidiary (Kirkland-Whittaker).

The expanding nature of discount market business may well necessitate a stronger capital base. Such a development is further reinforced by the authorities shift away from quantitative controls of the banking system. There is therefore a possibility that the ceilings which presently limit the houses business will be replaced by another form of regulation. Two controls presently exist: (1) the maximum permitted portfolio of each house is 30 times its true resources including inner reserves; and (2) within this ratio, calculated on a formula based on a three year average true resources, is a 20 times multiplier for 'undefined' private sector assets which comprise mainly commercial bills and bank C.D.s. Within the market opinions differ as to the extent to which these controls inhibit market operations. The chief problem lies in achieving adequate levels of profitability to fund the market's capital base. Some houses feel that the controls prevent the market making sufficient profits in bull markets to offset losses incurred in bear markets. Other market men argue that even though there may be surplus paper in the market and houses cannot absorb it because of multiplier limitations, that rates will rise anyway, giving higher earnings. The market expects that the authorities will eventually impose capital and liquidity controls similar to those already proposed for the banks.

A FUTURES MARKET IN FINANCIAL FUTURES

Proposals have been put forward (September 1980) for the formation of a financial futures market in London. A working party was formed comprising a number of individuals from institutions, including banks, stockbrokers, discount houses and commercial companies. The Working Party conducted a four month research study in Chicago, New York and London, the objective of which was to produce a feasiblity study for a London futures market. At the time of writing no firm decisions have been made but the development of a futures market in the City could consolidate its position as the world's most sophisticated financial centre. So far the

Bank has given no indication as to whether or not it would support a futures market but in the past the authorities have always given strong encouragement to new and innovatory developments which bring foreign business to London.

ORIGIN AND CONCEPT OF A FUTURES MARKET

Rapidly changing economic conditions, coupled with increased volatility of interest rates and exchange rates, has created considerable uncertainty in industry, commerce and finance, both domestically and internationally.

A futures market could provide an efficient method of redistribution of these risks, at a known price determined by open competition, which reflects anticipated changes in market rates. The market would also allow rapid reversal of positions and adjustments for sudden changes. Once fully established it should have lower transaction costs than cash markets. Confidence in the market would stem from the existence of a clearing house providing a central source of information and guarantee of performance to each member.

A futures contract is a binding agreement to buy or sell a standard quantity of a commodity (of known quality) at a definite date and specified price, on fixed conditions of delivery. In a financial futures market the commodity would be currency or financial paper.

The contract is fulfilled by either selling or purchasing an equal and opposite contract to offset his original deal (this is the most common transaction), or he can deliver the commodity against a sale contract or take delivery against a purchase contract.

It is also possible to transfer risk by establishing a hedge. This is done by buying or selling a future contract in the opposite direction to an existing commitment in the cash market. The cash market transaction is eventually closed by either a sale or purchase and the future contract is then reversed, settlement being made in cash. If the cash transaction shows a loss then the futures contract profit will mitigate it, or alternatively, if prices have moved in favour of the cash deal, then there will be an offsetting loss in the futures market. A number of working examples are shown in Appendix IV.

THE ADVANTAGE OF MARKET IN LONDON

The development of a futures market in London would enable the City to attract additional new business and broaden the scope of its existing activities. It should have particular attraction to operators in the money and securities markets and Euro-markets enabling them to hedge their risks in the futures market.

The market will enable participants in U.S. markets to trade in London before their own markets open.

Initially contracts would be limited to currencies, sterling interest rates, and Euro-dollar rates as there is a wide range of instruments in adequate supply with well-developed secondary markets. It is recommended that both the sterling interest rate contract and Euro-dollar contract should be based on Certificates of Deposit and that currency contracts be based on the $.

Possible later developments would include a long sterling interest contract based on Government securities but this would require the co-operation of the Stock Exchange and the Bank of England.

POTENTIAL OPERATORS IN THE MARKET

The market appears likely to appeal to institutions where future cash flows follow a predictable pattern of receipts and payments such as insurance companies, building socieities, investment managers, stockbrokers and money brokers, banks and local authorities.

CONCLUSION

The discount houses have established an enviable reputation for financial prudence and dexterity in the face of an extremely difficult operating environment, many features of which are totally beyond their control. The markets in which they operate have become increasingly competitive throughout the 1970s, the management of the houses is highly professional as is amply demonstrated by their record financial strength at the end of the last decade. They have introduced new services, developed new marketing skills and successfully operated within a background of highly volatile interest rates. This has been achieved without prejudice to their traditional functions of supporting the Treasury in raising short-term finance and providing the mechanism through which the authorities control the level of interest rates in the economy.

The discount houses success in the 1970s has obviously prepared them well to face what may well prove to be even more far-reaching changes in the 1980s.

The Markets compared

Table 42 attempts to indicate the growth of resources employed in each of London's money markets. It must be emphasized, however, that the figures merely provide broad indications of rates of growth in each sector. Unfortunately, we are not comparing like with like but the nature of each market's figures is shown against each section. Generally they represent stock concepts as distinct from flow concepts and as figures for turnover are not available it is even more dangerous to compare one market with another. The position is further complicated by numerous improvements which have been made from time to time in the official statistics since 1962. Following these reservations and bearing in mind the comments made in this respect in the chapters dealing with the Euro-dollar and inter-bank markets, we must nevertheless attempt to draw some tentative conclusions and comment on future prospects.

It becomes increasingly anomalous to refer to these markets as either new or secondary. They are certainly not new as many of them have been in existence for fifteen years or more. They are hardly secondary in size as some are far larger than the discount market whilst those that are smaller seem to be rapidly catching up.

The outstanding feature of the table is the staggering growth in the Euro-currency market. The market is now sixty times larger than in 1965 and liabilities in non-sterling currencies now exceed £126,726 M.

Part of this increase stems from the high levels of inflation experienced throughout the world since 1972. A related factor is of course the dramatic increases in crude oil prices by OPEC. This growth, especially in the last five years, has caused considerable

Table 42

COMPARISON OF RESOURCES OF
SHORT-TERM MARKETS

(£M.)	1960	1965	1970	1975	1979
Treasury bill (total issued)	3,489	2,652	2,244	4,221	2,604
Commercial bill (total issued)	272	795	1,461	1,463	3,585
Local Authorities					
(temporary debt)	900	1,700	2,000	3,666	5,384
Finance Houses	340	600	690	1,073	869
(deposits)	(1,962)				
Euro-currencies (U.K. bank					
liabilities in non-sterling					
currencies)	N/A	2,122	15,153	63,368	126,726
Inter-bank (liabilities to					
U.K. banks in sterling)	N/A	365	1,598	7,415	19,317
$ Certificates of Deposit					
(total outstanding)	–	–	1,653	6,509	19,775
£ Certificates of Deposit					
(total outstanding)	–	–	1,062	2,979	3,833
Inter-Company (estimated					
loans outstanding)			100/300	50/100	–
Discount Houses					
(total assets)	1,050	1,400	2,300	2,670	4,778

misgivings, in particular amongst central bankers throughout the world, and in West Germany and America in addition, concern is expressed over the inflationary implications of the growth of Euro-dollar credit.

The inter-bank market has shown considerable growth from small beginnings in 1960 to £365 M. by 1965 and £1,600 M. by 1970. Following the introduction of the new monetary arrangements in September 1971, the market has grown in size to some £19,300 M. This is only to be expected since the market provides the vital link between the other markets, overlapping frequently with the local authority, finance house, sterling Certificates of Deposit, and Euro-dollar sectors. The presumption must be, therefore, that this market will continue to expand as all the others grow. Reservations were expressed in Chapter 7 concerning the viability of statistics in the inter-bank market and much stess is made by all commentators on the presumption that double-counting overstates the size of this market. There is, however, one aspect of this complex statistical problem which has been largely ignored and would have the effect of reducing the size of the quoted figures. All the non-clearing banks maintain accounts with the clearing banks (in some cases accounts may be kept with several clearing banks). It follows that a fair proportion of inter-bank funds must, in fact, represent balances held on behalf of non-clearers by the clearing banks. By and large these balances would be kept to a minimum because they are not interest bearing, but even so in aggregate (there are approximately 150 banks) they must represent a substantial sum and should, therefore, be deducted from the total of £19,300 M.

The underlying reasons for the lack of growth in the finance house market were detailed in Chapter 10 and were chiefly attributable to official credit restrictions and ceilings on advances. The real boom period for this sector was 1958–60 and since 1965 hardly any expansion occurred until the end of 1971. The principal reason for the lack of growth in the finance house market lay in the central orders of the Board of Trade which specified minimum amounts of initial deposits and maximum repayment periods. Consequently, periods of low economic activity have a depressing effect on this market. The period from December 1970 and March 1972 witnessed the increase in total liabilities of the finance houses from £1,100 M. to £1,400 M. as competition in the financial sector increased. A factor which distorted the statistics occured in 1972 when the Bank of England recognized certain finance houses as banks and this charge accounted for a fall of some £700 M. in total liabilities.

The market in $C.D.s has grown over ten-fold since 1970 and is a useful extension of the Euro-market for both banker and investor. It is the dealings in the secondary market that are attractive as it is the equivalent of a call option enabling the holder to sell at any point and by 'riding the yield curve' avoid running his investment into a lower yielding maturity. The sterling C.D. market has however, shown something of a decline from the peak of £5,943 M. in 1973, but this is chiefly a reflection of the changing levels of interest rates brought about by the historically high levels of inflation. The market will no doubt rapidly expand again when the issuing banks see a marked advantage in issuing C.D.s to increase their deposit base when economic conditions permit.

Finally, consideration must be given to the inter-company loans market which emerged in 1969. The size of this market is possibly the most difficult of all about which to conjecture and it is well-nigh impossible to estimate its real resources. Various guesses have been made by brokers (and many loans are transacted directly between the companies themselves, thus bypassing the brokers) varying from £50 M. to £500 M. with a realistic estimate said to be in the region of £100–300 M. The market was established by companies which, because of credit squeezes were unable to obtain funds from the banks, consequently some observers thought that it would disappear when the ceilings on bank overdrafts were removed. This has not proved to be the case because of the many interrelationships between this sector, commercial paper, Certificates of Deposit, and inter-bank markets.

The total of Treasury bills issued varies tremendously from week to week, month to month and year to year depending on the residual borrowing requirement of the Government and the difficulties it faces in obtaining long-term funding in the market. The commercial bill market is also affected strongly by outside influences such as restrictions placed on bank overdrafts, the corset and other banking controls. The very high figures in 1979 reflected the 'acceptance gap' as the banks have encouraged their customers to issue commercial bills as a substitute for overdrafts, thereby circumventing the special deposits scheme.

An important general point to be borne in mind when comparing the total assets figures of the Discount Houses with the other segments of the market is that the portfolio comprises, in varying degrees, some proportion of all the other instruments shown in the table. Hence, there is an element of double counting.

Bank of England monetary arrangements

This appendix gives a brief summary of the monetary arrangements introduced by the Bank of England in September 1971. Readers should refer to the Bank's publications 'Competition and Credit Control', Volume II, 1971, and 'Competition and Credit Control: Further Developments', March 1973, for full details.

Readers should also note that at the time of writing (February 1981) the whole system of banking and monetary controls is under review and major changes may well be implemented.

(1) THE DISCOUNT MARKET

(i) The houses are to continue to apply each week for an amount of Treasury bills sufficient to cover the amount of bills offered at the tender. The former arrangement of the 'syndicated bid' by the market as a whole was revoked. In return for the houses' agreement to cover the Treasury bill tender, the Bank continues to offer exclusive last-resort facilities to the discount houses.

(ii) Members of the market were obliged to hold a minimum of 50% of their funds in public sector debt.

Public sector debt was defined as:

British government and Northern Ireland Treasury bills; local government bills and bonds; British government and local authority guaranteed stocks with not more than five years to run to maturity.

(The 50% P.S.D. ratio was replaced in July 1973 by a control which limits aggregate holdings of certain assets by each house to a maximum of twenty times its capital and reserves.)

(2) THE BANKING SECTOR

(i) The system of lending ceilings on clearing banks was removed.

(ii) The whole banking system, i.e. clearing and non-clearing banks is subject to a reserve requirement to maintain a day-by-day minimum ratio of reserve assets to eligible liabilities of $12\frac{1}{2}\%$. In addition, the clearing banks are required to maintain a day-by-day total of $1\frac{1}{2}\%$ of eligible liabilities in the form of balances at the Bank of England.

(iii) Special Deposits to continue to be used with the same percentage to apply to all banks. The percentage may be different on overseas deposits.

(iv) The clearing banks abandoned their cartel arrangements on interest rates.

(v) The Bank continued its policy of not supporting the market in government bonds of more than one year's maturity.
Eligible liabilities are defined as:

(a) Sterling deposits with a term of two years or less from U.K. residents other than banks, overseas residents, and overseas offices.

(b) Sterling deposits of whatever term from U.K. banks, less any sterling claims of such banks.

(c) All sterling Certificates of Deposit issued, less any holdings of such Certificates.

(d) The bank's net liability in sterling to its overseas offices.

(e) The bank's net liability in currencies other than sterling.

(f) 60% of net value of items in transit, i.e. 60% of credits less 60% of debit items in transit.

Reserve assets are defined as:

(a) Balances with branches of the Bank of England, but exclude notes and coins held in the bank's tills. Holdings of notes and coins are excluded from reserve assets.

(b) Company tax reserve certificates.

(c) Money at call with London discount market.

(d) British government stocks with one year or less to final maturity.

(*e*) Local authority bills eligible for rediscount at the Bank.

(*f*) Commercial bills eligible for rediscount at the Bank up to a maximum of 2% of total eligible liabilities.

(*g*) British Government and Northern Ireland Treasury Bills.

Defined assets are:

- Balances at the Bank of England
- U.K. and N.I. Treasury bills

Only those with not more than 5 years to final maturity {
- British Government Stocks
- Nationalized Industry Stocks guaranteed by H.M. Government
- Local authority stocks
}
- Local authority bills and other public board's bills eligible at the Bank of England
- Local authority negotiable bonds
- Bank bills drawn by nationalized industries under specific government guarantee.

'Undefined assets' are all assets held except those mentioned above.

Undefined assets multiple = 20 times a 3 yearly moving average of shareholders funds.

APPENDIX III

A review of the Bank of England's proposals for a change to a system of monetary base control and for regulating the liquidity within the banking system.

The inadequacy of existing methods of control of the money supply and the associated problems of prudential and other controls on banks have been discussed in Parts III and IV of the book.

The precise position remains unclear but the Bank of England published draft proposals in June 1981. This Appendix summarizes the Bank's proposals.

1. THE CASH RATIO

(i) The $1\frac{1}{2}$% of eligible liabilities formerly provided by the Clearing Banks to the Bank of England and held in non-interest bearing accounts is abolished and to be replaced by a uniform requirement on all banks and licensed deposit takers to hold non-operational, non-interest bearing deposits with the Bank. The objective here is that the new ratio will provide approximately the same aggregate total funds to the central bank.

The requirement will be $\frac{1}{2}$% of an institutions's eligible liabilities where these average £10 million or more over the latest period which the requirement is calculated.

(ii) Eligible liabilities are to be redefined in future, offsets will be allowed in the calculation of eligible liabilities in respect of:

(1) funds (other than cash ratio deposits or Special Deposits placed with the Bank) lent by an institution in the newly defined monetary sector* to any other;

---

* See Statistical changes later (No.5)

(2) money at call placed with money brokers and gilt-edged jobbers in the Stock Exchange, and secured on gilt-edged stock, Treasury bills, local authority bills and bills of exchange.

(iii) Eligible liabilities will be calculated in uniform fashion for all reporting institutions* except:

(1) members of the London Discount Market Association (LDMA), whose eligible liabilities will be calculated as the total of sterling deposits other than from institutions with the monetary sector;

(2) certain banks with money trading departments, who will be allowed to omit from their eligible liabilities secured money at call placed by other banks with these departments, up to a limit set by the Bank.

2. SPECIAL DEPOSITS

The Special Deposits scheme remains in place and will apply to all institutions with eligible liabilities of £10 million or more.

3. ELIGIBILITY

A bank may apply for eligibility at any time. The Bank will judge applications, by recognized banks wishing their acceptances to become eligible for discount at the Bank, according to the following criteria:

(i) whether the applicant has and maintains a broadly based and substantial acceptance business in the United Kingdom;

(ii) whether its acceptances command the finest rates in the market for ineligible bills;

(iii) whether, in the case of foreign-owned banks, British banks enjoy reciprocal opportunities in the foreign owners' domestic market.

UNDERTAKINGS BY ELIGIBLE BANKS

From a date to be announced, each eligible bank undertakes to

---

* The present arrangements for those finance houses which have observed a 10% reserve asset ratio since 1971 will lapse accordingly.

maintain secured money with members of the LDMA and secured call money with money brokers and gilt-edged jobbers – such that:

(i) the total funds so held normally average 5–6%* of that bank's eligible liabilities;

(ii) the amount held in the form of secured money with members of the LDMA does not normally fall below 3–4% of eligible liabilities on any day.

In relation to the above undertaking, each eligible bank will

(1) aim to meet the daily average ratio over either six or twelve month periods at its discretion
   and

(2) to provide monthly returns of its daily figures, which the Bank will use to assess the bank's performance relative to its long-term commitment.

Banks will only be expected to go below the minimum in exceptional circumstances and will be required to explain their position to the Bank of England.

In accordance with Bank of England's long standing practice of flexibility and consultation it will be prepared to review the arrangements in the light of working experience.

4. PRUDENTIAL CONSIDERATIONS

Discussions on developments in supervision are continuing and a separate paper on liquidity will be issued by the Bank when appropriate. In the meantime, after the abolition of the reserve ratio, banks will discuss any changes in their policies towards liquidity management with the Bank of England.

5. STATISTICAL CHANGES

The present banking sector, as defined for the purposes of calculating the monetary aggregates, currently contains those institutions

---

* The figure in this sub-paragraph will be calculated to produce an aggregate amount of around £3 billion and is expected to be around 5% of eligible liabilities as presently defined, or perhaps 6% on the new definition.

included in the statistical list of banks and the list of discount market institutions. These lists were drawn up prior to the Banking Act and are no longer appropriate to current circumstances. They exclude a number of recognized banks, many LDTs, and also the trustee savings banks.

A new monetary sector will therefore be defined, to include

   (i) all recognized banks and LTDs;
  (ii) National Girobank;
 (iii) banks in the Channel Islands and the Isle of Man, so long as they are subject to broadly parallel arrangements for a cash ratio.
 (iv) the trustee savings banks (TSBs)
  (v) the Banking Department of the Bank.

Although the population of the monetary sector will be considerably larger than that of the 'statistical list', the statistical effect will be comparatively modest since the present business of many of the new contributors is relatively small. In total, the initial once-for-all adjustment to the stock of the main monetary aggregate, £M3, will probably be of the order of £8 billion (13%), of which the TSBs account for around £6 billion ($9\frac{1}{2}$%).

6. THE TIMETABLE FOR CHANGE AND THE TRANSITIONAL ARRANGEMENTS

The key features of the new arrangements will be implemented quickly and The Bank will shortly specify an operative date when:

   (i) the Reserve Asset Ratio will be abolished;
  (ii) banks whose acceptances are eligible for discount at the Bank will begin to observe the requirements set out in 3 above;
 (iii) the agreement with the London clearing banks, whereby they keep an average of $1\frac{1}{2}$% of their eligible liabilities at the Bank, will lapse;
 (iv) the Bank will receive the first deposits under the cash ratio requirement.

APPENDIX IV

Financial futures in London

EXAMPLES OF THE USES OF FUTURES

One of the main aims of the seminars being organized by the Working Party is to illustrate specific ways of using the markets, but in general three types of examples cover the basic use of interest rate and currency futures.

1. LONG HEDGES IN INTEREST RATES

A long hedge can be used to protect against a fall in interest rates. A typical user would be anyone who expects to have funds available for investment in the future but wishes to invest at current rates.

Example (ignoring expenses)

A portfolio manager knows he will receive £1 M. in three months' time when he expects interest rates to have fallen. The futures market, although anticipating declining rates does not fully discount his views. He can therefore use the market to invest at rates approaching current yields.

	Cash Market	Futures Market
1.10.80	6-month £C.D.s are trading at 14½%	Buys 4 March 81 £C.D. contracts @ 86 (14% yield)
		Cost: £965,000
Interest rates do decline as he expected.		
1.01.81	Buys £1 M. 6-month £C.D.s at 13½%	Sells 4 March 81 £C.D. contracts @ 86½ (13½% yield)
		Proceeds: £966,250
	OPPORTUNITY LOSS £5,000	PROFIT £1,250

*Abstracted from *Financial Futures in London*, September 1980

Suppose, however, interest rates rise, contrary to expectations, between 1.10.80 and 1.01.81:

	Cash Market	**Futures Market**
1.10.80	6-month £C.D.s are trading at 14½%	Buys 4 March 91 £C.D. contracts @ 86 (14% yield)
		Cost: £965,000
1.01.81	Buys £1 M. 6-month £C.D.s at 15½%	Sells 4 March 81 £C.D. contracts @ 85 (15% yield)
		Proceeds: £962,500
	OPPORTUNITY GAIN £5,000	LOSS £2,500

2. SHORT HEDGES IN INTEREST RATES

A short hedge can be used by a corporate treasurer who will require to raise £10,000,000 in March 1981 through the discounting of bills of exchange. A significant increase in interest rates is anticipated prior to that date.

	Cash Market		**Futures Market**
20.09.80	Anticipated 3 month bill rate in March 1981—16% (yield 16.66%) (current rate 15½%)		Sells 40 March 1981 £C.D. contracts @ 83½ (16½% yield)
10.03.81	Treasurer discounts £10.0 M for 91 days @ 17% (yield 17.75%)		Buys 40 March 1981 £C.D. contracts @ 82½ (17½% yield)
		£	
	Proceeds:	9,576,164	PROFIT = £24,657
	Interest cost: less futures profit:	423,836 · 24,657	
		£399,179	

Overall cost of finance: 16.67% (Discount Rate: 16%).

If, however, in the above example, interest rates remain at current levels, the transactions on 10 March, 1981 would be as follows:

10.03.81	Treasurer discounts £10.0 M. for 91 days @ 15½% (yield 16.12%)		Buys 40 March 1981 £C.D. contracts @ 84 (16%)
		£	
	Proceeds:	9,613,562	LOSS = £12,328
	Interest cost: plus futures loss:	386,438 12,328	
		£398,766	

Overall cost of finance: 16.65% (Discount Rate: 16%).

3. CURRENCY HEDGES

A currency hedge enables an individual or institution with foreign currency commitments to buy or sell a currency forward in this opposite direction to his future exposed position.

Example (ignoring expenses)

A corporate treasurer in the U.K. will be receiving a dividend of U.S. $350,000 from a U.S. subsidiary in September. He decides in, say, mid-June to lock in to current exchange rates.

	£ increasing in value	
	Cash Market	**Futures Market**
Mid-June	Forward rate for Mid-September $2·28 = £1 eqv. £153,509	Buys 3 sterling Sept. contracts at $2·28 eqv. $342,000
Mid-September	Sells $350,000 on cash	Sells 3 sterling Sept.
	market at $2·33 eqv. £150,215	contracts at $2·33 eqv. $349,500
		PROFIT £7,500

If the dividend is expected sometime in mid-November the following would occur:

	£ depreciating in value	
	Cash Market	**Futures Market**
Mid-June	Forward rate for Mid-September $2·28 = £1 eqv. £153,509	Buys 3 sterling Sept. contracts at $2·28 eqv. $342,000
Mid-September	Sells $350,000 on cash	Sells 3 sterling Sept.
	market at $2·25 eqv. £155,556	contracts at $2·25 eqv. $337,500
		LOSS $4,500

For the purposes of these illustrations the forward has been assumed to be a premium for the dollar of 1 cent per month and the spot rate $2.31 = £1.

Further reading

PART I

(1) FURNESS, E. L. *An Introduction to Financial Economics*, London: William Heinemann 1972.
(2) REVELL, J. R. S. *The British Financial System*, London: Macmillan, 1980.
(3) SCAMMELL, W. M. *The London Discount Market*, London: Elek Books 1968.
(4) Committee to Review the Functioning of the Financial Institutions Report and Appendices, Command Paper 7937, June 1980.
(5) *Midland Bank Review*
   'The Banking Sector and Monetary Policy', Winter 1978.
   'Monetary Policy and Regulations Imposed on Listed Banks', Summer 1979.

PART II

(1) GILLETT BROS. DISCOUNT CO. LTD. *The Bill on London*, 3rd edition, London: Chapman & Hall, 1964.
(2) SAYERS, R. S. *Gilletts in the London Money Market 1867–1967*, Oxford: Clarendon Press, 1969.
(3) SCAMMELL, W. M. *The London Discount Market*, London: Elek Books, 1968.
(4) CHALMERS, E. *The Gilt-Edged Market*, London: Griffiths, 1967.
(5) *Bank of England Quarterly Bulletin*
   Commercial Bills, December 1961.
   Treasury Bill, September 1964.
   The Gilt-Edged Market, June 1979.

(6) *Midland Bank Review*
'The Treasury Bill – The Story of an Economist Invention',
February 1961.
'Managing the Gilt-Edged Market', May 1969.
'The Gilt-Edged Market and Credit Control', August 1971.
(7) *Barclays Bank Review*
'Money, The Base and Interest Rates' May 1980.

PART III

(1) Layfield Committee of Enquiry into Local Government Financing, Command Paper 6453, May 1976.
(2) HEPWORTH, N. P. *The Financing of Local Government*, 5th edition, London: Allen and Unwin, 1979.
(3) REVELL, J. R. S. *The British Financial System*, London: Macmillan, 1980.
(4) *Bank of England Quarterly Bulletin*
'The U.K. Banking Sector, 1952–1967', June 1969.
'Local Authority Finance,' November 1967.
'Sterling Certificates of Deposit', November 1972.
'Sterling Certificates of Deposit and the Inter Bank Market',
September 1973.
(5) *Midland Bank Review*
'Borrowing by Local Authorities', November 1973.
(6) KLOPSTOCK, F. *The Wiring of the Euro-Dollar Market*, Euromoney, August 1970.
(7) SHAW, E. R. *The Development of London's Money Markets*, *Institute of Bankers Journal*, October 1978 & August 1979.
(8) ANGELINI, A. & LEES, F. A. *International Lending, Risk and the Euromarkets,* London: Macmillan, 1979.
(9) LOMAX, D. & GUTTMAN, P. *The Euromarkets and International Financial Policies*, London: Macmillan, 1981.
(10) DUFY, G. & GIDDY, I. H. *The International Money Market*, London: Prentice-Hall, 1978.

PART IV

(1) COHEN, C. D. *British Economic Policy 1960–1969*, London: Butterworths, 1971.
(2) GOWLAND, D. *Monetary Policy and Credit Control*, London: Croom Helm, 1979.
(3) *Midland Bank Review*

'Annual Review of Monetary Policy', May annually.

(4) *The Banker*
'Annual Review of Foreign Banks in London'.

(5) GILLETT BROS. DISCOUNT CO. LTD. LONDON,   'Competition and Credit Control – a Banking Revolution', Report of a one-day conference 8.11.72 and also 5.12.72.

(6) 'The Development of International Short-term Money Markets'. Report of the two one-day conferences in Zurich and Geneva, 4 and 6 May 1971. Also a conference held in London 3.7.68 on 'Sterling Certificates of Deposit' by Allen Harvey & Ross Ltd., London.

(7) W. GREENWELL & CO. LONDON, 'Monetary Base Control' April 1980 (a paper).

(8) *Bank of England*
'Monetary Base Control', June 1979.

(9) WILSON, J. S. G. *The London Money Markets*, State Universitaire Européenne de Recherches Financieres (SUERF), 1976.

(10) TAYLOR, G. W. *New Techniques in British Banking*, Gilbart Lectures on Banking, 1973.

Index